£19.95

Integrity in Organizations

Integrity in Organizations

AN ALTERNATIVE

BUSINESS ETHIC

Gordon Pearson

McGRAW-HILL BOOK COMPANY

London · New York · St Louis · San Francisco · Auckland
Bogotá · Caracas · Lisbon · Madrid · Mexico
Milan · Montreal · New Delhi · Panama · Paris · San Juan
São Paulo · Singapore · Sydney · Tokyo · Toronto

Published by
McGRAW-HILL Book Company Europe
Shoppenhangers Road, Maidenhead, Berkshire SL6 2QL, England
Telephone 01628 23432
Fax 01628 770224

British Library Cataloguing in Publication Data
Pearson, G. J.
  Integrity in Organizations: Alternative
  Business Ethic
  I. Title
  174.4

ISBN 0-07-709136-1

Library of Congress Cataloging-in-Publication Data
Pearson, Gordon J.,
    Integrity in organizations: an alternative business ethic /
  Gordon Pearson.
      p.   cm.
  Includes bibliographical references and index.
  ISBN 0-07-709136-1
  1. Business ethics.   2. Integrity.   I. Title.
  HF5387.P4   1995
  174′4–dc20   95-1428
                                                                            CIP

12345 BL 998765

Typeset by BookEns Ltd., Royston, Herts.
and printed and bound in Great Britain
by Biddles Limited, Guildford

Printed on permanent paper in compliance with ISO Standard 9706

Contents

Preface

Business ethics, as it is taught in the world's business schools, is a disaster area. Despite the very substantial funding it has attracted in recent years, it remains of little practical value to either the student or the practising manager.

Some who make their living from business ethics don't even intend that it should be of practical worth:

> 'As an academic field it stands or falls on the quality of the research done in it, on the body of knowledge developed, and on its success as an academic, liberal arts subject.' Its legitimacy is not dependent on it 'being effective in changing the climate of business'.
>
> (DeGeorge, 1991, p. 45)

This 'liberal arts subject' has been constructed on a foundation of moral philosophy, stretching back to Plato, Aristotle, Epicurus and beyond. This provides an impeccable academic foundation for a weighty business ethics curriculum. However, the ancient Greeks and their successors, Bentham, Mill, Kant, etc., knew nothing of modern business and applying their theories in this alien context has proved fruitless. Moreover, as philosophers themselves acknowledge, there are no final answers, no ultimate truths. The most that philosophy can provide is an approach to the problem: a structured way of thinking about things, of balancing conflicting arguments. However, none of their ways of thinking takes business realities into account. And even if they did, they would still only provide a range of alternative views, with no definitive answers.

Business ethicists sometimes make the distinction between business ethics and ethics-in-business: business ethics being a purely academic pursuit, not related to, or dependent on, business itself. As such, business ethics is not an appropriate subject of concern for business schools. They were originally constituted, and continue to be funded, whether by industry or government, as a strategic investment in the improvement of the nation's business in its global competitive context. *Pure* academic endeavour has little part to play in this project.

Rejection of business ethics is, in this sense, surely no longer controversial. The great weight of opinion among practitioners and the world at large is now set firmly against the purely academic pursuit.

The orthodox approach to ethics-in-business is, however, also flawed.

The presumption that the methods of moral philosophy can be applied to business is only valid in an academic sense: ethical dilemmas can certainly be considered from different philosophical perspectives, but it is much less clear that anything of practical value will emerge. Moreover, the thrust of the ethics-in-business approach is to try to improve the ethical values of individuals in business, since the ethicists take the view that 'business ... can be no more ethical than the persons who run the firms' (DeGeorge, 1993). This view ignores the notion of organizational culture and the possibility of building corporate values which transcend the individual, just as it ignores any other factor that is business specific. Moreover, it leads to the attempt to develop managers with 'moral imagination and courage'—surely a project well beyond the scope of the typical 10- to 12-week MBA business ethics module.

Nevertheless, these approaches to business ethics and ethics-in-business are the existing dominant orthodoxies taught in our business schools. Their rejection, though long overdue, is not in itself of great significance. The more interesting question relates to what can be used in their stead. This is an important question because the world of business is very much concerned about ethical issues. Never before has there been such public awareness of business transactions and the impacts and side-effects of business operations; never before has there been such public cynicism of the motivations of business, particularly 'big business'.

The practitioners' main concerns are, as they always have been, with developing an organization of substance which might stand as a lasting memorial to their efforts. Increasingly they have come to recognize that an essential ingredient of such longevity is the integrity with which their organization conducts its various transactions. In the absence of a useful theory, practitioners have developed pragmatic approaches to ethics and integrity, based on common sense and moral scruple. In so doing the best practitioners clearly lead the academic field.

The lack of a theory that takes business realities into any account is the particular concern of this book. A theoretical model is introduced which is based on a recognition of the interdependent nature of modern organizations, a strategic view of business, and on the definition of different levels of integrity that might be expected to operate at different times and in different circumstances. It is an approach to the problems of integrity and ethics that has direct practical implications for managers.

The model is based mainly on existing theoretical and empirical work, including a project being carried out at Keele Management Development Centre at Keele University, the first results of which are reported herein.

The model focuses on the interdependence between and within organizations—both business and non-business. Interdependence is an increasingly dominant organizational idea: interdependence in the form of technological collaborations, joint ventures and strategic alliances of all kinds, rather than discrete, short-term profit-maximizing transactions; and interdependence between people, functions and specialisms within organizations rather than the former rigid, standardized, hierarchical structures. While the focus is mainly on business organizations, the ideas are applicable to all organizations—public and private, profit and not for profit—that seek the benefit of these long-term relationships.

The book has been written primarily for practitioners who are keen to have a rationale on which to base the ethical position of their own organization. It is also hoped that the book will interest those involved with management education courses, particularly MBAs, who might share the desire to give 'business ethics', as it is taught, greater practical impact.

Though the book is intended to be practical, it does not offer simple 'how to' prescriptions. Managements adopting this approach to ethics will still have to use their own experience and judgement. They will have to adapt the model to their own organization's particular circumstances. In some cases they will have to take unique initiatives and adopt quite distinctive responses. Moreover, whatever action they take will not last for ever. Integrity in organizations is a live and evolving concern; which is what makes it fun to work with and, hopefully, read about.

Plan of the book

The opening chapter provides some insight into the ethical ambiguities inherent in business. From start-up to maturity and decline, business is necessarily managed at the boundaries of ethical acceptability. Not surprisingly, people in business cross those boundaries from time to time. The inherent conflict between business and ethics needs to be understood if any approach to business ethics is to be of practical value. Chapter 2 outlines why the business ethics orthodoxy fails to work and why, therefore, there is a need for this alternative approach. Chapter 3 provides the basic outline of the alternative, value free, business-driven model and sets it in the present context of interdependent organizations. Chapter 4 develops the strategic perspective of business, emphasizing the dominance of strategic and business objectives and how these relate to the internal and external relations of the business organization. Chapter 5 examines the implications of the model for its transactions with each category of stakeholder and in pursuit of each of its business objectives. The examination further elaborates the business perspective and provides a number of actual examples of integrity in transactions with stakeholders. Chapter 6 sets out a number of essential linking concepts in the model. Finally, Chapter 7 highlights the practical implications of the whole model and shows how managements may use it to define an approach relevant to their own particular organization.

Acknowledgements

Various organizations have generously allowed me to reproduce material in this volume. I list them below in alphabetical order:

- Financial Times for permission to include extracts from three articles originally published in the *Financial Times*.

- Gee Publishing Ltd for permission to include the Cadbury Code of Best Practice reproduced from the Final Report of the Committee on the Financial Aspects of Corporate Governance, published by Gee, South Quay Plaza, 183 Marsh Wall, London E14 9FS.

- ICI for permission to include the ICI Group Statement on Business Ethics.

- Institute of Business Ethics for permission to include 'A model statement and code' which was originally published by the Institute as Part III of their 1988 publication, *Company Philosophies and Codes of Business Ethics* by Simon Webley.

- Newspaper Publishing Plc for permission to include extracts from several articles previously published in *The Independent* and *The Independent on Sunday*.

- Shell International Petroleum Company Ltd for permission to include their 1994 Statement of General Business Principles.

I believe the above inclusions have considerably enhanced the vitality and practical relevance of the text and I am most grateful for the permissions granted.

I am also grateful to the many people I have met who share my interest in business ethics, particularly through the European Business Ethics Network. In particular I acknowledge my debt, both at first hand and at arm's length, to Brian Harvey, Professor of Corporate Responsibility at Manchester Business School, and Jack Mahoney, Professor of Ethics at London Business School. While I am uncertain as to how far they would support the argument of this text, I am sure we at least share the common goal of enhancing the practical value of business ethics teaching and research.

Business and ethics

The popular perception is that society in general, and business along with it, is becoming less ethical. The evidence for this is largely based on an apparently increasing number of notorious cases such as Maxwell, Guinness, BCCI, etc., which came to the surface during the less-than-caring eighties.

Capitalism itself is based on a foundation which many regard as of dubious morality. Greed doesn't work for the mass of people; profit maximizing is in practice unfair in its distribution of resources. The moral position of competitive business is highly ambiguous. The entrepreneurial mentality pushes deliberately at the ethical boundaries. People in business are as ethical as any other group in society, but their professional predicament is complex and evolving, from the time a business is first set up through to its mature development as a large-scale organization.

The application of ethical standards to business can only have a practical value if it takes full account of these business realities. The aim of this chapter is therefore to examine the ethical ambiguities inherent in the ownership and management of business at the various stages of its evolution.

Introduction

There has always been a natural tension between behaviour which is broadly accepted as being ethical and the imperatives of a successful business. This tension has increased very substantially over the past decade or so. The 1980s, often caricatured as a decade of unbridled greed by the few at the expense of the many, certainly raised concerns among some that business was not being run according to currently acceptable ethical standards. Inequity and inequality seemed to rule the day.

Employees, weakened by high rates of unemployment, seemed sometimes to be treated as chattels, their union representatives derecognized, their employment contracts unilaterally renegotiated. High street customers, in Gerald Ratner's immortal words, were being sold 'total crap' and, should they get into financial difficulties, were exploited outrageously by high street banks. At a time of punitively high interest rates, suppliers with little bargaining power were mercilessly exploited by over-dominant customers continually delaying payments and even boasting openly about it. Exploitative pricing was exercised wherever monopoly power permitted, most notably in the case of the newly privatized utilities. And while all this was happening, company directors appeared to be paying themselves extraordinary remuneration for far from extraordinary performance, and if their incompetence became a matter for termination their severance payments were the envy of the working population.

This was not a purely British phenomenon; similar processes were highly visible in the USA, continental Europe and even Japan. Nor was it uniquely impacting on business; every walk of life, particularly including politics and the media, seemed to have become infected. Morally we seemed to be going to the dogs!

Of course, it has always been so. Since the ancient Greeks, contemporary observers have reported the same phenomenon. In what now seems a golden age of virtue and rectitude, Dr Johnson bemoaned the moral decline then to be observed all around. More recently, Harold Macmillan placed the blame on the fact that we had stopped going to church on Sundays. Perhaps we should really worry when we think we have at last established a virtuous social system based on improving moral standards, for then we should really know that our principles had finally disintegrated!

The evidence of moral decline is inconclusive. Many statistics suggest that the world is becoming more violent and more criminal, but, on the other hand, the average law-abiding citizen is more aware, more caring and more generous than ever before. There is no doubt more violence on television now than there has ever been before, but television audiences give more generously to charity than was ever previously dreamed possible.

In business, there may be more outrageous stories of fraud and crime than previously, but many of the acts—for example, insider dealing—which are now rightly treated as criminal, were just custom and common practice among the great and the good to whom we all turn for our example. There will always be crooks and a few of them will always get into powerful positions in industry as in other walks of life—we have even had crooked popes not to mention American presidents—but this does not mean the majority of business people are any less virtuous than people in other areas.

Over the past decade there has been a rising tide of anxiety and indignation among the media, seeking to influence the population at large, as to the rights and wrongs of business, particularly big, multinational business. This concern caught the attention of politicians and, even among businesspeople, it became a subject of much debate. As a result a number of steps were taken. Specific initiatives such as the Cadbury report on corporate governance and the adoption of codes of practice by the CBI and several of the professional bodies are symptomatic of the times. In addition, there have been some more general moves, such as the adoption of business ethics as a core topic by most MBA teaching programmes. World wide, the business schools now offer hundreds of courses in business ethics and literally scores of professorships have been established in the subject as well as many centres of academic research.

Society seems to be maintained, more or less, in a state of equilibrium through such checks and balances. The excesses of one era produce periods of reaction. Nevertheless, incremental changes *do* take place. In our own time, for example, new technological developments have provided fresh opportunities for both unethical excesses and improvement. From these there is no going back. Nor, one must suppose, will there be any going back to church on Sundays and consequent adoption of some exogenous value system that will mediate the behaviour of the mass of people. To this extent we are therefore in new territory.

Business ethics is certainly a fashionable idea, but it is unclear that any of the initiatives with which it is associated has had, or will have, any significant effect. It is not even clear whether that is their intention. A cynic might argue, for example, that as long as business is *seen* to be concerned, that will be sufficient: a well-publicized code of ethical practice may have far greater public relations impact than any actual improvement in ethical behaviour. Certainly, it seems extremely unlikely that teaching business ethics has, or will have, any effect at all, as long as the approaches currently adopted by most business schools are retained.

Business people operate in an area which explicitly and deliberately butts up against ethical boundaries. It is extremely easy for them to step over the boundary and in so doing enjoy substantial personal gains. Whether or not direct personal gain is involved, crossing the ethical boundaries may sometimes be obvious and overt, sometimes covert, sometimes not obvious, and sometimes even done unwittingly. Being innocently unethical, or even unethical but well intentioned, may be concepts which the media and the non-business public regard with some cynicism. However, the whole area is distinguished by shades of grey–the blacks and whites of fraud on the one hand and altruism on the other certainly exist, but it is the murky greys of normal business life that make this whole subject so problematic. Moreover, the greatest difficulty is in deciding between alternatives that contain both ethical and unethical aspects, and this distinguishes very many business decisions.

The search for a solution to ethical dilemmas using the methods of moral philosophy has failed. Moral philosophy provides no definitive answers, only ways of approaching problems. Moreover, managers are not, and, it is to be hoped, have no desire to become, philosophers any more than philosophers wish to be business people.

If an approach to business ethics is to be of any help to business people, or to have any relevance at all to the world of organizations, it must be firmly based in, and take full account of, the business perspective.

This first chapter, therefore, explores the fundamental and practical relationship between ethics and business. The tension referred to in the opening sentence is real enough. The idea of business, and of capitalism itself, was born out of this tension. Business people, whether they are executives, professional specialists or workers of any kind, operate in this ethically ambiguous business environment, continually pushing up against the boundaries, balancing the hard slog for the long-term good against the attractions of the easy short-term opportunity.

The increasing attention on achieving value for money and adopting commercial criteria in evaluating non-commercial activities means that all organizations, whether private or public, for profit or not for profit, are trying to follow the business example. Thus the approach taken here has a wider relevance than purely to businesses. This wider applicability will become more evident in later chapters as the focus intensifies on the increasingly interdependent nature of modern organizations.

Capitalist business

The spirit of capitalism was, according to Weber, 'a peculiar ethic' based on the simple idea that it is a man's duty to ensure the increase of his capital. Weber quoted Benjamin Franklin describing how it could be done:

> *Remember that time is money. He that can earn ten shillings a day by his labour and sits idle one half of that day, though he spends but sixpence during his diversion or idleness, ought not to reckon that the only expense; he has really spent, or rather thrown away, five shillings besides. Remember that credit is money. If a man lets his money lie in my hands after it is due, he gives me the interest, or so much as I can make of it during that time. This amounts to a considerable sum where a man has good and large credit, and makes good use of it. ... Never keep borrowed money an hour beyond the time you promised, lest a disappointment shut up your friend's purse for ever ...*   (Weber, 1920)

This *spirit of capitalism*, which actually predated the industrial revolution itself, was an ethos which seemed to impose on an individual the *duty* of profit maximization. The philosophy was summed up by Kürnberger in the words 'they make tallow out of cattle and money out of men'. The tension between ethical behaviour and business was apparent from the beginnings of the modern capitalist system.

'Greed works' was the 1980s expression of this same ethos. While at the micro level of the individual, avarice and selfishness are surely reprehensible, this ethos holds that through the workings of the market, they serve to optimize the allocation of resources to the benefit of all at the macro level. In theory, a perfect market of profit maximizers results in maximized social welfare.

Even though the theory required underlying assumptions that were wholly unrealistic, the idea of profit maximization remains extremely powerful. Thus, a finance director who paid a penny more to the tax authorities than was strictly necessary, a buyer who failed to achieve the greatest benefit from his or her suppliers, a salesperson who gave customers more value than they were prepared to pay for, a manager who pays people more than they require to work effectively, are all examples of waste that dissipate the company's resources and would progressively reduce its capacity to build a sustainable competitive advantage.

The idea of profit maximization is an abstraction from classical microeconomics, but the *spirit of capitalism* translated into operational terms, still guides the individual entrepreneur from the moment the business starts up.

Almost every business that exists has evolved through this initial entrepreneurial phase and has thus been set on its course with these same entrepreneurial imperatives. Old industries are in decline, but they are being replaced by a new generation of entrepreneurs starting a new wave of family corporate ownership. Moreover, even among those large mature public companies that appear to have orthodox public ownership and control, many still exhibit in their shareholders' registers substantial remnants of family control, and sometimes not just remnants. For example, the present chairman of Barclays Bank did not become chairman and chief executive simply on merit, but because of the strong family influence remaining in that business. The long tradition of the family-controlled business is far from dead and what remains true of Barclays is even more potent in many lesser firms.

The ownership and management control critically shape ethical behaviour in a business. When a business is started up the owner/manager owns everything. He or she not only has access to the till, but owns it. Even before that the liquid assets of the business are all kept in the owner's back pocket. As the business evolves its culture develops and new rules are established with its members or employees, ownership and management control are progressively separated, and the business refocuses on new objectives.

Many ethically charged issues arise as the firm moves through various stages of corporate ownership and management control and increases in size and maturity. As it progresses the business establishes various rules about how things are done, and these become embedded in the organization's culture. The following sections consider some of the ethical issues arising as this evolution process takes place.

Corporate evolution

There is a natural cycle in the development of most systems, whether biological, technological or social. It seems to apply to systems as diverse as single cells, lighted candles, human beings, products and businesses, even nation states. They all appear to follow the familiar pattern of birth, growth, maturity, decline and death and at each stage they appear to be driven by certain common goals, as summarized in Table 1.1.

In infancy, most successful systems are dominated by the need to survive. This is entirely natural and appropriate because of inherently high infant mortality rates. High infant mortality among human beings has been reduced primarily by state provision in such areas as public hygiene, health and other social aspects. Moreover, infant humans are usually nurtured by loving parents in a generally benign adult population.

The infant business has few of these benefits. The doting parent or founder may lack the competence to ensure that the fledgling survives. The wider population is by no means benign—if an infant business makes too much of a nuisance of itself it is likely to be squashed by its larger competitors. Moreover, state provision is extremely unreliable.

From time to time governments may make welcoming noises about small business, enterprise, etc., but few coherent attempts are made to provide a healthy environment. There are no state midwives, hospitals, doctors and health visitors for the infant business. The UK government has invested substantial sums in publicizing its various 'enterprise' initiatives, but its far more powerful policy on interest rates has, over many years, taken money away from the small, high-growth, cash-hungry business and

Table 1.1 Systematic corporate evolution

System phase	Company evolution	System goals
Birth	Start-up/entrepreneur	Survival to achieve maturity
Adolescence	Family control	Building strength to achieve maturity
Maturity 1	Public (quoted) company	Autonomy and control of environment
Maturity 2	Wholly owned subsidiary	Self-actualization and control of environment
Decline	Subsidiary or independent	Stability and longevity
Death	Disinvestment and liquidation	Survival

given it to the bureaucratic, cash-rich leviathans of industry which very often have no very good idea of what to do with the gratuitous wealth thrust upon them.

In such circumstances, an obsession with survival is vital for the infant business. If its survival is threatened, the infant business must take any necessary life-saving action and put other considerations, ethical niceties included, on the back burner. If it survives this first phase the adolescent will be able to turn its attention to growth and the development of functional strength. It progresses through adolescence being sharp, opportunistic and focused on satisfying customers' needs. It carries no spare weight, no passengers. It is lean and fit, quick on its feet and builds its strength through constant striving and exercise.

This phase sees the business change from being a one-person concern with a simple structure to employing an increasing number of professional specialists involved in the firm's technological development and the professionalization of its various management functions.

In a growing market the adolescent business has to run very fast in order simply to maintain its market position. If it fails to do this then in all probability it will not survive the first shake out when market growth starts to falter. In a static market there is not the same necessity to grow. Many businesses stay small, providing relatively stable employment for small numbers of people. Other businesses are more ambitious and grow rapidly in order to achieve the critical mass at which the new specialists can be profitably supported. Growth in static markets can only be achieved by increasing market share or by moving into new markets, both of which may be problematic in highly competitive situations. The overall aim at this stage of evolution is to compete effectively, i.e. to please customers more than competitors do and thereby to beat competitors. The focus on beating competitors may lead businesses to indulge in activities of dubious ethical worth.

To achieve maturity is the goal of all systems. Maturity is the phase when a successful system achieves maximum entropy, the most efficient process of energy conversion, the closest to self-actualization or fulfilment. In the case of a business, maturity is the phase when wealth creation is maximized, when the most surplus cash is generated and when the business achieves its position of greatest power and influence. Leadership in a mature market used to be an enviable position in which a business could expect to maintain the generation of surplus for many years. This is no longer true and successful businesses have to continue striving to maintain their dominance. They may do this by threat of competitive reprisal or through collaboration or collusion to exploit monopolistic power. These are the most obvious ways that mature businesses may use to control and stabilize their environments and where they may be tempted to cross over the borders of ethical acceptability.

In most systems it appears that ultimate decline and extinction are certain. In most cases they are entirely predictable. A candle, for example, follows all these system stages. When first lit, it may spit and sputter and possibly go out. If it remains lit, the flame quickly reaches its full size. This is its mature phase when it burns the maximum wax and gives off the greatest light. In due course, it starts to putter and flicker and thereafter fairly quickly declines and is extinguished. Depending on the size of wick and the diameter and length of the candle, its longevity is fairly predictable. Similarly, the longevity of a biological cell is also reasonably predictable. But social systems are less so. They are renewable in a way that living systems are not, and one of the aims of most social systems, and most managements, is to prolong the life of the system for as long as possible. Some succeed better than others.

For those that do not achieve continuous renewal, decline will ultimately set in. During decline the focus of attention moves once more back to a focus on survival, the preoccupation with which becomes totally dominant up to the point of extinction.

During these different phases in the natural evolution of a business, there are quite different pressures on the owners and managers of the business. Sometimes these will be totally dominant as in the infancy and extinction phases when a single-minded concern for survival may appear to justify almost any action, no matter how unethical. At other times, a more balanced approach may be sustainable. Even in maturity, however, there are natural pressures that may push the business to the edge. For example, the tendency for mature businesses to form protective cartels is natural but illegal and, for most people, would also be regarded as unethical and as an abuse of economic power to exploit the relatively weak, be they competitors or customers.

The natural evolution of business as a system thus suggests that business will naturally operate at the boundaries of what would widely be regarded as ethically acceptable.

Evolution and ethical rules

Business evolves naturally at this boundary of ethical acceptability and as it does so develops certain ethical rules of behaviour related to ownership and management control. These can be inferred from the custom and practice of the individuals concerned in their business setting. They are ethical in the sense that they are value loaded, pertinent to ethics, rather than having a particular ethical value themselves.

As a company grows and as the form of its ownership evolves, so the rules, customs and practices in which ownership is embedded also change. The customs and practices of the entrepreneur/owner may be radically different from those of the professional manager, but the dilemma is not simply of the differences between ownership and management of the business. Ethical rules that are applicable to a sole trader may not be relevant to a small entrepreneurial business. Rules that apply to the entrepreneur may not be appropriate for a firm being managed by the second or third generation of the owning family. Rules that apply to a publicly owned but family-controlled business may not be applicable to the same business if it becomes the wholly owned subsidiary of a larger quoted company.

The points of change in ownership may themselves be discrete and explicit events, but the change in ethical rules implied by the change in ownership often remains implicit. In practice, changes in ethical rules may be both delayed and gradual. However, if the change in ethical rules is too delayed and too gradual, the result is likely to be a dissonance and cultural breakdown. The resultant behaviour patterns and standards may not merely cease to bind the social group together, as predicted by White (1984), but may have the strategically decisive effect of breaking it apart.

The evolution of ownership typically follows the stages set out in Table 1.2. The six phases identified are those where the change in ownership and control have the most direct implications for the relevant ethical rules, both directly and through concomitant changes in the organization's culture and the psychological contracts of people working within the organization. The phases also tend to coincide with a strategic refocusing of the business, which again may have implications for the ethical dimension.

In the following sections these phases in Table 1.2 are illustrated by reference to a company named S.T.P., which is a composite of a number of real companies, the issues highlighted all being drawn from the real antecedents of S.T.P.

Table 1.2 Phases of ownership and control

Phase	Control	Form	Ownership
1	Start-up	Sole trader	100% founder/entrepreneur
2	Entrepreneur	Private company	90%+ founder/entrepreneur
3	Family	Private company	100% founder's family
4	Family	Public company	Large family holding
5	Public	Quoted company	Smaller family holding
6	Parent company	Private company	100% owned by parent company

Start-up

Box 1.1 illustrates the early formation of the first ethical rule to which most rational individuals would be likely to subscribe. Although, of course, it is

Box 1.1   Start-up

Eric Kirtchin set up Scientific and Technical Papers (S.T.P.), to make impregnated technical grades of paper mainly for electrical applications. He asked Maurice Hope, of Hope & Ellis, to act as his accountant. He had known Hope for many years and knew he would give good, sound advice. The first thing Hope had suggested was that they agree with the tax authorities a financial year ending April 30th so that they would get an extra eleven months before having to pay any taxes. He also suggested that Kirtchin employ his wife, Ann in some nominal capacity so that they could maximize their joint tax-free earnings. These were perfectly orthodox arrangements, but Eric was reassured that Hope & Ellis had his best interests at heart.

The accountants had been retained to advise Eric how to keep his records efficiently, to prepare his financial accounts and, above all, to smooth his path with the tax authorities, with whom Hope & Ellis had 'a good and trusting relationship'.

Hope & Ellis negotiated a number of items with the tax authorities about allowable expenses to be charged against the business. These included 20 per cent of the cost of running Eric's house (rates, water, gas and electricity) plus 50 per cent of his home telephone bill, the full cost of running Eric's car including his personal use, and a proportion of his wife's motoring expenses. In addition Eric kept all invoices that might be considered in any way related to the business and these were charged in his quarterly VAT returns and then passed to Hope & Ellis along with all the other documents for preparing the company's accounts. Some items included in this way were probably not much to do with the business, e.g. various items that went down as subsistence, also some books, personal stationery and other consumables.

Emergent ethical rule

The business should be so arranged, by agreement with the tax authorities, as to keep tax payments to the minimum. It is thus sensible to charge every feasible item against the business in order to minimize the payment of taxation.

highly incomplete it seems clear that such an ethical rule is an early influence in the 'behaviour patterns and standards' that are subsequently built up over many years to form a 'unifying philosophy, ethic and spirit'— in short, an organizational culture (White, 1984).

By the time the first *financial* accounts are being prepared the entrepreneur may have been in business for over two years. During this time certain systematic ways of operating have been developed which embed the initial ethical rule ever more firmly in the organization. The crux of the rule is simply to minimize payment of tax, a very basic concept which commands widespread support yet which sets the tone of what has been referred to as 'the business predicament'.

The establishment of this basic ethical rule is directly in line with the spirit of capitalism. Few people would suggest that there was anything unethical in the specified behaviour as long as it is agreed with the tax authorities. All management training and education would support this, both in the specific case of taxation and on a broader front in relation to all the firm's interactions. Suppliers are not paid more than they invoice and are not paid early; employees are not generally paid more than the 'going rate' and are rarely paid for nothing; customers are not provided extra bells and whistles unless they want them and are prepared to pay for them. To behave in any other way would be eccentric, even irresponsible.

Subsequent phases of development serve largely to reinforce and elaborate this early ethos.

The entrepreneurial phase

The second, entrepreneurial, phase sees the business grow rapidly and start to take on additional employees who typically carry out simple routine tasks or work under the entrepreneur's instructions. The founder/entrepreneur retains 100 per cent ownership of the business and 100 per cent management control. Every decision of any significance is taken by the entrepreneur who is answerable to no one except the customers and the tax authorities. This is what Handy referred to as the 'power culture', where control is exercised largely by one individual (Handy, 1976).

The entrepreneur's contract with the business is limitless. Typically he or she works all the hours of the day and including every weekend. The young business has a voracious appetite for cash. Very probably the entrepreneur will have put up all personal wealth as collateral on the firm's borrowings, very often including the family house. The personal investment in the business in terms of finance, psychological commitment, time and effort is total. Many marriages do not survive the entrepreneurial phase!

Without this manic level of commitment by the entrepreneur few businesses would survive. But there are compensations, as suggested in Box 1.2. The emergent ethical rule seems to be moving the entrepreneur a stage closer to using the business for personal ends.

However, since the business is legally 100 per cent his and since his psychological contract with the business is completely open ended, it does not seem that at this stage that any serious moral issues are raised.

Box 1.2 Entrepreneurial phase

S.T.P. grew rapidly but, in its early years, was perpetually short of cash for both capacity building and for financing working capital. Over several periods, Eric Kirtchin was living on a knife edge wondering if the bank would bounce his wages cheque. On one occasion he risked the entire enterprise by making a large opportunistic purchase with no certainty at all of being able to pay the bill. He knew that if the deal didn't work out, the consequences for suppliers, customers and employees would be disastrous and he would not only lose his house but probably be charged with fraud. During a particular 48-hour period he lied to his bank manager and to two major creditors. In the event the deal was successful and generated much needed funds for the company's future growth, but for years its failure was one of Eric's recurrent nightmares.

One of his lifelong interests, apart from the business, was vintage motor cars. He possessed a 1911 Daimler and in the past had entered the London–Brighton run on several occasions. The setting up and early growth of S.T.P. had required not only the signing away of the freehold on his house, but also the reluctant sale of the Daimler. For a number of years Eric had put his hobby aside. However, he still retained an ambition to set up a really well-equipped workshop where he could renovate old cars. It was his dream for retirement should he survive.

S.T.P. continued to grow rapidly and was profitable. One of the first luxuries that Eric permitted himself when the survival of the business seemed assured was the equipping of the machine shop to standards well beyond what was strictly required for the business. His intention was, when time permitted, to acquire an old automobile and renovate it using the company facilities. This in due course he did, recruiting a craftsman charge-hand who was able to carry out the renovation work. The costs incurred on this venture were indistinguishable from the ordinary machine shop costs and no attempt was made to separate them out.

As the company grew Eric's motoring interests were further gratified and included visits to several of the Formula One Grand Prix race meetings in combination with some genuine sales visits. It was agreed with the accountants that these should be treated as overseas sales trips, with Eric's wife travelling as his secretary.

Eric's personal expenditure (e.g. old cars and race meetings) could be paid for either out of his salary which was paid by the business, or by charging it directly to the business as an item of business expense. Either way, as 100 per cent owner of the business, he would ultimately pay. it was generally more tax efficient to charge items of personal expenditure as business expenses and, consequently, Eric charged personal items to the business unless the tax authorities objected.

Emergent ethical rule

The entrepreneur/owner's commitment to the business is total. It is sensible to use the most tax efficient way of repaying this commitment by charging personal items of expenditure directly to the business if it is acceptable to the tax authorities.

The family business

The aim of most successful entrepreneurs is not to maximize profits but to build a business of substance that will survive and prosper. For some it is important that they develop something that could be handed down to their children and at the same time offer a little bit of immortality. This is the true spirit of capitalism, according to Weber.

The change from entrepreneurial to family business is usually a progressive development. At some stage the company ceases to be the sole possession of the original entrepreneur and becomes a family business. The change may be symbolized by some ritual such as the son or daughter formally taking on the role of chief executive, or the assumption of life presidency by the founding entrepreneur, but the real process may be much less perceptible and occur informally and progressively (Box 1.3).

Box 1.3 Family business

The company was very profitable and grew rapidly, soon employing several hundred. Eric agreed to bring his daughter and two sons onto the board of S.T.P., all three being employed in the business. Annette was made marketing director, Peter became production director and Charles, administration director responsible for accounting and personnel matters.

In the past Eric had tended to charge things to the business if he felt that a reasonably legitimate case could be made for it. However, now that other members of the family were involved he felt it would be better to be more systematic about what personal expenditure by family members should be charged to the business. Consequently he agreed a list of such items with the accountants. This included the following:

- 'Top hat' pension scheme for himself.
- Bentley car for himself and Porsche for his wife.
- Executive cars for directors (all family).
- Furnished company houses for all directors.
- All directors' motoring expenses, including petrol for personal mileage.

- Overseas 'sales' trips for himself and wife.
- Generous general expenses.

Emergent ethical rule

It is rational and ethical to maximize the 'family take' subject to agreement with the tax authorities and the company's financial capacity.

Nevertheless the metamorphosis from entrepreneurial unit to family business is of critical importance. Often the entrepreneur's children or other succeeding relatives fail to share his or her passion for and commitment to the business. Often there is not just one inheritor—there may be two or more progeny among whom the business will be ultimately divided.

Different family members are therefore likely to have different psychological contracts with the business, some possibly replicating the founding entrepreneur's while others may be based solely on what they can extract from the business while putting little into it other than retaining their inherited share (Box 1.4).

Box 1.4   Family management

In due course family roles became further differentiated. Annette married and started a family and ceased working in the firm but retained her shareholding. Her husband took her position and in due course became a director. Peter Kirtchin appeared not well suited to management and became something of a passenger with a professional works manager nominally reporting to him but in reality doing the job. Charles became managing director and devoted all his energies to the business just as his father had.

These developments caused considerable strain among family relationships. So far as 'family take' was concerned the rules did not change. However, the justification for them changed radically, with Annette and Peter both taking substantially from the business while putting little back. In due course they no longer enjoyed the benefit of being able to claim significant expenses. Eric and Charles being both fully dedicated to the firm, continued to enjoy their former emoluments.

Thus a distinction was made between those family members involved in managing the business and those who were not. 'Family take' became the preserve of family managers rather than shareholders. The behaviour patterns and standards that had been built up over the years were embedded as family custom and practice and formed an important part of the organization's culture.

Emergent ethical rule

Family members who are also managers of the business are entitled to the full 'family take' from the business because of their role as managers. Family members not also managers forfeit this 'right'.

The rules of the business therefore change somewhat as indicated in Box 1.4 and a distinction is made which appears to entitle family managers to 'take' from the business in ways that are not legitimized for either non-managers or non-members of the owning family.

This distinction is further complicated when the company enters its next stage of evolution and gains a public quotation.

The quoted company

In a publicly quoted company there is no formal role for family members; there are simply owners, directors and employees. The position of family managers or directors is therefore no different from non-family members and they fulfil the tasks or roles of either shareholders, executive or non-executive directors and/or professional managers or employees. The system makes no legal distinction between family shareholders, directors and employees and non-family members; indeed the law specifically lays down that all shareholders should be treated exactly alike.

In order to obtain a quotation a business must meet certain criteria of substance and have a reasonably long and successful track record. For most businesses this means that, by the time they go public, the customs and practices, behaviour patterns and standards, have become well formed, fixed and embedded in the culture of the organization. For many companies, these behaviour patterns and practices may conflict with the legal requirement to treat all shareholders alike. Clearly the family managers are not treated like other shareholders, nor like other managers. This is typical and widespread: the Barclays example has already been quoted of family dominance, and vestiges of family influence on quoted company boards of directors is extremely common. Nevertheless, at the stage when the company achieves its public quotation the former customs and practice of family managers are starting to appear less acceptable, both to the institutions of its new financial environment and, as illustrated in Box 1.5, to employees.

Family managers may still, perhaps quite wrongly but perhaps understandably, behave according to ethical rules which were applicable at earlier stages of the company's evolution. For example, they may still operate within the mindset which suggests it is not particularly important

Box 1.5   Quoted company

Eric Kirtchin achieved his ambition when S.T.P. achieved its public quotation. It set the seal on his achievement: a substantial business that would survive for the benefit of succeeding generations. Eric was regarded by employees in a variety of ways. He had not been a particularly charismatic leader, but he had been conscientious and hard working as several company stories testified.

However, there were many other, less benign symbols of his leadership. One is described below:

During the late 1960s Eric had spent a holiday in West Germany and had, rather unexpectedly, ordered a 2.5 metre wide paper machine. This was a much wider machine than they had ever used before and there did not seem to be much justification for purchasing such a big unit. The machine was eventually delivered in thirteen huge packing cases, which were unpacked while Eric was on a visit to America. The engineers were surprised to find that the contents of case number 7 was a large bodiless vintage Mercedes-Benz ready for restoration. The 2.5 m machine proved to be a white elephant that was never adequately utilized. The story was told and retold that Eric had bought the machine because an 84 in. machine could be packed into cases that were too small to contain the Mercedes. While rational reflection would suggest this story was untrue, it was nevertheless a much repeated symbolic tale, the meaning of which shed light on 'management's' concern for the company and its fortunes.

The sequel to this story was that the Mercedes was renovated at great and obvious expense in S.T.P.'s remarkably well-equipped machine shop, often referred to as 'Mr Eric's folly'. The car did later run in the London–Brighton and some acknowledgement of S.T.P.'s 'sponsorship' was made.

These stories, and many others of similar ilk, were told by successive employees because of their obvious symbolic meaning. The importance of this symbolism was increased in the mid-1970s when the company barely survived a four-year recession in its main markets. Amid redundancies and cutbacks such symbols of extravagance and exploitation caused considerable alienation among employees.

Emergent ethical rule

The previous rules which seemed initially acceptable, now appear unacceptable, but it is not necessarily clear where the line of acceptability should be drawn.

whether they benefit from the firm in terms of salary or 'family take', i.e. if the latter is more tax efficient then it is acceptable. Certain elements of 'take' that are not specifically prescribed in the new situation–for example, director's expenses–may continue as previously, but the fact that family managers might be slow to adapt their customs and practices to the new situation does not arise because they are uniquely wicked. They may be equally slow to behave as ordinary employees in terms of the amount of personal effort and commitment they continue to give to the business and the loyalty they continue to display. This slowness to adapt to the new stage in the company's evolution is one source of ethical ambiguity which impacts most businesses at some stage and its impact is cultural and long lasting. It is not simply restricted to family businesses, or even to family members in former family businesses, but impacts all stakeholders in those businesses. What is acceptable in the behaviour of one director is clearly also acceptable in another. Over time, the culture created is likely to affect the behaviour of professional, non-family managers, just as much as it does family managers and the overall impact, for good or ill, will be on the organization as a whole.

The incident described in Box 1.6 is apparently an example of clearly dishonest and unacceptable behaviour. It is unacceptable in business terms: not only is the company being defrauded, but the behavioural impact on other people in the organization might be very considerable. It looks like a simple black-and-white situation. However, the process by which such an incident comes about, though it is extremely common in business, is not simple. The one time founder/entrepreneur/owner of the business has given his life to it, risked everything for it and worked all hours to nurture it. Labelling that person, the perpetrator of such a transaction, as a crook does not help the real position to be understood. Understanding the business predicament is the first vital step to its being managed effectively.

The wholly owned subsidiary

Should the quoted company be taken over by another group the ethical rules become somewhat clearer. In these circumstances the wholly owned subsidiary has to operate to the rules of its new owners. An incident such as the one described in Box 1.6 becomes much less ambiguous. The perpetrator can have no vestige of doubt that what he is doing is a straightforward criminal act of theft. Nevertheless there are still areas of doubt. For example the acquiring company may be family managed or controlled and bring its own ambiguities to the new subsidiary.

Another real business issue is competition. During the early stages of a firm's evolution, it is predominantly fighting for survival, but once

Box 1.6   Internal dealings

Charles Kirtchin, managing director, exercised management control through what he called the Executive Committee, which comprised the executive directors of the company. After one of these monthly meetings Charles asked Gerald Smith, the new chief accountant, to stay behind a moment after the others had left the room. They talked a moment or two about some cost calculations, then Charles casually pushed a piece of paper across to Gerald and said,

'Code this to the works canteen, would you, Gerald.'

Gerald looked at the piece of paper. It was an invoice for a domestic refrigerator. Gerald knew full well that no such item had been purchased for the works canteen. He looked across the table at his boss who was already turning his attention to other things. He mumbled something incoherent, picked the paper up and hurriedly left the room. He knew exactly what was afoot. It was a straightforward fiddle. In itself it was trivial, but what else did it symbolize? Gerald knew also that in not questioning it immediately he had passively condoned it.

From that moment on Gerald felt that his relationship with Charles Kirtchin had changed irrevocably. Charles, on the other hand, was wholly unaware of the impact of this relatively routine transaction, which, though not strictly above board, was a trivial 'perk' in comparison with the total dedication he had given the company over very many years and continued to give.

Emergent ethical rule

The rules are clear, but the situation that leads to their disregard needs to be understood if the rules are to be obeyed.

---

established it is necessarily concerned with competitive issues. A successful business inevitably becomes the focus for competitive attack.

In competition, normally accepted rules cease to apply. An analogy can be made with boxing. In normal circumstances we would regard punching colleagues as an unacceptable procedure. However, in the boxing ring different rules are adopted. Similarly in competition, knock-out punches are highly regarded so long as they are legal. Box 1.7 illustrates the point.

Being a wholly owned subsidiary is likely to provide the business with additional financial strength which it can use to take advantage of its weaker competitors.

Box 1.7 Competition

In its mature years S.T.P. attracted considerable competition both from within the UK and subsequently from a Pakistani company. The British company lacked S.T.P.'s financial strength and the S.T.P. management decided that the most effective response was to mount a two-pronged attack promoting their own products as highest quality while pricing aggressively with the specific intention of driving the competitor out of the market. The strategy was expensive, but ultimately successful, the competitor being driven utlimately into receivership and out of the market.

S.T.P.'s approach with the Pakistani business was to continue to emphasize its own quality image while at the same time mounting a covert campaign to discredit the competitor's quality. While there was some truth in S.T.P.'s claims, the management did not shrink from exaggerating the quality problems some customers had experienced with the Pakistani product. This strategy too was largely successful. While the competitor did not withdraw from the UK entirely, it was left with only a very low price segment of the market.

The net result of these competitive strategies was a substantial long-term economic gain for S.T.P., but overall a reduction of jobs in the industry and possibly a loss of benefit for the customer as a result of the reduced competition.

Emergent ethical rule

All is fair in competition.

Evolution of culture and psychological contract

The evolution of ownership as the business progresses from start-up through public quotation to wholly owned subsidiary is one perspective on business. The purpose of taking this perspective is to understand how business works in relation to ethical issues. The changing pattern of ownership has direct consequences for the 'philosophy, ethic and spirit' of a company. What is acceptable at one phase may be unacceptable at another. But ownership is not the whole story. There are other aspects which influence the acceptability of 'behaviour patterns and standards'.

For example, during the early stages of the company's evolution it is completely dependent on the owner/entrepreneur, whereas by the time the company has gained its public quotation it has established its own critical mass as an institution, with structures, rules and regulations which make it no longer reliant on any individual. The entrepreneur's psychological contract with the business, which starts out completely open-ended based on his or her achieving 'self-actualization' in the business itself, becomes progressively less open as the business develops, being what Handy called 'co-operative' (Handy, 1976) in the typical family business and rather more 'calculative' by the time the business goes public. This progression is mirrored by the changing organizational culture which is dominated by the entrepreneur from the start in what Handy referred to as a 'power culture', and progresses through a phase of 'task culture' and ends up as a large company 'role culture'. To a substantial extent it is the changes in culture and psychological contract that change the ethical acceptability of the behaviour patterns described. These changes are summarized in Tables 1.3 and 1.4.

As has already been noted, the behaviour patterns and standards that are shaped by the culture and psychological contract only change slowly after a change in ownership and control. During this lag, the behaviour patterns, which are likely to be well known and understood by employees within the organization, will be widely perceived as inappropriate, and are likely to be seen as symbolic of low ethical standards.

The progressions outlined in Tables 1.3 and 1.4 are typical of how many businesses have developed in the past. However, the calculative contract and role culture appear to be less appropriate to organizations operating in volatile and fast-changing environments. The current high rate of technological innovation is impacting on most businesses and, as a consequence, they are having to find alternative forms of organization that can remain flexible and responsive to change. The most appropriate forms of organization seem to be smaller, team-based, network organizations, rather than the traditional large-scale monolithic structures that were effective in mass-producing industries. This suggests that the psychological contracts and cultures may not change as suggested above, but remain in, or even return to, the entrepreneurial phase, thus adding further to the complexity of maintaining appropriate ethical rules in response to the evolving business organization.

Table 1.3   Control and the psychological contract

Ownership stage	Control	Psychological contract
Start-up Entrepreneur	Entrepreneurial control	Self-actualization
Family	↓	Co-operative
Family/Public		
Wholly owned subsidiary	External/Plc control	Calculative

Table 1.4   Control and the organizational culture

Ownership stage	Control	Organizational culture
Start-up	Entrepreneurial control	Power culture
Entrepreneur		
Family	$\downarrow$	Task culture
Family/Public		
Wholly owned subsidiary	External/Plc control	Role culture

Conclusion

Companies are set up and evolve in a way that deliberately pushes at the boundaries of what is widely regarded as ethical acceptability. This is endemic to the capitalist system. *The spirit of capitalism* stressed the importance, to the economy in general and social welfare in particular, of the duty of entrepreneurs to maximize their profit.

Even though the classical microeconomic model on which this idea was based is almost wholly unrealistic, profit maximization, and all that is supposed to flow from it, has nevertheless been a highly influential idea. If a firm focused wholly on short-term profit maximization it would behave in ways that we would all find unacceptable.

Business is set up in a way that is deliberately pushing at the boundaries of ethical acceptability and evolves naturally along a path of ethical ambiguity. This does not arise because of the intrinsically low integrity of the entrepreneur or top manager, but because of the genuinely ambiguous position of entrepreneur/owners. Moreover, the ambiguity is compounded by business imperatives, notably to survive and to compete, which give both start-up entrepreneurs and mature business managers more pressing concerns than ethical niceties. As business evolves a system of implicit but perfectly rational, ethically pertinent *rules* emerges which seems to lead inexorably to the adoption of low ethical standards.

So what are the checks and balances that constrain businesses to behave in any way ethically? There are two broad schools of thought.

The first approach suggests that an ethical business depends crucially on the ethical standards of the individuals who take the critical decisions. According to this view, the business environment continuously offers opportunities for profit from unethical behaviour whether it is theft, fraud, deception or exploitation of some other form. The only way such activity will be constrained, in a profit-maximizing world, is through the moral courage and imagination of people in business. This is the orthodox business ethics approach, broadly supported by the academic and religious communities with some support from a minority of practitioners.

The second school of thought is based on the assumption that ethical behaviour in business is required for long-term prosperity. Therefore, enlightened self-interest requires that businesses do behave in ways that would be considered ethical by most people. This view is given more credence by practitioners, but has not been very well formulated in terms that practitioners can use. Some of the assertions in this category have been naive statements that 'good business is good business', or irrelevant suggestions that there are exciting market opportunities in being green. However, there is more substance to enlightened self-interest than this. The unique contribution of this book is to describe a particular model of enlightened self-interest which has a theoretical pedigree, some empirical support and, above all, is of practical use to those responsible for managing organizations. This is an unorthodox approach to ethics in business which stands in stark contrast to the theoretical business ethics examined in Chapter 2. The reader who is already familiar with this orthodox business ethics perspective may choose to skip Chapter 2 and proceed straight to Chapter 3 which examines the enlightened self-interest approach.

The business ethics movement

In response to the apparent decline in ethical standards of business, academics, business people and spiritual leaders have combined to create the business ethics movement. This chapter reviews the movement, its purpose, its approach, its considerable impact and its inevitable failure.

The aim of the movement is to raise the ethical standards of people in business. It has grown rapidly and scored many direct successes, but its effectiveness in raising moral standards is unproven.

Business ethicists attempt to apply the concepts of moral philosophy to business. Two main thrusts are consequentialism–having regard to the consequences of an action–and universalism–being concerned with the principles involved and the motivation behind an action. Neither approach provides definitive moral answers, though both provide structured ways of examining the moral content of actions.

Introduction

People in business operate in an ethically ambiguous environment. Many of them–executives, managers and professionals of all kinds–enjoy considerable autonomy and freedom to exercise their own personal value systems, for good or ill. Being ordinarily frail human beings, inherently neither more nor less ethical than the rest of the population, their behaviour varies and some are seduced by the easy opportunities for theft and fraud. Over the past few decades there seems to have been an increasing number of notorious cases.

There have been two main responses to this apparently deteriorating situation. First, there has been a statutory response, particularly affecting the financial sector. The notion of self-regulation has come to be regarded with increasing scepticism and much legislation has been introduced over the past 20 years to replace voluntary constraint. This process is ongoing. However, the law will never be wholly effective in eliminating transgressions, and even where it does seem appropriate–for example, in cases of fraud–its application is often extremely cumbersome and expensive.

A second response to the apparent increase in the unethical behaviour of business has been the rise of the business ethics movement. This explicitly aims to modify business behaviour, especially in areas of discretion where the law would seem not to be appropriate, by focusing on values. The main thrust of the business ethics movement is to *raise* the ethical values and behaviour of people, particularly senior people, in business, so that the ethical performance of business as a whole will be raised.

The movement has had a great deal of success in raising the general awareness of ethical issues in contemporary organizations, but has not been of much practical help to practitioners. This is largely because the orthodox business ethics approach relies heavily on unworldly philo-sophical argument and is largely innocent of modern business realities. It is nevertheless currently the dominant perspective in this area and does offer some insights into ways of thinking about ethical issues.

This chapter provides a brief excursion into the field of business ethics, not with the intention of providing any detailed analysis, but merely so that the reader might recognize the general approach and appreciate some of the issues raised.

The business ethics approach

The phrase 'business ethics movement' might seem to imply that there is some formal organization which gives those involved some overall coherence, but this is not the case. People in the movement come from various directions and may have somewhat different approaches to the basic agenda. This is seen most clearly when the various interest groups come together, for example, at a business ethics conference. On such occasions there are usually three quite distinct groups of delegates: the first group will comprise senior managers from business and commerce, some delivering papers concerned with issues in their own particular industry or confronting the role of industry in society at large; the second group will consist of academics, from a variety of disciplines, some already in the field of management studies, many from other areas such as philosophy, science and mathematics, even literature, drawn together by the rapidly growing interest in business ethics as a *new* academic field of endeavour; and the third group, surprisingly substantial in numbers, will come from various religious backgrounds, mainly from branches of the Christian churches, but also some from other cultures.

These three groups are not wholly separated; many individuals belong to more than one constituency. Moreover, many share the same broad aims though their detailed agendas may have been somewhat different in emphasis.

The religious community seek both to learn and to proselytize. Their underlying motivation for attending such a conference is presumably to increase their understanding of the ways in which the world of business functions, or malfunctions, so that their efforts to improve humanity's moral worth, and in particular the ethics of business operations, might be better informed and more effective, so that they might increase their beneficial impact on the world.

The academic community, though perhaps lacking the driving force of religious conviction, share many of these long-term objectives, but approach them by a fundamentally different route. For the academic, business ethics is a field of study whose day has come. In America, and increasingly now in Europe also, business ethics is a taught subject on both first and higher degree courses such as management science, business studies, business administration, etc. The ultimate aim, one might presume, is to work for the practical benefit of the world of business, though academic purists among business ethicists strenuously deny this, claiming that business ethics need have no relevance at all to the practice of ethics in business.

The agendas of these groups are implicit, if not covert. Many of the business delegates to such conferences are bemused by the plain clothes clerics and the academics. There is, of course, the inevitable language barrier between three such disparate groups, especially arising from the use of the language and vocabulary of philosophy. But beyond this, there is confusion as to motivations. The business people attend simply because they want to try to do something to improve the ethical standing of business in general, and their own organizations in particular, and so offset the bad press from the rest of the world when it comes to ethics and morality. Business scandals such as Guinness, Bophal, Maxwell, etc., do not mean that every business is run by dishonest, exploitative rogues. Most are convinced that their business success is necessarily based on a reputation for high ethical standards and they have a code of ethical practice by which they try to live and they may be interested to share this experience, learn from other parallel examples and help others learn from it too.

The business practitioners are sometimes puzzled, even dismayed, to find their concerns being hi-jacked by clerics and academics and turned into a subject which they do not understand and which seems to have little relation to practical business situations. Appealing to people to behave in a certain way because the creator of the universe wishes it so, is not helpful if most of the population do not believe in the existence of a superior being. Similarly, appeals to ethical behaviour on the often subtle and obscure grounds advanced by moral philosophers, may have only limited effect on managers who are largely unconcerned with philosophy.

The business ethics movement contains these three main separate strands which nevertheless are bound together (with the exception of the academic purists) on the fundamental issues:

- the ethical performance of business needs to be improved;

- this improvement is dependent on raising the ethical values of people in business; and

- this will only be achieved by a process of education.

Thus education is of prime importance to the business ethics movement. The teaching curriculum is unusually well endowed from an academic point of view. It is acquiring an accepted curriculum, the theoretical roots of which stretch back to the ancient Greeks and beyond, whereas most management subjects have a lineage that barely reaches back to the Second World War. Moreover, it is a subject which naturally lends itself to interesting and stimulating, participative, student-centred, learning methods.

Most business ethics courses (over 90 per cent according to a recent unpublished survey conducted by Huddersfield University) are heavily focused on the use of case studies. These are often quite short and typically centre on some topical, real-world, ethical dilemma relevant to people in business. Students may then be asked questions such as: 'Is it ethical?', 'What *should* be done?' and 'What would *you* do in the circumstances?'

These are questions that serve to sharpen up the student's perception of ethical issues and to identify their own values explicitly to see how they relate to the ethical performance of business in many different circumstances.

Typically, business ethics courses expose students to such dilemmas from the start. Initially, the students have only their own, possibly intuitive, values plus their own common sense and intelligence to bring to bear on analysing the cases. Most ethical issues used for this purpose are genuine dilemmas, not just black and white but more a quagmire into which the unwary and untutored rapidly sink. Thus, students quickly perceive the need for a more structured method of thinking and analysis. This is provided by introducing some training in moral philosophy to provide the analytical frameworks and conceptual tools required to make finely balanced ethical judgements. Thus, the student is better equipped to answer the questions 'Is it ethical?' and 'What should be done?'. Finally, after further exposure to philosophical ideas and experience of this form of dilemma and analysis, it is hoped that the students' own ethical standards and awareness are raised and so the cumulative experience finally impacts on their answers to the final question, 'What would you do in the circumstances?' It is a process which, according to feedback from students themselves, provides both enjoyment and a valued learning experience.

Impact of business ethics

The question arises as to how successful the movement has been. Clearly there is a problem in measuring success. The basic question to be addressed is 'Has business become more ethical?' Attributing this to the efforts of the business ethics movement may be more problematic, but just seeing whether business has become more ethical is the first question. The simple fact is, even accepting commonsense interpretations of 'ethical', that the answer is not known. There is no agreement as to what would be a suitable objective measure. Measuring the level of convictions for illegality would rather miss the point. Data on more searching measures of ethical performance are simply not available, though gut feel, based on media stories, etc., might suggest that the movement has not been overwhelmingly successful.

Some empirical work has sought to identify business practice in relation to business ethics. There have been a number of surveys of attitudes to ethics (e.g. Burke *et al.* , 1993; Adams *et al.* , 1991) and of codes of ethics (e.g. Webley, 1988, 1992), but so far there appears to be relatively little empirical evidence of the underlying management motivation and of management action taken to ensure that the espoused ethical standards and codes of practice are upheld and acted on, Burke and Hill (1990) being an exception in this latter regard, but their survey being concerned solely with environmental issues.

The problems with such research are that responses may be unusually difficult to interpret. As far as codes of practice are concerned, most research does not distinguish between (a) the organization that has a code and puts a lot of effort into making it effective, (b) the organization that has a code more or less as an item of window dressing, and (c) the organization that has a code as a deliberate part of the marketing image. Similarly, there are problems with interview surveys. Interviews with chief executives and senior managers are always susceptible to bias in the sense that the respondents may be prone to wishful thinking–'they would say that, wouldn't they!'

As yet there is no body of empirical qualitative evidence on the ethical performance of business, much less how it has changed over time or identifying the causes of the change. However, there are other measures of achievement. The business ethics movement has grown very significantly in the few short years of its existence. A number of specialist academic journals–seven in the English language to date–have been started, exclusively serving the field of business ethics, and there are now more than thirty textbooks in the field. More than twenty professorships and a growing number of substantial research centres have been established–at least sixteen in the US alone according to Dickson (1993b)–and significant research programmes commenced. There are now literally hundreds of degree and diploma courses which include business ethics as a core subject (more than 500 in the US alone) and hundreds more which offer it as an option at first and higher degree levels as well as postgraduate diplomas and most notably including almost all MBA courses. In short, the whole paraphernalia of building academic peer group reputations is now in place and the area is seen as a potentially fertile field for academics from a variety of different disciplines.

The religious community too has been highly active, taking a major role in forming and organizing leading European business ethics organizations, including the European Business Ethics Network (formed out of the European Foundation for Management Development), the International Society of Business, Economics and Ethics, the Society for Business Ethics, and the Institute of Business Ethics which was founded by the Christian Association of Business Executives and has leading religious figures as patrons, including the Archbishop of Canterbury, the Cardinal Archbishop of Westminster, the Chief Rabbi, the Imam of the London Central Mosque and others. Their motivation is clearly normative, to encourage business to exercise altruism and run itself according to the precepts of religious morality.

These are solid achievements and it would be surprising, and certainly disappointing, if all this activity did not have a significant impact on the way businesses are managed. At the same time, it is as well to recognize that although management education itself has expanded substantially this has not reduced the pressure on business schools to make their education and training more practical and relevant to business realities and rather less academic. Thus, the growth of the business ethics movement in education is no guarantee that the movement is being successful in achieving the changes it seeks. As far as that is concerned, the evidence is limited; however, we can look at the main thrusts of the business ethics argument and perhaps draw some conclusions about their worth as practical management tools.

Normative ethical theories

The forms of analysis used in business ethics are mainly those borrowed from moral philosophy. They are necessarily borrowed in somewhat abbreviated form—managers and management students are not expected to become philosophers of any substance on their way to achieving their master's degree. There are obviously problems in this abbreviation and the philosophical explanations offered on most management courses are clearly superficial and limited. To the philosopher these shortcomings may be crucial, but to the management practitioner they are not so important since philosophy itself does not provide definitive answers, only different ways of looking at questions.

The business ethics movement, because its main aim is to change peoples values, is largely concerned with the application of normative ethics. Its focus is, as far as possible, on practical issues. It is not concerned with descriptive ethics which avoids judging matters of right and wrong. Nor is it concerned with the field of meta-ethics, which is concerned with the analysis of the meanings of crucial ethical terms, such as 'right', 'obligation', 'virtue' and 'responsibility', the logic of moral reasoning and the nature of moral justification.

General normative ethical theories seek to formulate and to defend a system of fundamental moral principles and rules that determine which actions are right and which are wrong. Since the ancient Greeks, people have tried to define a set of ethical principles that would apply to all situations at all times. The *golden rule* (e.g. 'do unto others as you would have done unto you') is one such endeavour; Kant's categorical imperative (e.g. 'what if everyone did it?') is another. Not surprisingly there has not been a single principle or truth, but a variety of approaches and theories. Among this great variety there are certain broad streams that have been widely adopted in business ethics. One such, the consequentialist approach or utilitarianism, is concerned with the consequences of an action, while another broad approach, sometimes known as universalism, is concerned more with acting on principle or out of duty, i.e. the motivation underlying an action, rather than its consequences. These represent different perspectives that can be used to answer the question 'Is it ethical?'

Utilitarianism

Utilitarianism asserts that we ought always to do whatever has the best consequences. It was originally based on the idea that actions are right in proportion as they tend to promote happiness and wrong as they produce the reverse of happiness.

A more modern formulation holds than an action is right if it produces, or if it tends to produce, the greatest amount of good for the greatest number of people. Alternatively, we ought, in all circumstances, to produce the greatest possible balance of value over disvalue for all persons affected (or the least possible balance of disvalue if only bad results can be brought about).

These various formulations are simple enough concepts to understand at face value, but rather more difficult to apply in practice. The immediate problem is how to define 'pain' and 'pleasure', or 'good' or 'value' in meaningful terms. Whatever instrumental value some action may have, its ultimate justification must be that it contributes towards something that has *intrinsic* value, i.e. it is valuable for its own sake, such as providing health, happiness or freedom from pain.

Hedonistic utilitarianism claims that there is ultimately only one intrinsic value: that is, pleasure or happiness. Bentham defined happiness as intended pleasure and absence of pain:

> Nature has placed mankind under the governance of two sovereign masters, pain and pleasure. ... The principle of utility recognises this subjection and ... approves or disapproves of every action whatsoever according to the tendency which it appears to have to augment or diminish the happiness of the party whose interest is in question.
>
> (Bentham, 1789)

Mill also defines utilitarianism as

> the creed which accepts as the foundation of morals, Utility, or the Greatest Happiness Principle, (which) holds that actions are right in proportion as they tend to produce happiness, wrong as they tend to produce the reverse of happiness. By happiness is intended pleasure and the absence of pain; by unhappiness, pain, and the privation of pleasure.
>
> (Mill, 1861)

Although both Mill and Bentham regard happiness and pleasure as synonymous, Mill was at pains to point out that happiness does not just mean 'a continuity of highly pleasurable excitement', but rather happiness must be understood in the broader sense of satisfaction, or contentment or being rewarding. The primary objection to hedonistic utilitarianism is that it is by no means obvious that everything we do is simply to attain pleasure and to avoid pain.

Pluralistic utilitarianism replaces this monistic idea of intrinsic value with a range of possible goods which are thought to be good in themselves, such as friendship, knowledge, courage, health, and beauty. On this view moral rightness is to be assessed in terms of the total range of intrinsic values ultimately produced by an action. The difficulty of determining what has intrinsic value has, however, led to the use of the concept of preferences. On this view, what is intrinsically valuable is what individuals prefer to obtain, and utility is translated into the satisfaction of those needs and desires that individuals choose to satisfy.

A major problem with this approach is that some individuals' desires will be morally unacceptable and it is unclear whether these should be excluded from the calculation. Other preferences may be based on ignorance or false reasoning, or be affected by sour grapes or unrealistic expectations. Defenders argue that morally unacceptable preferences would be ruled out by their being inconsistent with other firmly established group preferences, while others argue that the correct principle should be based not on actual preferences of agents, but on their 'perfectly prudent preferences', i.e. what someone would desire if fully informed and unconfused. This then begins to look as if utilitarianism will not necessarily allow anyone to achieve his or her own desires, only those of some 'ideal observer' who does not actually exist.

Controversy has arisen over whether the principle of utility is applied to particular acts in particular circumstances or to *rules* of conduct that themselves determine which acts are right and wrong. *Act utilitarianism* asks, 'What good and evil consequences follow from this action in this circumstance?'; *rule utilitarianism* asks 'What consequences follow from this rule being generally obeyed?' Act utilitarianism regards such rules as 'tell the truth' as useful guidelines, for while they may offer a rule of thumb about what is most likely to produce the best consequences, they do not always predict what will actually bring about the general good and therefore can always be overridden in particular situations. Rule utilitarianism suggests that if the general rule of truth telling produces the greatest good, then that rule should be followed, even in circumstances when it would appear that the good is not maximized.

Act utilitarianism has been criticized for producing results which, intuitively, seem to be wrong. For example, it seems to condone breaking promises when someone can do so undetected, or acting unfairly when in so doing one maximizes benefits. Rule utilitarianism avoids these unfortunate consequences of act utilitarianism, but runs into problems of its own, for example, when exceptions to the rule are clearly justified. If we never allow exceptions then all our actions will be controlled by unchangeable, general laws, which would be inflexible and quite unable to respond to the exigencies of particular circumstances. On the other hand, if exceptions are allowed, then rule utilitarianism collapses back into act utilitarianism.

It is important to note that in utilitarianism no rule or action is ever absolutely wrong in itself. A rule's acceptability in the system of rules depends strictly on its consequences. Even rules against killing may be overturned in circumstances when permitting killing would maximize value. There is in principle no objection to any action until the consequences of that action have been assessed. This may be seen as an advantage, in that no appeal is made to a 'transcendental' source of moral right (such as a deity) or to an authoritative source (such as holy scriptures) and it seems to hold out the hope of a flexible policy based on empirical investigation of what will maximize welfare. But equally the possibility that anything might be justified in particular circumstances may seem abhorrent to those who think there are moral rights and wrongs which are unchanging and overriding.

Also, there is a difficulty in assessing concepts such as pleasure, pain, good and value. This is important in business since many, if not most, business decisions contain elements of both pain and pleasure. In order to assess whether an act is ethical it would be necessary to define both pain and pleasure and measure the amounts resulting from the act in question.

Only if the act produced a net increase in happiness it would be adjudged ethical.

These problems of definition and measurement are in practice very substantial and the approach by no means presents the non-philosopher manager with an answer that can be confidently applied to the real situation. Moreover, even if these problems did not arise, there may still be difficulties of simple justice. We might assume that all people are to be valued equally in measuring aggregate pleasure and pain, but what if an action produced a large increase in pleasure for a large number of people, but extreme and prolonged pain for a minority? How such injustice should be handled remains unclear.

These practical problems with utilitarianism will not apply to every act or decision. Some business actions may have no consequential downside. However, such decisions present no ethical dilemma and so the application of ethical theory would not arise in the first place. Where a dilemma does arise, it is surely useful to think through the consequences and try to assess some net effect, but that would be reducing utilitarianism to simple common sense and philosophy is not just common sense. Thus there is no alternative but to conclude that if utilitarianism is to be used at all it should be used rigorously, with all the detailed implications identified and the logical consequences understood. However, in the case of business, this only seems to provide solutions where no problems exist, but none where they are most needed.

Universalism

Universalism or deontology (from the Greek term referring to duties or obligations of individuals) is the other main strand of ethical theory applied to business. This approach is based on the idea that the moral worth of an action is dependent on the intentions of the person taking the action. Thus, duty is the foundation of morality and some acts are morally obligatory regardless of their consequences. Examples of the kinds of principles that are widely accepted include 'tell the truth, keep your promises, aim at the happiness of those around you'. These 'moral axioms' are ones that we can 'see' to be moral by a kind of 'intuition' or 'moral vision', though such vision may be culturally defined and does not apply equally at different times and in different places.

The claim that certain moral principles are self-evidently true is made in the opening words of the American Constitution:

> We hold these truths to be self-evident; that all men are created equal; that they are endowed by their Creator with certain inalienable rights; that among these are life, liberty and the pursuit of happiness.

Similarly, some modern theorists on human rights suggest the following as self-evident:

■ The right not to have one's health impaired or threatened by the careless manufacture or design of a product available for sale.

■ The right not to be sexually harassed by a fellow employee or boss.

■ The right not to have personal property invaded, undermined, damaged, or degraded by the activities of a company.

It is argued that where someone has such rights then this entails that others *ought* to respect the rights of the right-holder. So from a claim about what rights we possess is entailed a view about what actions we ought or ought not to perform. However, there is the problem of determining what our moral rights are. Moral philosophers have attempted to provide rational procedures for determining what is right. Kant, who was writing at the end of the eighteenth century, was a most important influence on deontological ethics. Kant's theory suggests that

1. The rightness of an action depends on the person acting for the right reasons, it does not depend on the consequences of the action.

2. Nothing is intrinsically good except a *good will*. Other things may also be good—like happiness, wealth, courage, etc., but these are not unconditionally good, because unless they are accompanied by the good will they can be worthless or even evil.

3. The good will shows itself in a sound disposition to do your moral duty—to do what is right because you want to do what is right, and for no other reason than that it is right. When agents act like this they do so out of *duty*, and this is the only moral way to act. It is not just a matter of acting in *accordance* with duty—one has to act out of duty.

4. If duty or obligation is to have absolute moral force it cannot be based on anything contingent, but must be absolute.

5. All human action is purposive and based on 'maxims'—that is, rules for what to do in set circumstances. Most maxims are hypothetical, but the moral law is *categorical*—that is, it applies in all circumstances, and is the principle upon which rational beings necessarily act.

Kant thus derived the categorical imperative, for which he provided several varying formulations:

Act only on that maxim through which you can at the same time will that it should become a universal law.

Act as if the maxim of your action were to become through your will a universal law of nature.

Act in such a way that you always treat humanity whether in your own person, or in the person of any other, never simply as a means, but always at the same time as an end.

Act only so as to be able to regard yourself as both a subject and a law-giver in a kingdom of ends.

These variations suggest that the key concepts of Kantian ethics are:

■ *Universality*—moral principles are general rules which apply universally. A modern version of this is Hare's idea that 'universalizability' is a necessary characteristic of morals, i.e. we can only treat as moral those principles which we are prepared to 'universalize'.

■ *Impartiality*—moral principles apply impartially to all moral agents. All persons deserve equal respect and consideration.

■ *Rationality*—we decide what is right by the prior application of reason. This gives us absolute and objective rules to follow.

■ *Autonomy*—the goal of ethics is to recognize and maximize each person's freedom.

This is a clear and unambiguous statement, but not one that is comfortable to live with. Wrongs, such as lying or murder, are not merely negatives that enter into a calculation of net good and might be outweighed by the concurrent good that might be done or bad that might be avoided. They are absolutely, unequivocally and universally wrong and must not be done in any circumstances. The apparent simplicity and unambiguity may, however, in some cases be an illusion. Murder is clearly always and absolutely wrong and as a consequence British law accords the murderer a mandatory life sentence. However, there are murders and murders. Consequently, there are life sentences and life sentences ranging from a few weeks to a whole lifetime.

Universalism has been closely associated with the 'laws' of religion. Thus, for a Christian as for many others, the 10 commandments are regarded as fundamental statements of right and wrong. In any circumstances, breaking any of the commandments would be wrong.

This simplicity and lack of ambiguity has always been a source of great difficulty. An early statement of the position on lying was made by St Augustine:

It is evident that speech was given to man, not that men might therewith deceive one another, but that one man might make known his thoughts to another. To use speech then for the purpose of deception, and not for its appointed end, is a sin. Nor are we to suppose that there is any lie that is not a sin, because it is sometimes possible, by telling a lie, to do service to another. (St Augustine: *The Enchiridion*)

Even before Augustine the absolute wrong of lying had been difficult to live with. Ways round it had been widely practised. Augustine himself allowed of different categories of lie: they were all sins but some were more sinful than others. Others had practised equivocation—the use of ambiguity in order to induce a belief in something in another sense from that in which it was understood by the equivocator. Mental reservation was the practice of saying, for example, that one did not do such a thing (though one did) but adding silently that one did not do it on a particular day. These primitive, to our minds simply childish, methods of deceit without telling lies, just indicate the problems with deontology. It was not easy to live with in the Middle Ages, and it is no easier in a modern business.

Kant's assertion is even more absolute than St Augustine's.

Truthfulness in statements which cannot be avoided, is the formal duty of an individual to everyone, however great may be the disadvantage accruing to himself or to another.

Moreover, Kant does not allow of any different categories of lie: they were all equally wrong. The customary argument against such an absolutist position, specifically considered by Kant himself, is when a known murderer enquires whether 'our friend is in the house?'. Should you lie to save a friend's life, or should you tell the truth? Kant was consistent and said you should tell the truth, though simple common sense suggests otherwise.

The universalist approach can thus clearly lead to behaviour which, under utilitarian analysis, would seem to be obviously wrong. Similarly acts that lack any ethical motivation but have a good utilitarian consequence might by this approach be regarded as unethical. There are many examples of such incompatibilities, especially those deriving from religious philosophies. For example, traditional Catholics who follow the teachings of the Church as currently promulgated, might believe that the production and open sale of contraceptives is universally unethical, whereas, the utilitarian view of the consequences for the world's population might be regarded as highly ethical.

Universalism cannot be interpreted at a commonsense level. It does not advocate general norms of behaviour such as 'whenever possible be honest with your stakeholders'. It is precise and absolute. If it is interpreted at a commonsense level then it reduces to something which in business decisions either is not relevant, or in those particular difficult decisions where some philosophical guidance would be most useful, it retreats into an ivory tower purity which is impervious to attempts to extract any intelligent utility.

Application to business

Looking at ethical dilemmas from the dual perspectives of universalism and utilitarianism sheds light on the question 'Is it ethical?' and such consideration may help towards an informed view of 'What should be done?' However, there are problems in applying either approach and little guidance as to how to respond when the two produce conflicting interpretations. Moreover, the more thoroughly these philosophical approaches are applied, the greater appear to be the difficulties.

Because the aim of ethicists is to 'raise' the ethical values of individuals in business, they are necessarily concerned with the morality of individuals and, in some situations, morality apparently conflicts directly with business. For example, all ethicists attribute value to altruism, i.e. the notion that an individual should do good because it is right or because it has consequences that benefit others, not because the individual will derive any benefit. In itself this is unexceptionable, but it is the departure point for the academic purist which quickly leads to conflict with the simple, basic tenets of business itself. This has been expressed simply as follows:

> To be ethical as a business because it may increase your profits is to do so for entirely the wrong reason. The ethical business must be ethical because it wants to be ethical.   (Anon. quote in Stark, 1993)

Philosophically it is quite clear and understandable, and a great many people in business do in fact behave altruistically with considerable frequency. There is no reason to suppose that business people behave any less altruistically than philosophers: when one thinks of the names of the world's benefactors, far more business people than philosophers spring to mind. Nevertheless, this suggestion that an act is only ethical if it is done for purely altruistic reasons is where the academic purists cease to claim any relevance to business practice. People in business have to make profits if their organizations are to survive. When altruism and profits clash, it is not particularly helpful to practitioners to simply admonish them to be altruistic. Yet this is where moral philosophy leads.

The position has been succinctly demonstrated by Stark (1993). The ethicists' approach implied by the various statements quoted below leads inexorably 'to the untenable conclusion that managers cannot be genuinely ethical unless what they do in no way serves their own interests', i.e. as Stark put it: 'ethics has to hurt'. The various items quoted below all emanate from academic business ethicists. Stark quotes them to highlight the problem, as he sees it, of the increasing uselessness of the orthodox business ethics approach. The main points are paraphrased below:

- Managers should try to ensure that their organizations are places in which employees can be fully free to express themselves as unrestrained human beings, liberated and achieving. Managers should not be directive or repressive, managing their organizations as places of oppression and denial.

- The first obligation of every manager is to provide meaningful work for the employees in the organization.

- If being ethical means cutting into a company's profits then managers should unhesitatingly cut profits, and have no regrets about it.

- Even if it means the company closing down as a result, managers must still do only what is ethical.

- The only way an organization can be ethical is by being wholly altruistic, i.e. with no self-interest. The presence of any element of self-interest automatically and inevitably eliminates the possibility of the action or decision being ethical.

- No organization can be truly ethical unless it has eliminated all forms of external motivation for its employees. (NB: by 'external motivation' is meant such orthodox management practices as the exercise of authority or power, the use of incentives or professional modes of leadership.) These practices are simply sophisticated forms of coercion and are therefore morally wrong. If organizations cannot be run without resort to these practices then it would be preferable that the organizations did not exist.

- Similarly when 'ethical' behaviour is encouraged by 'external stimuli', e.g. by senior managers providing a model of proper behaviour or provide others with incentives to behave ethically, then the behaviour isn't really ethical.

- Capitalism itself is ethically unjustifiable. Socialism may be ethically preferable.

These statements lead a long way from the world inhabited by business people and are not helpful to those practitioners concerned, for whatever reason, with trying to help their organizations to run on ethical bases.

This is a major difficulty with the application of philosophy to business. Philosophy is about giant intellects grappling with unworldly issues; where things that might appear irrelevant to lesser mortals are accorded huge significance and where what may be commonly regarded as important might be dismissed as utterly trivial. Philosophy seeks to address the truly great questions. It contributes to man's progress in many different fields and underpins pure research of almost every kind. The problem is not with philosophy as such, but whether it is appropriate to this particular project.

Conclusion

The business ethics project seeks to *raise* the ethical values and behaviour of people in business. It is not content simply to enlighten and suggest feasible solutions, but seeks also to indoctrinate. Whether ethicists are justified in trying to change the moral values of managers is an interesting question—a moral dilemma in its own right. For ministers of religion this is explicitly their main task, but for management theorists the position is much less satisfactory.

Justified or not, these efforts appear doomed to failure, despite the considerable success in building a strong academic position. The contribution of moral philosophy to ethics in modern business, currently so much emphasized, may in due course come to be regarded as merely a transitional position while the real project was getting established.

Business ethics is unlikely to cut much ice with practising managers when its leading proponents express the views quoted in 'Application to business' above. Moreover, managers may not have the time or the inclination to go into the philosophical issues in sufficient depth to gain much benefit, if benefit were available. Even this last point is unclear—it seems the more mature the philosopher, the more modest his or her claims for philosophy.

The main benefit apparently on offer from orthodox business ethics is the capacity to assess whether an act is ethical or not. But this is not management's main problem. The business ethics movement asks the wrong questions. It is not so much whether or not an act is ethical, but whether or not business should be ethical, and if so to what degree and how can management achieve the required performance?

These are the questions that are crucial to organizational integrity and are the concern of the remainder of this book.

Organizational integrity

Businesses necessarily put business success before altruism. Nevertheless, business practitioners clearly recognize that being ethical is an essential ingredient of business success. Some businesses (e.g. Start-rite) are based on a happy coincidence of altruism and profit seeking, but for most firms, enlightened self-interest is a more generalized concept.

To make the concept more specific, interest is focused on the organization's interactions with its various internal and external stakeholders, where these interactions form part of an ongoing relationship, rather than simple once-only transactions. A simple example of this mutual interdependence is provided which shows how it is necessary to be seen as trustworthy, i.e. as having integrity, before being invited into these mutually advantageous relationships.

Ongoing relationships in the form of collaborations and alliances of various forms, networks and teams are increasingly crucial to the success of the (post) modern organization. Successful business is no longer the monolithic structure seeking to maximize profits from each transaction, but a series of partnerships so arranged as to benefit all parties over the long term.

The concept of integrity is identified as being one of degree and different levels of integrity are defined using Kohlberg's approach to individual moral development. Whereas business ethicists seek to raise the level of moral development of individuals in business, the integrity model seeks to understand perceptions of integrity, from the perspective of people in business.

This chapter outlines the main features of the organizational integrity model of enlightened self-interest, which is an alternative to the orthodox business ethics approach.

Introduction

The previous chapter examined some of the issues raised by business ethicists and concluded that their orthodox approach was failing as a practical project related to ethics in business. This chapter proposes an alternative approach based more on enlightened self-interest than on philosophical considerations.

The following section examines why ethical performance is important to organizations and in particular to businesses. Subsequent sections outline the organizational integrity model which is intended to help managers define and implement standards of behaviour that are appropriate for their organizations. The model is based on four main foundations:

1. Appreciation of organization as a set of partnerships

2. Requirement for integrity between partners

3. Definition of different levels of integrity

4. Identification of critical aspects of an organization's particular circumstances.

A deliberately value-free perspective is taken in defining this model, avoiding as far as possible the use of any extraneous value system. The main features of the model are therefore derived, as far as possible, from the business predicament itself.

The importance of ethical standards

Business, particularly big business, is often not credited with the possibility of altruism. When evidence of the profit motive is revealed the media greet it gleefully as evidence of the degenerative nature of business.

'Firms reveal they put profits before ethics,' was one headline response to a Co-operative Bank sponsored survey entitled 'How Ethical is British Business?'.

> The new values of the caring 1990s have largely failed to penetrate the UK boardroom, which still believes firmly in the greed-driven motives of the past, according to the first extensive survey of business ethics to be conducted in Britain.
>
> Researchers found that businessmen showed little desire to serve the community, and although they displayed a high degree of ethical awareness, many would jettison their principles if they affected their company's profitability.
>
> ... the survey found only minority support for helping the poor ... 39% said helping the poor was not a matter for their company ... while 90% said business should pay for causing environmental damage, only 7% would insist on their company having a recycling policy. ...
>
> (Hotten, 1993)

The survey apparently caused surprise that business people had still taken on board so little of the business ethics message and remained solidly 'greed-driven'—a journalistic phrase, but it reveals how the business community is regarded in some quarters.

More mature reflection might give some comfort that only a minority regarded helping the poor as a matter for their company. Helping the poor might be regarded as no more the concern of business than competing with the Japanese is a concern of the Church. Clearly if businesses pay too much attention to helping the poor, to recycling policies, and the whole paraphernalia of 'social responsibility' they risk losing their competitive way and may well end up being unable to fulfil clear responsibilities even to their immediate stakeholders.

But this does not mean that business cannot be run in a way that combines both making profits and benefiting mankind. There is a lot of common interest in being ethical in business and being profitable. Many businesses focus specifically on ethical aspects for both business and altruistic reasons. They would cheerfully ignore the moral philosopher who asserted that such a coincidence is impossible because the element of benefit to oneself makes the action necessarily unethical. The coincidence of altruism and self-interest would be better regarded as an ideal rather than impossible. The chairman of Start-rite, children's shoe manufacturer, was asked which came first in his business: profit or concern for children's foot care?

> *Neither. They work simultaneously. We're a business. We're unasham-edly out to make a profit **and** we're very concerned about the health of children's feet and posture. We run the business on both concerns.*
>
> (Nash 1990, p. 152)

The perception that Start-rite care about the health of children's feet is no doubt an important consideration both in their market success and as a value which affects the behaviour of those working in the business. This combination of profit seeking with an element of altruism might be regarded as a form of enlightened self-interest. It can clearly be successful as the 'Winning Streak' studies of successful British businesses confirmed:

> *One of the surprises in our interviews at chief executive level and below was the passion with which our successful companies embraced integrity as an essential part of their culture. This clearly was not window dressing. Each company was convinced that without absolute integrity the business simply could not operate.*
>
> (Goldsmith and Clutterbuck, 1985, p. 123)

A 1994 survey among 100 leading UK companies (see Appendix I) also confirmed this concern among practitioners for the achievement of high ethical standards. Many of these leading firms devote a great deal of effort to the achievement of certain levels of ethical performance. Their initiatives are considered in greater detail later, but the measured tones of Sir Richard Greenbury, chairman of Marks & Spencer, represent the views of many leading organizations:

> a large number of companies, of whom I would like to think we are one, do their best to run their businesses efficiently, profitably and successfully on behalf of shareholders, customers and employees alike. ... we would never put short term shareholder interests before the long term interests of customers and employees. Furthermore on the way to achieving these objectives there is clearly a right way of doing things through high standards and integrity, that fosters a culture within the business which believes that success and profitable growth are only worthwhile if achieved within the aforementioned parameters. Although we in Marks & Spencer are by no means perfect and make many mistakes, we are always doing our best to run the business in a responsible manner.
>
> (Greenbury, 1994)

Sir Denis Henderson, chairman of ICI, makes the same point rather more tersely,

> ICI takes the question of integrity in business extremely seriously. ...
>
> (Henderson, 1994)

Enlightened self-interest

The Start-rite example quoted above is a happy marriage of self-interest and altruism which is the key to the long-term success of that particular firm. But not many businesses are so based. Marks & Spencer and ICI, for example, though sharing Start-rite's concern for ethical standards, do not to the same extent enjoy their happy coincidence of interests. For such organizations a more generally applicable model is required.

A general model must focus on two issues. First, ethical content is only of significance in the organization's actual behaviour. The notion that a business might sin in thought is not very useful; what matters is what the business actually does and how it actually affects the other parties to its transaction. Jimmy Carter's admission that he committed adultery in his mind is not a concept that can be transferred to the business situation. Business people might consider whether or not to carry out an unethical transaction, but what matters is what the business actually does as a result. Considering unethical behaviour is only to be deprecated inasmuch as it increases the probability of unethical action.

Second, ethical content is only significant in the organization's transactions with its various stakeholders. Where there is no transaction, there is no content for any ethical judgement. If no transaction has taken place there can be no consequences. This generally applicable model of enlightened self-interest must therefore focus on the various transactions of the business.

These transactions have been modelled in various ways, notably by using games theory. This might be a particularly pertinent way of looking at transactions between partners because the rules of behaviour so derived are not based on any extraneous value system. A widely quoted examination of this approach was carried out by Robert Axelrod (1984).

Axelrod begins his analysis using the prisoners' dilemma model. In this situation, two prisoners are correctly accused of a crime and the jailers so arrange the pay-offs to encourage each prisoner to confess. If neither prisoner confesses, both are given fairly short jail sentences of, say, one year. If one prisoner confesses while the other remains silent, the first goes free while the other receives a long sentence of, say, ten years. If both prisoners confess, both get a heavy sentence, but with time off for good behaviour—say, five years. Neither prisoner knows what the other is going to do.

Clearly, each player does better by confessing than by remaining silent. If one confesses and the other doesn't, the first is freed immediately. If both confess, they each get five years instead of ten. So the question is, why would either remain silent? How is it, when the two are unable to communicate and collude, that cooperation could ever get started?

The answer lies in repeated play. Prior to Axelrod, it had been noted that the tendency to cooperate in prisoners' dilemma games increased dramatically whenever a player was paired repeatedly with the same partner. In this situation a tit-for-tat strategy emerged: cooperate on the first move, then follow suit on all subsequent moves; cooperate when your partner cooperates, defect if he or she defects, at least until the end of the game is in sight.

The tit-for-tat strategy is one of cooperation in the first period and from then on mimics the rival's action from the previous period. In effect it is a game theory expression of the Old Testament injunction 'an eye for an eye, a tooth for a tooth', or do unto others as they have done onto you.

> Tit-for-tat embodies four principles that should be evident in any effective strategy: clarity, niceness, provocability, and forgivingness. Tit-for-tat is as clear and simple as you can get. It is nice in that it never initiates cheating. It is provocable, that is, it never lets cheating go unpunished. And it is forgiving, because it does not hold a grudge for too long and is willing to restore co-operation.
>
> (Dixit and Nalebuff, 1991, pp. 106-7)

Axelrod showed that players adopting the tit-for-tat strategy would seek each other out and go on to accumulate higher scores than other players who adopted more short-term strategies of defection. This conclusion was repeated again and again both in computer tournament results and from computer simulations as well as being paralleled in biological systems.

Axelrod's model is widely applicable. Businesses really do cooperate in many different ways with all the different agencies with which they transact. For example, they extend each other reciprocal credit as long as their business relationship is expected to continue. However, if liquidation of one of the parties looms, then cooperation will be terminated no matter how long the history of previous cooperation. The assumed continuity of the relationship is crucial to its viability.

There are several theoretical objections that can be raised against this game theoretical approach. Rather than getting side-tracked into a turgid academic discussion, a simple alternative is proposed. This model, expounded by Gauthier (1991), no doubt also has problems, but it also has the great benefit of simplicity and simple outcomes, while at the same time retaining most of the essential characteristics.

The model involves individuals interacting with each other, each having their own 'schedule of preferences or values that relate to the various possible outcomes that can be brought about by their actions'. Importantly, for the present purpose, they do not need to subscribe to any particular view of morality, whether religious or philosophical—in fact, it is assumed that different persons will have different values and different preferences. It is also implicitly assumed at the outset that persons involved in the transactions take an egocentric, utterly self-interested point of view. The model assumes that we live in circumstances of variable scarcity and adopts the idea of society being a cooperative venture for mutual advantage. The cooperative aspect is particularly pertinent to contemporary business organizations as is highlighted later in this chapter.

Gauthier's simple example involves two neighbouring farmers, one with a crop ready for harvesting immediately and one shortly. If they work alone to harvest their crops it will take 20 hours each; if they work together on each other's crops it will take 25 per cent less time.

Cooperation would clearly be of mutual advantage. However, when the first farmer's crops are harvested, he would then have no incentive to help his neighbour. This assumes he would be acting rationally as a short-term profit maximiser with no particular view of morality. However, if the transaction was part of an ongoing relationship, the situation would obviously be different. If the farmers were to be in the same position the following year, then long-term profit maximizing would require cooperation. The difference in timescale, implied by whether or not the transaction was a one-off or part of a stream of such transactions, makes the crucial difference.

If the first farmer was going to retire before next year's harvest he would have no incentive to cooperate beyond his own harvest. However, if the second farmer knew of the impending retirement he would have no reason to cooperate in the first place. In these circumstances a contract would be required to which both farmers would adhere. A legal contract might be impractical and expensive, but an informal agreement to which both farmers were committed with each knowing the other was also committed, i.e. on a basis of trust, would work very well.

However, unless each person in the transaction of mutual advantage believed the other person in the transaction had internalized the principle of trust, neither would enter into the transaction with the other person. Thus, people who are not believed to have internalized the principle of trust would be excluded from transactions of mutual advantage. As Gauthier suggests,

> we understand the role of ethical principles as principles which constrain what would otherwise be the rational pattern of decision making in ways that enable persons to reach mutually advantageous outcomes, overcoming the temptation to 'free-ride' when such behaviour would on the face of it prove profitable to the individual concerned.
> (Gauthier, 1991, p. 60)

The idea of exclusion from transactions of mutual advantage if the principle of trust were absent is both powerful and increasingly applicable in today's international or globalized and increasingly technological business world.

Gauthier's model has clear similarities with the games theory model, many examples of which were examined by Dixit and Nalebuff who emphasize the importance of the ongoing relationship:

> There is no solution that achieves reciprocal co-operation in a one-time game. Only in an ongoing relationship is there an ability to punish, and thus a stick to motivate, co-operation. A collapse of co-operation carries an automatic cost in the form of a loss of future profits. If this cost is large enough, cheating will be deterred and co-operation sustained.
> (Dixit and Nalebuff, 1991, p. 100)

There are some exceptions to this general rule; for example, if the ongoing relationship has some natural end, such as when one of Gauthier's farmers retires. Cooperation then breaks down in the final transaction. Since both parties can predict breakdown in the final transaction, they will not be prepared to cooperate in the penultimate transaction. Logically, it would be expected, therefore, that ongoing relationships that have some natural termination would not be conducted on the basis of cooperation in the first place. As Dixit and Nalebuff point out, the real world is characterized by episodes of successful cooperation. This could be explained by the existence of some 'nice' people who will cooperate despite the apparent material advantages of cheating. 'Nice' people are those who have internalized the principle of trust, but as Dixit and Nalebuff point out (not to mention Groucho Marx) credibility of 'niceness' is crucial. Without credibility, trust will not be perceived and cooperative transactions will not be entered into.

> *Establishing credibility in the strategic sense means that you are expected to carry out your unconditional moves, keep your promises and make good on your threats. ... Credibility must be earned.*
>
> (Dixit and Nalebuff, 1991, p. 143)

These models suggest that, in a strategic time frame (i.e. in an ongoing relationship), the internalization of the principle of trust leads to engagement in cooperative transactions (from which otherwise the actor would be excluded) of mutual advantage and thereby, it is suggested, to an increase in long-term profitability above the level that would be achieved by short-run profit-maximizing behaviour.

The old City motto 'my word is my bond' was based on nothing more than this. Rees-Mogg (1987) bemoaned the demise of 'old City standards':

> *There is no incentive to good conduct stronger than stability. If you have been doing profitable business with the same man for 25 years and hope to do it for another 25; if your house has done business with his house for 150 years and hopes to do it for another 150, there is no smart short term gain which can possibly be worth the long term loss to the relationship.*

Concern for ongoing relationships between autonomous units is particularly relevant to contemporary business which is increasingly based on technological collaborations and other strategic alliances among networks of specialist organizations. Moreover, this focus on ongoing relationships is also highly pertinent to the fast-moving deconstructed team-based organizational forms which, with the help of computers and information technology, are now replacing the hierarchies and mechanistic monoliths of the past. The next two sections examine these contemporary external and internal developments which seem to further emphasize the importance of the principle of trust.

Collaborations and alliances

The twin thrusts of rapid technological development and the globalization of markets are together threatening the viability of the isolated, autonomous business unit. Firms are having to form collaborations and alliances with other units in order to remain competitive. The basic motivation for collaborating with other businesses is to 'gain additional access to new competencies, to markets, to technology or to specific resources in order to sustain its competitive advantage' (Lorange *et al.*, 1992) which sets the business apart and makes it distinctive in some way.

The current rapid rate of technological development and its equally rapid rate of adoption across the globe make it essential that all businesses, large and small, take a global view. Even a localized business, with no global pretensions, must take full account of global developments in markets and technologies potentially relevant to its products and customers. This global awareness is essential to the maintenance of technological position (Clark, 1989).

No longer can firms ignore technological change, wherever it occurs, because its diffusion is comprehensive and affects all industry and society. Neither is it any longer feasible for an individual firm to remain at the forefront of all the technological developments impacting a particular sector. The technologies are diverse, but their impact is general. Thus there is an urgent need to collaborate with other organizations in order to maintain and extend the firm's own distinctive competence.

The ever-increasing scale of investment required by advancing technology means that there must be a rapid exploitation of that technology in order for it to be profitably exploited. The required speed of exploitation means that the fruits of technology must be sold to ever larger markets, and ultimately to the whole world. The assiduous pursuit of a global market results inevitably in convergence of consumer tastes (Ohmae, 1989): and changes in the global environment arise directly from global technology development (Miller, 1990). Just a few decades ago, the cultural differences between, say, Japan and Britain, meant that it would be difficult to envisage the same consumer product succeeding equally in both markets. Now, tastes for many technically advanced consumer durables clearly coincide and the same product can be marketed in London and in Tokyo with only superficial differences.

The globalization process appears irrevocable, the globalization of technology both facilitating and requiring globalization of markets at an ever-increasing rate. Thus firms are tending to become ever more expert in ever more tightly defined technologies. In order to maintain this rapidly developing expertise, they need to focus all their efforts on the core technologies. They therefore find it both necessary and profitable to buy in those technologies which they have not defined as core to their own business. The notion of focusing on core competences, and outsourcing all others, has developed as one of the strategic orthodoxies for the 1990s, essential to survival in this era of rapid innovation. The approach is based on simple principles:

> *Focus on those components that are critical to the product and that the company is distinctively good at making.*
>
> *Outsource components where suppliers have a distinct comparative advantage—greater scale, fundamentally lower cost structure, or stronger performance incentives.* (Venkatesan, 1992)

The original theory behind this approach can be traced back to orthodox economic theory of international trade, used by Porter in his approach to international business (Porter, 1990). Moreover, it is the basis also of Drucker's assertion that concentration is the key to economic results (Drucker, 1964). Unless there is the determination to outsource non-core components or technology there will be little chance of concentrating effectively on the core and achieving leading edge competence. Reliance on external organizations for non-core, though nevertheless essential, elements in the business process results in the establishment of various forms of strategic alliance.

Evidence of these global alliances is not restricted to the professional/ academic literature. Hitachi took full-page advertisements in the *Financial Times* to explain their approach under the title: 'Localising the Multinational: Globalisation Holds the Key.'

> In our efforts to source more components and raw materials outside of Japan, Hitachi recently established an 'Asia Procurement Programme Centre' whose task is to locate suppliers of parts in countries such as Singapore and Hong Kong that can provide our manufacturing operations–both inside and outside Japan–with components ... earlier this year we reached an (OEM) agreement with IBM to market three types of personal computers in Japan ... we are also supplying mainframe computers to Germany's Compalex and Italy's Olivetti on an OEM basis and have licensed our 1-megabit and 4-megabit DRAM technology to Goldstar Electron of Korea. ... Hitachi has established seven overseas R&D bases including Dublin, Düsseldorf and Milan ... development of a single electron memory device (in the order of 64Gb) which we developed jointly with Cambridge University ... working with Hewlett Packard (UK) to develop an artificial intelligence software program ... working with Trinity College, Dublin, we have developed an artificial retina.
>
> (Hitachi, 1993)

Hitachi is an archetype of the modern multinational. Collaborations are not restricted to friendly supplier–customer relationships or the essentially unthreatening industry–academe transactions. Fierce competitors are increasingly forced to collaborate for their future survival and prosperity. Hamel and Prahalad (1989) documented the ways in which Canon acquired technology from Xerox while establishing itself in photocopiers and how Komatsu acquired, and improved on, the technology of its main competitor Caterpillar. Both of these were examples of collaborations motivated by the need to learn–to acquire key technological competence. This is perhaps the most powerful motivation of all, particularly among Japanese collaborative partners. Such alliances can be both offensive and defensive in their ultimate aim.

Lei (1993) reviews several multinational-based strategic alliance systems. Eight American firms in the semiconductor industry having 25 such alliances with mainly Pacific Rim firms to achieve a variety of aims. Lei's examination of AT&T reveals alliances with 17 autonomous, mainly foreign, firms some aimed at learning new core technologies, some at penetrating new markets, some at a combination of both. A similar examination of IBM's alliance strategy revealed no less than 40 such strategic alliances.

It is worth re-emphasizing that these are all genuinely strategic alliances, not simple one-off transactions. They are planned to last for a considerable time and in many cases may be regarded as indefinitely 'ongoing'. As such they all meet Gauthier's essential criterion. All parties to these strategic alliances must necessarily therefore be able to demonstrate that they have internalized the principle of trust, otherwise they would have been excluded from such mutually advantageous collaborations, left only to participate in those where the gains were strictly short term.

New and ever more surprising collaborations are continually being reported. Renault, Saab and Fiat, fierce competitors in the European executive car market, joined forces to develop and tool a new car body. Kodak and Xerox, erstwhile sworn enemies in photocopying technology, agreed to pool resources and work together on new products. Ford and Volkswagen, world competitors in people carrying, united to produce a new generation 'people carrier to beat Renault's Espace'. The list of such strategic alliances is surprisingly long and is growing with great speed. British Aerospace, Aerospaciale of France and Deutsche Aerospace, part of Daimler Benz, have come together to form the European Supersonic Research Programme with the aim of developing technology to offer potential American and Japanese partners in the project the opportunity to develop a successor to Concorde (itself the product of such a technological alliance). Amersham International, Hitachi and Molecular Dynamics of California formed an alliance to exploit the growing demand for instruments with which to 'sequence' or analyse genes—all three companies already having products and expertise in the market.

A contrast between the traditional, vertically integrated monolithic organization and the newer more fragmented organization of alliances and collaborations can be seen in the aggregate 1989 comparison of Toyota and GM shown in Table 3.1.

Just as globalization impacts all businesses, great and small, so does the need to establish long-lasting alliances. It is advantageous for the major multinational firms to collaborate, but it is crucial for the minnows to do likewise and forge relationships that help them leverage up their meagre resources. Only in this way can they hope to maintain any shred of even localized leadership in their core technologies.

Globalization and rapid technological change are the dual pressures forcing firms to establish long-lasting relationships in order to achieve two objectives. The first is to concentrate all their resources, efforts and

Table 3.1 Outsourcing and insourcing at Toyota and General Motors (*Source*: Womack *et al.*, 1990)

Measure	Partner system (Toyota)	Mass production system (GM)
Volume	4 000 000	8 000 000
Number of employees	37 000	850 000
Volume/employee	108	9
Costs incurred 'in house' (%)	27	70
Bought in components/ services (%)	73	30
No. of employees in purchasing function	337	6 000

enthusiasm on their core competences. Only by such concentration will they achieve leadership and superior economic results. This is done by deliberately buying-in the non-core competences—in practice, one of the most difficult of strategic decisions to implement. The second is to replicate the speed and flexibility of small organizations so that they can be innovative and ensure that their leadership positions are maintained despite a rapidly changing environment. This is done by managing through networks and teams rather than through hierarchies and functions.

Networks and teams

The deconstruction of the old machine-like bureaucracies and the creation of new team-based, fragmented forms of organization is currently a fashionable area for consultants and academics alike.

> For more than a decade, pundit after pundit, from Tom Peters to Harvard economist Michael Jensen, has sounded the death knell for large companies. The real world has appeared to bear them out: action by governments, shareholders and managements themselves has broken up all sorts of established dynasties, both sensible but unwieldy business monoliths such as AT&T and illogical conglomerates such as ITT. Other big companies have reacted by stripping themselves 'back to basics': concentrating on their core businesses, and divesting or 'outsourcing' the remainder. A fashion has even developed for voluntary demerger.
>   In the marketplace, lumbering giants, from IBM, Sears Roebuck and General Motors to the American TV networks, have been overtaken by

more sprightly upstarts–Microsoft, WalMart, Toyota, CNN–and been attacked by hordes of smaller innovators.

Small is now beautiful it seems–at least until, like Microsoft, you become big enough to join the ranks of the bad and ugly. In his new book, Global Paradox, John Naisbitt, the futurologist who made his name with Megatrends, declares that 'the bigger the world economy, the more powerful its smallest players'. He claims that 'we have moved ... from bigger is better to bigger is inefficient, costly, wastefully bureaucratic, inflexible and, now, disastrous'.   (Lorenz, 1994)

This is the orthodox wisdom and Lorenz highlights its dangers. Being big is not all bad news–there are benefits as well as costs. Being big does not necessarily mean being inefficient. ABB, Hewlett-Packard and 3M, for example, are all big in their chosen markets but exceedingly lean in the way they are managed. The same applies to a growing number of large multinationals which, stripped back to their core businesses and focusing on their key technologies, are managed increasingly like a collection of small businesses–but with the difference that they also share various degrees of management skills, research, design, development and purchasing, as well as aspects of distribution and service. Bigness can certainly bring benefits.

The key to achieving these benefits is to exercise the optimum degree of coordination and integration: too little and the benefits do not accrue; too much and all the dysfunctions of large-scale bureaucracy will be experienced. Management of this balance, always a key issue in the study of management, is currently the focus of much debate among practitioners and academics.

The study of management was originally very much concerned with large-scale organizations, employing large numbers of semi-skilled and unskilled labour. This was the focus of classical management, principles of which were defined by Henri Fayol whose practical experience had been gained heading up the French mining industry at the end of the last century. Taylor added 'scientific' methods to management, based on his study of work, and in no small way facilitated the establishment of mass production methods first achieved by Ford and on which much of the world's industrial wealth has been based. These huge organizations, employing masses of labour performing standardized tasks to produce standardized products, were the dominant industrial form of organization through this century.

The change, as mass labour was progressively replaced by machines and as the old 'smoke stack' industries were replaced by new knowledge-based industries, was examined by Burns and Stalker (1961) who described two organizational categories: mechanistic and organismic. Their contribution is worth a brief examination here since their categories lie at the bottom of much of the current debate about contemporary organizational forms.

Burns and Stalker studied the attempts to implant the fledgling electronics industry in parts of Scotland which had only previously experienced the old heavy industries of coal, steel and shipbuilding. The job of management in these older industries was broken down into specialist functions, each with its precisely defined task. There was a clear hierarchy of control, with the reins firmly held at the top. Communications flowed down the line and occasionally back up, but rarely across the organization. There was an emphasis on loyalty to the company and obedience to one's superior. The result of this bureaucratic system was that individuals in the organization were not committed to its fundamental business aims, only to obeying the rules and fulfilling their (strictly limited) employment contract and enjoying whatever perks such a regime might offer. Burns and Stalker found the system ill-suited to handling change and innovation and labelled it 'mechanistic'.

Croome described mechanistic organizations as demanding that everyone shall have one job, clearly defined and delimited, with responsibility running up to a recognized limit and stopping there. The employee was not isolated, but was part of the organizational machine. In so far as 'he' had to think at all about 'his' relations with other parts of the machine, 'he' saw them as outside 'his' job. They were necessary to the job only as tools are necessary.

> For some data needs he can appeal to the slide rule, for others he may appeal to another individual; some tasks can be performed by a tool, others by an order to a subordinate.   (Croome, 1960)

But the clear definition of 'the job' and the simple set of outside relationships, broke down when conditions changed. New situations did not exactly match the traditional frontiers of responsibility. The individual no longer knew just what instructions were needed or where to seek them; 'he' had to consult with, rather than merely give orders to, 'his' subordinates.

The organismic organization was at the opposite end of the spectrum. It lacked rigid structure, lived by a process of continual adaptation, often involving the redefinition of individual tasks. Communications occurred in any direction as might be required at any particular time, and the commitment of employees was open ended and generally dedicated to the achievement of organizational aims. As one might expect, organismic systems were well suited to handling the new and unfamiliar: they were highly effective innovators.

According to Burns and Stalker, the work of the manager under the organismic system was much more exacting:

> He must give up his safe, cut and dried, contractual relationship with the

firm—a relationship with an impersonal, immutable 'they'—for member-ship of a body kept going by a shared creative activity; for the limited commitments of the 'nine to fiver' he must substitute the general open ended commitment of the professional. (Burns and Stalker, 1961)

They did not suggest that there was 'one best way' of organizing. If the mechanistic system was adequate, then so much the better because it was the most efficient. However, as Croome suggested, 'when the firm is tackling new tasks, whether commercial or technical, this system of differentiated responsibilities must be elastically shared' (Croome, 1960). Every effort must be made to encourage the sense of the business as a whole with objectives and goals common to all its members, rather than a complex of 'separate jobs'. The stronger this sense, the more there will be resource to lateral consultation. This should be recognized and facilitated, and not regarded as a mere semi-legitimate supplement to vertical channels of command.

Clearly, the organismic system, or some modern form of it, will be much more appropriate to the rapidly changing business world we now enjoy. The question is 'What form is most appropriate?' Over the past few decades there have been various attempts at concurrently achieving the benefits of both systems. Some have advocated various forms of matrix management where individuals enjoy more than one reporting link on either permanent or temporary bases. Others have advocated setting up various forms of organization within an organization, such as a 'new ventures' division or department where an organismic culture is encouraged while a more mechanistic system is retained for the main business. None of these attempts to combine mechanistic and organismic systems has been wholly satisfactory. Peters and Waterman's (1982) assertion that matrix management merely creates confusion no doubt contains some truth. Their advocacy of 'skunkworks', 'boot-legging corporate resources' to work on the new, nevertheless has a ring of desperation about it. An effective organization should be able to progress by more positive means than turning a blind eye.

The elimination of mass unskilled and semi-skilled labour has largely removed, for good or ill, the problem of bigness in terms of numbers employed. This does not mean that companies do not employ large numbers, but individual units no longer have to manage mass low-skilled labour which is almost inevitably alienated by the meaningless nature of their work. At least this is largely the case in the advanced economies. Less-developed countries, such as India and China, still have responsibility for mass labour without any apparent pain-free solution.

The benefits of bigness claimed by Lorenz are nevertheless being enjoyed by many organizations, a widely quoted exemplar of the modern organization form being ABB of Zurich. ABB is a big company in any terms.

It employs around 225 000 people (including 25 000 managers) in more than 1200 subsidiary companies and 5000 profit centres. This is the key to its organizational form: a multiplicity of semi-autonomous subsidiary units, connected to their parent by computerized umbilical cord. Potentially this organizational form could achieve an ideal balance between the benefits of scale and the advantages of being small. The force of ABB's anti-bureaucratic style can be seen by the no doubt far from painless reductions in numbers employed in their various subsidiary head offices. For example, Stromberg's head office staff was reduced from 880 to 25, Mannheim from 1600 to 100, Combustion Engineering of Stamford from 600 to 100. ABB's group headquarters comprises no more than 100 people.

The modern business is essentially a processor of knowledge. Drucker suggests that the key economic resource is no longer labour, capital or land, but knowledge; the central wealth-creating activity is no longer the allocation of capital and labour to production processes but the allocation of knowledge to productivity and innovation; the key groups in this new 'post-capitalist' society are the knowledge workers who know how to allocate their knowledge to this productive use and who will own both the means of production (through their pension funds) and the tools of production (i.e. knowledge) (Drucker, 1993).

Hogg (1986) provided an early illustration of how this process occurs in practice. Former large-scale employers have automated away unskilled and semi-skilled work, but have created new, highly specialized and skilled work to develop and maintain the new technology. Increasingly, the robots which replaced shopfloor workers are not maintained by full-time employees of the firm, but by small specialist firms on maintenance contracts to ensure the robots achieve agreed levels of performance in terms of down-time, availability, etc. This process was clearly underway a decade ago and has continued apace, increasingly involving the operation of new technology as well as its development and maintenance.

The impact on the nature of work and the nature of organizations are already felt, but the total picture is still only emerging by stages. So far governments have been able to avoid facing up to the social implications, but in many industries businesses have been forced for their own survival to face the organizational implications.

The new organisation consists of bits and pieces of various firms, plus an array of independent contractors, which the partners gather like members of a movie company for a limited time to perform a discrete task.

(Peters, 1994a)

Various models of this new organismic organizational form have been proposed. Drucker suggests the symphony orchestra as the prototype of the new knowledge-processing organization and his general thrust is paraphrased below:

For him an organization is a human group, composed of specialists, working together on a common task. It is purposefully designed and intended to endure. It is always specialized, defined by its task and is effective only if it concentrates on one task—a symphony orchestra does not attempt to cure the sick!

The function of organization is to make knowledge productive. This is done by making the best use of specialists. The best specialists are effective as specialists not generalists—neurosurgeons get better the more they practise neurosurgery, not by being promoted into general administrative work as often happened in hierarchically based organizations. In order for them to practise their specialism and to produce results, organization is needed. In the symphony orchestra, each of the players is a specialist. While each is playing a part towards the overall mission, each subordinates his or her speciality to the overall task, and they play only one piece of music at a given time.

The results of organization are always external. Results for an orchestra is the music heard by the audience; results of a hospital are cured patients returned home; results of an army are wars deterred or won. Thus results may be a long way away from the individual specialist organization member. An absolute prerequisite of an organization's performance is therefore that the task or mission must be absolutely clear and results must also be clear, unambiguous and, if possible, measurable.

Membership of an organization is optional. Thus organizations need to market membership—they have to attract people, hold people, recognize and reward people, motivate, serve and satisfy people. Because organization is organization of knowledge specialists it has to be an organization of equals, of colleagues, **a team of associates**, rather than an organization of ranks and hierarchies.

Organizations have to be managed. There must be people who are accountable for its mission, its spirit, its performance and its results. They must direct the organization, not command it.

Organizations must be autonomous, free to do their own thing.

The organization of the post-capitalist society of organizations is essentially destabilizing. Its function is to apply knowledge to tools, processes and products, to work and to knowledge itself and therefore it is continually creating change. 'It must therefore be organised for constant change. It must be organised for innovation (what Schumpeter referred to as creative destruction), for the systematic abandonment of the established, the customary, the familiar, the comfortable whether products, services and processes, human and social relationships, skills or organizations themselves.'

As well as being organized for the systematic abandonment of the established, organizations also need to be organized for the creation of the new; first, by continuous improvement (kaizen); second, by exploitation of knowledge (i.e. by developing applications); and, finally, by innovation. Unless the knowledge-based organization achieves this continually it will soon find itself obsolescent, losing the capacity to perform and to attract suitable specialists.

Thus the new organizations constantly upset, disorganize and destabilize the community. It is the nature of the organization's task which determines the culture of the organization, not the culture of the community, i.e. the organization has to be dominant if it is to survive.

The post-capitalist society is a society of employees, i.e. whether or not they are legally employees or self-employed they are dependent on access to an organization to make their contribution (or living). There are two sorts of employee: the low-skilled service workers and knowledge workers. The dignity and welfare of service workers is a central social problem for government; the productivity of knowledge workers is the crucial managerial problem. They have the means of production in their heads, they are highly mobile and they cannot be supervised.

(Paraphrased, in précis form, and with apologies to, Drucker, 1993)

Drucker's 'team of associates' is widely held to be the most effective organizational form for today's knowledge-processing, learning organization. This is a stage further than organismic organization. The replacement of hierarchy with teams and of mechanistic structures with networks has been widely reported (e.g. McGill *et al.*, 1992). The ABB example quoted earlier shows how effective a very large organization can be in minimizing hierarchy, using a team-based structure with strong networks throughout the firm to exploit the advantages of bigness.

Team-based organization facilitates the individual knowledge worker's contribution in a form of 'collaborative individualism' (Chorn, 1992) focused on the task in hand. This implies a fluidity of organization where individual contributions to different teams will vary over time as the relevance of their particular knowledge specialism varies. The permanent organization form is an arrangement of networks of teams of associates for which various metaphors have been used:

Quinn called them 'spider's web organisations' ... Weick, a researcher at the University of Michigan, likes the improvisational theatre metaphor. Charles Savage, management guru from Digital Equipment, cottons to jazz combos.   (Peters, 1994a)

Gavaghan (founder of First Direct, Midland Bank's electronic telephone banking service) looks outside the business world to find models for the virtual company. A surgeon's team ... a film production unit ... the Desert Storm force in the Gulf War.   (Bowen, 1994)

Even within a traditional monolithic organization there is an increasing reliance on networks. A network is not simply a group of communicators. Such a group may be connected at random to exchange information of an undefined nature. They may well lack the essential purposive element. 'Have a nice day' is a communication—or at least it meets most of the requirements of an orthodox definition of a communication. Its purpose is, however, limited.

> *The term network is the communications analogue of the sociological concept of 'group', but 'network' is distinct from 'group' in that it refers to a number of individuals (or other units) who persistently interact with one another in accordance with established patterns.* (Mueller, 1986)

Corporate networks take many different forms. The informal grapevine is a communications network, in most organizations fulfilling the very clear purpose of communicating corporate information which has not (yet) been communicated by official channels. Mueller describes a semi-formal network which he used to great effect; what he called his 'GWRK File'—a listing of contacts ('Guys Who Really Know'). This was really a networking system comprising various subnetworks which might serve particular purposes. For example, within the GWRK file there would be specialists on the market, on technology, on government, etc. The GWRK network system was set up carefully and very deliberately by Mueller to help him fulfil his managerial purpose more effectively.

Networks may be internal, connecting individuals and departments that have no other formal organizational links. They may have a physical form, as with electronic networks, operating as important aids to communications. Or they may be external, connecting the organization with its existing and potential customers, competitors, and technology suppliers, or other external system, e.g. financial markets. The science park concept derives its strength from networking. Silicon Valley is not just a geographical area, but a network.

Networks are systems of communications links which overlay the formal organization and are increasingly replacing it. They may be informal and be activated only irregularly, but they are persistent and, most important of all, they are clearly purposive.

External communications, i.e. networks involving customers and technology suppliers, both existing and potential, as well as other networks concerned with competitors though not necessarily involving them directly, are crucial to the achievement of an effective business. Without such networks, the firm's strategy will be based on an inadequate understanding of customer needs, a lack of knowledge about technological developments and an ill-formed view about competitive strengths and weaknesses.

Networks are set up directly with the sources of primary information such as customers, suppliers, technology suppliers, or less directly related experts who may be useful in providing strategically relevant information in one field or another. As the speed of technological development increases and markets become more global, so the inadequacies of the individual organization are exposed and the networks become more important, to the extent that they may take over parts of the organization where their expertise gives them an advantage.

Morgan (1992) illustrated the six stages in organizational evolution from mechanistic bureaucracy to loosely coupled networks of autonomous teams, and finally used the spider plant as his favoured metaphor for the modern organizational form. Handy uses the shamrock organization to similar purpose.

Networks and teams and collaborations and alliances are all part of the same process: the deconstruction of the purpose-built modern organization of the mass-production era to the fragmented postmodern organizational form of today and tomorrow.

Organizations and managers are now utterly dependent on the voluntary but ongoing relationships between autonomous parties from which both draw mutual benefit. Exclusion from such ongoing relationships would prove crucial, as it would for Gauthier's farmers, whether the exclusion was from an external collaboration intended to assist the acquisition of technological competences, or whether it was internal in the form of being unable to recruit and retain the right technologically specialist knowledge workers.

More than ever before businesses must be able to engage in such relationships and so must establish the principle of trust.

Levels of integrity

The idea of interdependence between enlightened but self-interested partners needs to be firmly based on an understanding of the modern fragmented business organization. The model needs to incorporate the means for potential partners to understand how trustworthiness will be perceived for different organizations in different situations. This can be done using Kohlberg's theoretical work on moral development (Modgil and Modgil, 1985).

Kohlberg's theory is based on certain assumptions which need to be acknowledged at the outset.

First, moral judgements must be understood from the subject's own perspective, rather than assessed on the basis of some extraneous value system. It is important that moral judgements are seen as reasonable and rational in their own terms, rather than treated as irrational, emotional or subconsciously based expressions. It is important, for example, when understanding the moral judgements of business managers that their business situation is fully understood, rather than trying to interpret their judgements from the point of view, for example, of a fifteenth-century cleric as some business ethicists might do.

Second, Kohlberg's approach focuses more on the way people arrange their thinking (i.e. their general moral world view) when making moral judgements rather than on the actual content (i.e. the specific moral beliefs or opinions) of the moral judgement. In order to understand the structure of their thinking it is again essential to adopt their point of view and so understand the meaning moral arguments have for them.

Third, Kohlberg recognizes that throughout our thinking, acting lives we construct meaning for ourselves. When events occur, we interpret and reinterpret reality. When events recur we create new interpretations and reconstructions of reality, each interpretation being determined or constrained by our current level of development.

Following these three assumptions Kohlberg then seeks to identify in individuals and groups what he refers to as their 'sociomoral perspective'. The sociomoral perspective defines and unifies six stages, as outlined in Table 3.2.

> [These] *levels of moral perspective provide a general organisation of moral judgement and serve to inform other more specific moral concepts such as the nature of the morally right or good, of obligation or duty, of fairness, of welfare consequences, and of moral values such as obedience to authority, preservation of human life, and maintenance of contracts and affectional relations.*   (Colby and Kohlberg, 1987)

The six moral stages are grouped into three levels:

■ Preconventional level (Stages 1 and 2)

■ Conventional level (Stages 3 and 4)

■ Postconventional level (Stages 5 and 6).

Business organizations also behave at different levels of 'moral development', as outlined in the following chapter. Levels of moral development are indicative of levels of integrity and it is therefore worth examining the original application to individuals in rather more detail to appreciate the relevance to organizations and integrity in organizations.

The preconventional level is the level of most children under age 9, some adolescents, and many adolescent and adult criminal offenders. The conventional level is the level of most adolescents and adults in modern society. The postconventional level is reached by a minority of adults and usually only after the age of 20–25. As noted earlier, the term *conventional* does not mean that individuals at this level are unable to distinguish between morality and social convention but rather that morality consists of socially shared systems of moral rules, roles, and norms. Individuals at the preconventional level have not yet come to really understand and uphold socially shared moral norms and expectations. Those at the postconventional level understand and generally accept society's rules, but acceptance of society's rules is based on formulating and accepting the general moral

Table 3.2 Six stages of moral development (based on Kohlberg, 1976)

Stage of moral development	Content of stage		
	What is right	Reasons for doing right	Sociomoral perspective
Level 1: Preconventional *Stage 1:* Legalistic morality	To avoid breaking the law or rules backed by punishment, and avoiding physical damage to persons and property.	Avoidance of punishment and the superior power of authorities.	Self-centred. No consideration for the interests of others. Fails to recognize that other people's interests differ. Actions are considered physically rather than in terms of psychological interests of others.
Stage 2: Individualism	To comply with rules only when it is in someone's immediate interest; to meet one's own interests and needs and to allow others to do the same. Right is what's fair, an equal exchange.	To serve one's own needs or interests but at the same time to recognize that other people have their interests, too.	Aware that everyone has his or her own interests to pursue and these may conflict, so that right is recognized as a relative concept.
Level 2: Conventional *Stage 3:* Mutual, interpersonal expectations	Living up to what is expected by people close to you or what people generally expect of people in your position. 'Being good' is important and means keeping mutual relationships through trust, loyalty and respect. Also having good motives and showing concern for others.	The need to be a good person in your own eyes and those of others. Desire to maintain rules and authority which support stereotypical good behaviour.	Aware of shared feelings, agreements, and expectations which take primacy over individual interests. Relates points of view by putting yourself in the other person's shoes.

Stage 4: Social system and conscience	Fulfilling the actual duties to which you have agreed. Laws are to be upheld except in extreme cases where they conflict with other fixed social duties. Right is also contributing to society, the group, or institution.	To keep the institution going as a whole, to avoid the breakdown in the system 'if everyone did it'.	Differentiates societal point of view from interpersonal agreement or motives. Takes the point of view of the system that defines roles and rules.
Level 3: Postconventional **Stage 5:** Social contract and individual rights	Being aware that people hold a that most values and rules are relative to your group and these relative rules should usually be upheld because they are the social contract. Some absolute values and rights like life and liberty, however, must be upheld in any society and regardless of majority opinion.	A sense of obligation to law to make and abide by laws for the welfare of all and for the protection of all people's rights. Concern that laws and duties be based on rational calculation of overall utility, 'the greatest good for the greatest number'.	Perspective of a rational individual social attachments and contracts. Integrates perspectives by formal mechanisms of agreement, contract, objective impartiality, and due process. Considers moral and legal points of view, recognizes that they sometimes conflict and finds it difficult to integrate them.
Stage 6: Universal ethical principles	Following self-chosen ethical principles such as the equality of human rights and respect for the dignity of human beings as individual persons. When laws violate these principles, one acts in accordance with the principle.	The belief as a rational person in the validity of universal moral principles, and a sense of personal commitment to them.	The moral perspective from which social arrangements derive. That of any rational individual recognizing that persons are ends in themselves and must be treated as such.

principles that underlie these rules. These principles in some cases come into conflict with society's rules, in which case the postconventional individual judges by principle rather than by convention.

> *One way of understanding the three levels is to think of them as three different types of relationships between the self and society's moral rules and expectations. From this point of view, Level I (preconventional) is a perspective from which rules and social expectations are something external to the self; in the Level 2 perspective the self is identified with or has internalised the rules and expectations of others, especially those of authorities; and the Level 3 (postconventional) perspective differentiates the self from the rules and expectations of others and defines moral values in terms of self-chosen principles.* (Colby and Kohlberg, 1987, p. 16)

These levels and stages have been identified in long-term research studies of individuals and groups of individuals examining their responses to basic ethical questions as they change over the years. A number of these longitudinal studies are reported in Colby and Kohlberg and some examples are quoted below in order to further illustrate the meaning of the different stages and levels.

One of the questions asked in Kohlberg's longitudinal study was 'Why shouldn't you steal from a store?' One of the respondents, at age 10, gave the following preconventional level response:

> *It's not good to steal from the store. It's against the law. Someone could see you and call the police.*

This is a response from a clearly egocentric sociomoral perspective. Seven years later the same respondent answered the same question as follows:

> *It's a matter of law. It's one of our rules that we're trying to help protect everyone, protect property, not just to protect a store. It's something that's needed in our society. If we didn't have these laws, people would steal, they wouldn't have to work for a living and our whole society would get out of kilter.*

This is a conventional level answer where the respondent is clearly concerned with the good of society with which he clearly identifies strongly. A further seven years later, the same respondent, now 24, gives a clearly postconventional or principles-based response:

> *Why shouldn't someone steal from a store?*
> **It's violating another person's rights, in this case to property.**
>
> *Does the law enter in?*
> **Well, the law in most cases is based on what is morally right so it's not a separate subject, it's a consideration.**

What does morality, or morally right, mean to you?
Recognizing the rights of other individuals, first to life and then to do
as he pleases as long as it doesn't interfere with somebody else's
rights.

How does this approach relate to business? From Kohlberg's opening assumptions it is clear that we must understand the general sociomoral business perspective as it is perceived by people in business. The opening chapter aimed to assist this process: in some aspects, business is deliberately set up and managed at the margin of ethical acceptability. Moreover, the *spirit of capitalism* further reinforces the requirement that business seeks to maximize their technical efficiency, often measured in terms of profitability, and in order to compete necessarily operates at the margin of ethical acceptability. However, the margin is indistinct—the clear definition of what is acceptable, and what is not, is yet to be made, despite the efforts of the business ethicists.

Most businesses, most of the time, might be expected to operate at Kohlberg's conventional level at which something is considered to be wrong because it is generally considered wrong. They would behave in such a way that they would be perceived as generally trustworthy and suitable partners for their stakeholders. Such organizations could be defined as exhibiting the conventional level of integrity.

An attempt to raise such organizations to the postconventional level, which is the project of most business ethicists, is doomed to fail. The alternative approach is to accept that an act is sufficiently ethical if it is generally accepted as being ethical. If an act has to be worked through in detail, using the tools and frameworks of moral philosophy, to assess whether or not it is ethical, it probably doesn't matter from the business point of view. Perhaps it is not important if people in business are not interested in being any more precisely ethical than that. Using normative moral philosophy to assess whether or not an act is ethical is in any case a fruitless exercise only resulting in alternative views.

This alternative, integrity focused approach, recognizes the realities of a conventional level of integrity and accepts that different business organizations operate at different levels at different times and in different situations in order to be most effective in achieving their organizational aims. The role of management, then, is to set up those structures and processes within the organization that would result in the organization behaving at the level of integrity at which it would be most effective. It is not a question of what actions would be ethical in a particular circumstance, but what businesses should do to achieve the required level of integrity.

Conclusion

Applying moral philosophy to business is problematic, mainly because philosophy is unaware of modern business. The absolutes of Kantian philosophy are simply unrealistic in a business context. Business ethicists seeking to raise the ethical values of business would risk the destruction of competitive business and the desertion of all its stakeholders. Organizations require an approach to ethics that takes account of the business context and recognizes the need for organizations to operate in their own best interests.

In this vein, Gauthier has provided a model of cooperative business behaviour which requires businesses to establish their credibility as being trustworthy. Perceived trustworthiness, or integrity, makes individuals and organizations attractive partners in mutually advantageous cooperative arrangements. Such collaborations and alliances are increasingly crucial to the strategic success of modern business.

These considerations apply to all transactions between organizations and are also increasingly important within organizations as the old monolithic hierarchies which enabled mass employers to be mass producers of standardized products are breaking down. If organizations are to be effective knowledge processors they must adopt flexible, fragmented, network- and team-based organizational forms which can relate people and initiatives and encourage their unlimited contributions. Such organizational forms cannot rely on orders down the line, but require the principle of trust to be recognized among equals.

The boundary between the networks and teams within an organization and its external collaborations and alliances is becoming increasingly blurred. The modern business is based on layers of relationships, internal and external, which will only continue on the basis of trust, i.e. on perceived integrity. It is therefore vital to know how such perceived integrity can be achieved.

One way of assessing this is to establish at which of Kohlberg's levels of integrity does business need to be in order to achieve its organizational goals most effectively. The credibility of integrity is vital if firms are to be invited into the mutually advantageous partnerships; its reality is crucial to their continuity.

To examine the application of this integrity model further, it is essential to understand the moral judgements that business people are under pressure to make, i.e. to understand their sociomoral perspective. This was first examined in the opening chapter. The next chapter looks in further detail at business goals and how these might complement or conflict with the organization's perceived level of integrity.

The business perspective

This chapter examines the strategic business perspective, as opposed to short-term profit maximization so that organizational integrity can be better understood and the model applied in practical situations.

The strategic view is concerned with business focus and concentration of resources on achieving strategic aims. In this context, a *primary* concern with ethical issues could only serve to reduce focus and concentration.

Business objectives are examined in terms of a hierarchy which shows how a business interacts with its various stakeholders and what it seeks to achieve in these interrelations. This indicates the different levels of integrity to be expected in the relations with different stakeholders in different situations.

It is therefore important to be able to identify the 'different situations' and this is done by diagnosing the 'strategic health' of the business, i.e. by defining the hierarchy of objectives and recognizing which level of the hierarchy is operative.

Introduction

Integrity can only be understood in context. For example, if a patron of the RSPCA was attacked by a pack of hungry hyenas it would be understandable if he or she, at least temporarily, accorded animal rights a fairly low priority. The perspective of the subject is crucial. To understand organizational integrity, it is important to understand the organization's perspective. This chapter examines the perspective of business organizations—something that business ethicists singularly fail to do.

The starting point is intended to be, as far as possible, value free—i.e. not based on any extraneous value system, but having regard only to the best interests of the businesses and organizations themselves. It is recognized that, in today's harsh and competitive environment, businesses must focus on business aims to ensure that they are successful in business terms. Social responsibility is a side issue—it is not a primary role of business to put funds on one side to, for example, help the urban poor.

Business ethicists, on the other hand, suggest that always putting profit first is not somehow 'good'. More than this, they suggest that businesses should deliberately undertake non-business-related expenses, whether it is employing more people than is strictly necessary, or perhaps contributing to the welfare of the local community in some way. Ethicists would have social responsibility added to the list of management tasks. They do not envisage social responsibility as a preconventional level phenomenon—i.e. something that should be done because it's the law and if it is ignored, you will be found out and punished. For them, social responsibility refers to something over and beyond what is legally necessary and they suggest that managers have a responsibility to ensure that their businesses voluntarily undertake these optional investments.

Clearly, there is a clash between two different cultures. Looked at from the perspective of the business, investments in social responsibility are essentially wasteful. They go against everything that the professional business manager has learned and experienced from the time the business was first started. Suggesting that such investments should nevertheless be made, because of an unanswerable Kantian argument, is not very convincing from the business perspective.

These opposing arguments, from the business and ethicist viewpoints, appear irreconcilable. Understanding the different perspectives is the only possible way to achieve any resolution. Gauthier and the games theorists showed that short-term profit maximizing leads to long-term failure and that a more appropriate version of the business perspective would be one that takes account of the need to engage in ongoing relationships, rather than simply one-off transactions, i.e. they suggest a strategic perspective.

This is not to deny that businesses based on one-off transactions exist, or that short-term profit maximizers can make a quick killing. The wild west peddler coming into the frontier township on the wagon train selling his patent medicine, knowing that tomorrow he will be on his way again, certainly has his modern counterpart. Why should he be honest and admit the medicine will cure nothing? The only reasons you might trust him is because he is a man you know to be of deep religious or other philosophical conviction, or because you know he'll be coming again next week and will need to sell some more. Otherwise you would be prudent to assume he is in business for a swift buck.

Most businesses are intended to last, to have some substance, to be able to recruit and retain high-calibre professional specialists and managers, and to enter into long-term relationships with other organizations. We need to understand this strategic perspective of such businesses if we are to be able to understand the level of integrity at which they will be most effective.

Business strategy

Strategy is concerned with long-term prosperity and long-term asset growth, not short-term profit. Focusing on short-term profitability, to the exclusion of strategic considerations, leads organizations to make short-term opportunistic decisions which, while financially rational in themselves, may lack any coherence or consistency and lead to the business becoming widely diversified, highly complex and in the end unmanageable.

Businesses need strategy in order to ensure that resources are allocated in the most effective way. This is particularly important when it comes to major resource allocation decisions such as large capital expenditures, disposals or divestments and all forms of diversification, including acquisitions. When such major decisions arise, consideration of the strategic issues involved is more or less unavoidable. Such decisions themselves serve to clarify strategic thinking and overtly planned strategy usually focuses on these major resource allocations. However, resources are also allocated by a thousand and one minuscule decisions, mainly taken by default, every day by every organization member. Cumulatively these decisions may be far more important than the occasional one-off large-scale investment. The important question is whether all these thousands of mini 'strategic' decisions get taken in a way that reinforces the organization's strategy, or they get taken more or less randomly with regard to strategy.

The strategist's role can be seen in terms of the corporate navigator and the strategic plan as the charts by which direction is set and progress measured. This is perhaps the most commonly used analogy. We wouldn't leave London along the Edgware Road in a random attempt to get to Canterbury.

Thus, the familiar idea underlying the cyclical strategy process:

'Where are we now?
Where do we want to get to?
How can we get there?
    Start moving,
How are we doing?'

The directional idea is far from being the whole story, but it is nevertheless surely crucial. Once the direction is set, it becomes possible to take decisions in a consistent manner with regard to strategy. Only when direction is set is it possible for all members of the business to know which way they are headed, and only then can they shape their own efforts accordingly. With no direction, members may well allocate their efforts and enthusiasm in random and conflicting directions and investments may be made similarly.

Setting direction sounds simple, but is difficult to achieve in practice. The main difficulty is that it requires management continually to reject other courses of action–products, markets, technologies, etc.–which in themselves look perfectly sensible, profitable strategies. It requires determination and commitment on the part of management to overcome the natural 'Pareto' type processes which result in a thin spread of resources across a wide front. It requires that management reject an apparently natural attitude to risk, the risk of putting all your eggs in one basket. It requires courage to overrule the almost inevitable resource allocations suggested by orthodox accounting and administrative processes which otherwise control the business.

Setting direction and concentrating all efforts on that direction is the key purpose of strategy. Drucker and others have continuously highlighted the power of concentration.

Concentration is the key to real economic results.   (Drucker, 1964)

Managers must concentrate their efforts on the smallest number of products, product lines, services, customers, markets, etc. Such statements have continuously highlighted the power of concentration and the need for strategic focus.

Concentration applies both to the small number of large-scale capital investments, and also to the plethora of mini-decisions about apparently unimportant jobs and work priorities that are taken every day by people at every level in an organization. The strategic importance of the big decisions is difficult to ignore, but the cumulative weight of the mini-decisions is less frequently recognized as being truly strategic and, as a consequence, in most firms they are taken pragmatically with little regard to strategy and receive little attention unless catastrophe threatens.

Concentration seems to be one of those concepts about which there is a high degree of consensus; but, with very few exceptions, businesses continually fail to put it into practice. The 80 : 20 rule is a monument to the failure to concentrate. Resources tend to get misallocated and spread thinly across all activities, products, customers, etc. No other principle of effectiveness is violated as constantly as the basic principle of concentration.

The reasons for lack of concentration are various. The most difficult aspect of concentration is the very positive management decision not to do things. If there is a known market, which a business could satisfy using existing competences and which looks highly profitable, then why not go for it? Very few managers would be able to mount a very persuasive argument for not doing so, and even fewer would be prepared to stand by it and insist that the opportunity is passed up, just in order to stay focused. This is one of the most difficult of all managerial decisions.

Porter (1988) interviewed John Rollwagon, CEO of Cray Research, world leader in supercomputers. Cray had identified the then looming market for mini-supercomputers, worth many millions of dollars. Cray, itself, had a prior position technologically and also in marketing terms. Cray's customers wanted the company to enter the market. The company developed a detailed plan and the whole thing looked highly profitable. But in the end it decided to turn down the opportunity, just in order to stay focused as the manufacturer of the world's most powerful computer. Rollwagon pointed to this decision as the key to Cray's success.

Concentrating was difficult for Cray. It was a decision not to do something that looked in itself highly profitable and made a lot of sense. But if it was difficult for Cray, how much more difficult is it to take a decision to stop doing something in order to focus. This is the situation for most businesses. In these cases, stopping doing something means accepting a reduction in sales volume and most often a reduction in profit, at least a reduction in contribution to overheads. How can such a decision be justified? The example of Skil (see page 77) shows that such decisions can be extremely effective; that concentration is, as Drucker said, the key to economic results. However, in the Skil case, the management had one distinct advantage. Skil had just been acquired by Emerson so the executives concerned in the decision to concentrate were not burdened by having been associated with the old Skil business. There were no long-standing psychological investments to be jettisoned when the decision was taken to give up a substantial proportion of the market and some of the company's product range. Nevertheless, the decision was difficult—the first problem was simply being believed! Skil and Cray both had another advantage over the vast majority of businesses. They both had a very clear strategic direction. Without clear direction there can be no concentration simply because there will be no agreement as to what to concentrate on. Most organizations do not have simply stated, unifying strategic objectives such as 'the most powerful computer in the world'. Few businesses really understand what their particular specialism is. Most formally stated strategies are not simple, but reflect the complex world in which the business operates. As a consequence, strategy statements often appear to convey conflicting messages and strategic managements seem reluctant to acknowledge the simplicity of effective strategic concepts.

Peters and Waterman found it was a prime requirement of 'excellent' business performance (Peters and Waterman, 1982): operate with a simple structure and a lean staff so that efforts can be concentrated on 'the knitting', i.e. the core business. Concentration remains one of the key determinants of business success, but with no direction there can be no concentration.

A third main purpose of strategy is to provide consistency. All that has been said of concentration applies to consistency. Consistency is simply concentration over time. Like concentration it applies to the big one-off investment decisions and it applies to the myriad mini-strategic decisions which determine how an individual's time, effort and enthusiasm will be allocated.

Without consistency the organization will continually change direction, flitting like a butterfly from one project to another, developing no critical mass of expertise or even proficiency let alone any form of leadership position.

Direction, concentration and consistency, extremely simple ideas in themselves, are the essence of strategy. An appropriate direction on which resources are consistently concentrated is the key to long-term prosperity. It can lead to the establishment of a leadership position, based on a continually developing body of knowledge, skill and expertise which generates real economic results.

The successful behaviour patterns that are regularly reinforced, the successfully established position and effective culture of the organization gradually become more deeply imprinted on organization members and more rigid and automatic. Individual members become expert and make heavy personal and psychological investments in their expertise and the organization as a whole accumulates substantial investment in, and commitment to, the existing and successful technology, customers, competitive positions and ways of doing things. The successful strategy has a built-in obsolescence and will tend gradually to blinker the organization and render it less capable of noticing, let alone creating, change.

As Drucker (1964) pointed out, 'any leadership position is transitory and likely to be short-lived' and 'what exists is getting old'. If it was true in 1964 it is far more true in the 1990s, and the need to be flexible and responsive to these changes is more vital than ever before.

Strategy needs to set direction, concentrate effort and provide consistency, but at the same time, it needs also to ensure organizational flexibility. The concepts of direction, concentration and consistency are simple, perhaps too simple, but flexibility is rather more complex. A flexible strategy may be almost a contradiction in terms, yet this is the other main purpose of strategy.

Direction, concentration and consistency do not arise from any natural process but require determined management action for their achievement. And when achieved, they militate against flexibility. Thus the purpose of strategy is rather subtle: a balance between commitment to a successful direction and the ability to change direction when required.

Some recent research on the UK textile industry suggested that the maintenance of strategic focus was critically affected by the level of corporate integrity perceived by members within the organization. Integrity was one of the essential factors that determined the commitment of all members of the organization to an effective business strategy (Pearson *et al.*, 1989).

The impact of low integrity is illustrated by the case of Falcon Computer where top management went through the motions of creating a corporate culture based on highly laudable aims. However, the reality differed so far from the official version they were trying to elaborate, that all management's attempts were counterproductive and only resulted in increased cynicism and alienation among employees.

> *Everyone knew the operative values at Falcon Computer were hierarchy, secrecy and expediency–regardless of what the official culture said.*
>
> (Reynolds, 1986)

All attempts to articulate a coherent strategy and to 'secure essential services' of individuals in pursuance of that strategy were rendered completely ineffective because of the perceived lack of integrity.

Businesses need to make absolutely certain they are not distracted from their primary business purpose by any extraneous pressures, whether they are the apparent, but elusive, attractions of diversification or the humanly appealing blandishments of business ethicists.

Business objectives

If strategic focus is to be achieved then it must be expressed in some readily communicable form, so that people inside and outside the organization know and understand what it is about. Such expression usually takes the form of a set of objectives against which performance can be measured.

The debate about objectives has continued right through the history of management literature, and before that the literature of classical economics. Objectives play a key role in the strategic management of any business. However, no really coherent theory of objectives has ever achieved any consensus.

Classical economics was based on the mathematically convenient concept of profit maximization. The entrepreneur was held to equate his or her marginal revenue with marginal cost, at which point the level of profit would be maximized. The beauty of this was its mathematical simplicity–for economists, basic calculus solves the problem of management. However the theory only works if it is accepted that (a) the only factors of importance are the price of the product and the volume produced and sold; (b) that the entrepreneur's costs are identical to the costs of everyone else; (c) that the product is also identical; and (d) that the entrepreneur knows every one else's volume, price and cost, and all the other underpinnings of perfect competition. The purpose of this completely unreal theory remains obscure to the management theorist or practitioner.

Slightly more realistic ideas were developed, such as sales revenue maximization (Baumol, 1959), management utility maximization (Williamson, 1963) and so on. At each stage *en route* to reality the economists lost something in mathematical tractability, until they ended up with the behavioural model of Cyert and March (1963) which indicated that major decisions tended to be made by compromise between coalitions of managers aiming to satisfy at least the minimum requirements of all interested parties—a process referred to as satisficing. While seeking to be realistic this behavioural model defied any attempt to make it mathematically, or practically, usable.

Accountancy has had a major impact on both the theory and practice relating to business objectives. Accounting considerations lead to multiple financial objectives which may have an internal focus such as return on assets, asset turnover, margins on sales, etc., or an external focus such as share performance targets (price earnings ratios, dividend yields, etc.) Increasingly these objectives are being adopted by economists and financial models of the firm are becoming part of economic orthodoxy.

In practice, objectives have remained more diffuse. Since the days of Henri Fayol, whose main working experience was in the last century, multiple objectives have been the common ground. More than 30 years ago Drucker (1955) cited the necessity for objectives in the following eight areas:

■ Market standing

■ Innovation

■ Productivity

■ Physical and financial resources

■ Profitability

■ Manager performance and development

■ Worker performance and attitude

■ Public responsibility.

This practical approach to multiple objectives presents a complex picture where often objectives will be in opposition to each other. Maximizing one would inevitably mean failure with another. A balance has to be achieved, but there is no indication as to how this should best be done. Drucker's concept was an unstructured check-list. Management's job was to achieve the balance between conflicting objectives, but they were given no guidance as to how this should be done.

The systems approach (Emery and Trist, 1965) presented the firm as a complicated open system having a constantly changing relationship with its various environments. These are the firm's product markets, its suppliers, technological, financial and labour environments, government and society. Management's job was to control the boundary conditions of the firm, i.e. its relationship with these various environments.

The idea of boundary management and of constantly changing relationships cast some new light on the subject. The idea of managing the firm's relationship with, for example, its financial environment, implies managing the firm's share price. This would not simply be a matter of maximizing the shareholders' wealth, but managing the share so that its performance was sufficient to permit adequate performance in other boundary areas. Increasing the shareholders' wealth by more than is necessary would be just as wasteful as over-designing a product (i.e. giving the customer something he or she neither wants nor is prepared to pay for). The idea of balancing the firm's performance in its various, and often competing environments, still implies management's role is basically a balancing act.

Unstructured multiple objectives, which require trading off against each other, only serve to confuse and paralyse. What is required is a system of objectives that can be used to focus effort and guide the firm towards a unified strategic approach.

Translating boundary ideas into a set of objectives might produce targets in each of Drucker's eight objective areas. The systems approach implies that the firm ought to set financial objectives, for instance, that would ensure that the share price performed well enough to safeguard the firm's continued independence, together with its ability to raise such finance as would be required to perform on other objectives, such as market standing and innovation. These corporate objectives would be required to be achieved, in order that other objectives could be aimed for.

This seems to imply a hierarchical ordering of objectives, analogous to Maslow's model of intrinsic human needs (1943). Maslow suggested a hierarchy of needs going from the lowest level of physiological needs (food, sex, sleep, etc.) through safety needs, love needs, esteem needs, up to the highest level, what he called the need for self-actualization. As each need level in the hierarchy was satisfied, so the next higher level became potent. Thus if physiological needs were satisfied, the need for safety became dominant, and if at any time a lower level need ceased to be satisfied then that lower level need would again become prepotent. Maslow's model has often been criticized as lacking empirical support and subsequent motivation theorists suggested that needs were not necessarily ordered hierarchically and that more than one level might be active at the same time. Nevertheless, the Maslow hierarchy remains intuitively plausible.

Business objectives seem to follow a similar pattern, as shown in Figure 4.1, and in this case the hierarchical ordering is the common experience of anyone who has worked in a business that, for example, runs short of cash.

The objectives system of a business is a means of the business concentrating its efforts and resources on achieving success over different timescales, in different situations and with respect to different criteria. Management has to do more than simply balance these multiple objectives; it has to express the objectives in a hierarchical form which remains valid consistently in different situations and timescales, so that they do not have to be continually revised thus confusing organization members.

The strategic aim, or mission, is what the business exists to achieve, the lower level objectives are means to this end. If any of the lower level objectives cease to be satisfied they become prepotent, and the lower the level the stronger is its dominance when not satisfied. Thus, when the organization's survival is threatened, all higher level objectives are ignored.

The strategic aim is not expressed as a generalized mission statement specifying the organization's espoused values and other cultural variables. It is a concise statement which clearly identifies the organization's strategic direction expressed in a form that is readily communicable and capable of motivating people in the organization to concentrate their efforts on the identified intent.

The term 'mission' is often used in quite a different context from the present one. There is a tendency to dwell on values and cultural issues that

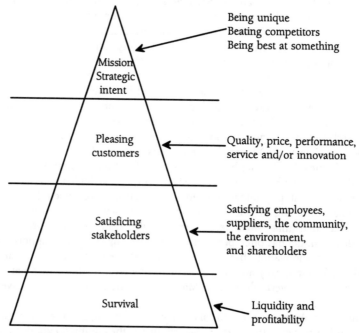

Figure 4.1 *A hierarchy of objectives.*

have little to do with focus. A good example of this brand of mission statement was published by the Zale Corporation some time before it filed for protection from its creditors. Zale's document, said to be a summary statement of company mission (Pearce, 1982), included the following:

Our ultimate responsibility is to our shareholders. Our goal is to earn an optimum return on invested capital ...

We feel a deep, personal responsibility to our employees ...

We are committed to honesty and integrity in all relationships ...

We are demanding but fair.

We recognize community involvement as an important obligation ...

We believe in the free enterprise system and in the American Democratic form of government ...

This mission statement spells out the creed by which we live.

(Pearce, 1982)

This variety of mission is more a statement of pious belief than a tight definition of the real strategic focus of the business.

The following are rather more useful statements which define the strategic focus of the business:

Coca Cola: 'Put a Coke within arm's reach of every consumer in the world.'

NEC: 'Exploit competence in computing and communications.'

Komatsu: 'Encircle Caterpillar.'

Canon: 'Beat Xerox.'

NASA: 'Put a man on the moon by the end of the decade.'

(Pearson, 1992)

These have obvious attractions in terms of their definitive direction and also in terms of communicability. Moreover, they are also transformational or motivational. But they also have one other great virtue: they are sufficiently precise that an analytically sound set of milestones can be defined leading to the achievement of each. These milestone sets include very specific dated, target achievements, in some cases extending over a 10-year period.

The strategic aim is what should drive the business at all times. When other objectives intervene, the business is being blown off course. This applies even to the next objective down, pleasing the customer. The model suggests that the customer must be pleased before the business can focus on its real strategic aim. However, many successful businesses remain stuck at this level on the hierarchy. Peters has suggested that you should have a passion for your customer, but this is not entirely rational. The supplier–customer relationship should not be passionate, but calculated. Providing the customer with an overabundance of some product attribute is itself simply wasteful and may be directly counterproductive. Sticking at this level inhibits the unique achievement of a strategically focused firm.

Other firms never seek to progress beyond the second level objectives and mistakenly regard these not as *satisficing* objectives, but *maximizing*. The notion of maximizing shareholders' wealth, for example, has had many adherents. Ironically, many studies have shown that such a focus rarely achieves for the shareholder a return that compares with the strategically focused business. Again maximizing performance at this level is wasteful. For example, providing the shareholder with greater returns than is necessary to achieve the required share performance is a form of liquidation which suggests a paucity of strategic aim.

Liquidity and profitability are measures of performance which define minimum levels necessary to permit the business to focus its attention on the higher level objectives.

The idea of social responsibility is at an intermediate (i.e. satisficing) level in the hierarchy. It is clearly not the main purpose of the business to maximize the amount of social good it does. Nevertheless, a complete disregard for social responsibility is not a valid strategy. The business should aim to satisfy the minimum needs of society, wherever there is a direct contact, and having done sufficient to satisfy those needs, address itself to the higher level objective.

Apart from the strategic objective, none is a maximization objective. They only require some minimum level of achievement in order that the business may then seek to satisfy the next higher level in the hierarchy. Thus the business is focused on achieving its top level, strategic objectives. Anything more than satisfaction of needs at lower levels merely serves to inhibit the firm in its attempts to satisfy the business strategy objectives. From time to time the lower level needs become prepotent and then the firm has to shift its attention, for example, away from the long-term strategy on to short-term survival. This is a common enough experience when managements may find it prudent to ration capital, postpone long-term developments, slash R&D expenditure and so on. In an accounting culture, such actions can take on an almost heroic aspect, almost as though the aim of the business is to cut costs and operate efficiently. In reality these are the means to the end. Sometimes they become dominant, but they should be recognized as an interruption in the pursuit of the strategic goal.

The hierarchical view of objectives provides a systematic way in which a firm may balance the conflicting priorities of various opposing interests. In particular it helps management to balance the long-term interests of the business itself against the short-term interests of the firm's financial environment.

It may also be apparent that this examination of the hierarchical organization of objectives coincidentally also considers each of the other agencies with which the organization interacts. These are the agencies with which the business will seek ongoing relationships and which are the actors in Gauthier's model. With each of these stakeholder groups the business needs to establish credibility of having internalized the principle of trust so that they will be invited into mutually advantageous collaborations. The next chapter looks in more detail at this aspect of the hierarchy.

Strategic health and performance

This brief examination of the business perspective has made a general assessment of the main strategic issues that business managers have to confront. Each organization does so differently. Each business has a unique mission or strategic aim and they each express different lower level objectives. So the business perspective contains both general business factors and other factors that are unique to the particular company. To understand the moral judgements made by people in business, it is essential to understand both aspects of the business perspective.

The general perspective is adequately defined by the hierarchy of objectives. The unique aspects of the perspective demand a means of measuring the strategic performance of the particular business. Orthodox financial measures will not do. Accounting methods only measure past performance–reported profitability is not even a measure of short-term health and performance. Accounting, with impeccable logic, accords the greatest value to the quickest gain: a pound now is worth more than a pound in a year's time. But strategy is concerned with a five- or ten-year horizon or even longer and it is crucial to have an adequate measure of strategic health and success.

Porter (1988) examined this issue with the CEO of Skil Corporation, the power tool business taken over by Emerson Electric in 1979. Five years after the acquisition Skil was still not very profitable and had lost market share over the period. However, during that five years a lot of action had been taken. The product range had been rationalized to standardize on far fewer components. The number of components in each product had been slashed. Three-quarters of the production factories had been closed. Production facilities had been radically upgraded or replaced with modern flexible plant. Stocks and work in progress had been largely eliminated. The distribution channels had been radically reorganized and Skil had taken the brave decision to stop supplying mass merchandisers. These represented around 40 per cent of the total market. The company had been given a new highly focused strategy and management had put a lot of effort into communicating this strategy both inside and out of the company so everyone knew what Skil was about. Nevertheless, after five years' hard work, Skil was still not very profitable and had still lost market share. From an accountant's perspective the situation would have looked desperate. But from the strategic perspective things looked good. The company had a clear strategic aim. It had focused on its core technologies and was outsourcing components where it had no advantage; it had improved its quality and at the same time slashed its costs; it had developed an excellent relationship with its key distributors which were the fastest growing in the industry. It was poised for great things, but, as Porter suggested, 'if you had come in from Mars you would have thought Skil was not doing very well'.

Clearly, the strategic health and strategic performance was far more important to Skil than its short-term financial performance. In that particular case, the development of close relationships with specialist distributors was the key to Skil's subsequent success. Skil had around 7 per cent of the US market against Black & Decker's 40+ per cent. Skil's wholesale prices to its specialist outlets were higher than the retail price of its products through mass merchandisers. The same applied, of course, to Black & Decker, but because of their scale of operation Black & Decker were unable to adopt Skil's strategy which was essentially the decision to stop supplying mass merchandisers and deliberately create a position of mutual dependence and loyalty between itself and its specialist distributors. The establishment of this Gauthier-like relationship was the basis of Skil's strategy and the source of its success which ultimately, after several years, showed through in enviable profitability.

Strategic considerations frequently result in very different evaluations from those produced using orthodox accounting criteria. For example, when Blue Circle Industries put its sand and gravel business up for sale in 1982, the business had a balance sheet total net asset value of around £9m. A professional revaluation of the land and minerals in the business produced a surplus over book value of almost £10m, implying an asset value of £19m. An alternative valuation was made by estimating the maintainable level of earnings multiplied by the then current sector PE ratio plus a 50 per cent premium to reflect the bid situation. This produced a valuation of almost £20m. A third valuation was based on an estimate of future cash flows from the business discounted at 15 per cent to a present value of £16.8m. These three different methods of valuing the business showed an average valuation of £18.6m. The business was actually sold for around £30m.

The justification for the premium was strategic. The Blue Circle Aggregates business included huge deposits of minerals in the West Midlands region. Many of these were not currently being exploited—some appeared unlikely to be used for as long as 40 years. The present value of £1 in 40 years' time, discounted at 15 per cent, is a mere 0.373 pence. The strategic value of having a secure business for the next 20 years is immense. Strategic value, whether it is invested in minerals under the ground, long-term research and development or a structural or positioning change in the business as with Skil, is not measurable in orthodox financial language.

The measurement of Skil's strategic health, for example, could only be achieved by analysing the viability of its strategy, and measurement of its strategic performance in terms of its progress in achieving its strategic objectives. Skil's strategy and strategic objectives were clearly unique to itself. There are no universal measures of strategic health and performance: they are always unique to the individual business and its particular situation. Thus the assessment of strategic health and performance must be made by understanding two particular issues which are unique to the individual business:

- First, the strategic aims of the business as expressed in a hierarchy of objectives, and including the practical milestones derived from the statement of strategic aim or mission, and

- Second, the level of objectives on the hierarchy which are operative at any particular time; for example, it is vital to understand whether the business is able to attack its strategic objective or is forced to be concerned with survival.

Conclusion

A basic assumption of Kohlberg's approach was the recognition that integrity could only be understood in its sociomoral setting. If we are to understand how people in business perceive the integrity of organizations, we must take the business perspective fully into account. The business perspective focuses not on short-term profit maximizing but on the achievement of strategic goals.

Management's task is to ensure that business pursues its strategic goals, whatever they are, and gets side-tracked as little as possible from this overriding aim, i.e. that lower level objectives in the hierarchy do not become prepotent and force attention away from strategic aims.

When a business is first set up the dominant objective is likely to be survival. The high rate of infant mortality among new businesses suggests that this focus is rational. Thus, from start-up businesses focus on being deliberately efficient, i.e. not wasteful of resources. This is the presumed result of *the spirit of capitalism*, and inevitably leads to business behaviour at the boundaries of ethical acceptability. In the opening chapter this was exampled through the series of snap-shots depicting the development and evolution of the generic company, S.T.P. Ltd.

It is management's job to ensure that the avoidance of waste is comprehensive. Businesses should not pay more taxes than they have to;

they should not carry more stocks and work in progress than is strictly necessary; they should not employ more people than are required to perform the business task; and so on. This emphasis on efficiency is so strong that professional specialists are hired, from the earliest days of the business's existence, to ensure that no such waste occurs. In many successful companies the emphasis on cost control and waste avoidance is built into the culture of the firm, so that all employees are imbued with the idea and behave accordingly.

More than this they are charged with the extremely difficult task of making sure their businesses achieve a concentration of all available resources, efforts and enthusiasms on the strategic aim. Professional managers are therefore conditioned to avoid side issues or non-business investments in such things as social responsibility.

The question remains as to how far these business objectives conflict with the requirement to behave with integrity. The business perspective suggests there may well be conflicts from time to time. In most situations, businesses operate at Kohlberg's conventional level of integrity. This is the level at which firms would be recognized as suitable or desirable partners in the mutually advantageous collaborations and alliances on which businesses increasingly depend; the level at which they would appear attractive as members of cooperating networks and teams. At other times, businesses may find that their position on the hierarchy of objectives changes, and in those circumstances they may be forced to adopt a different level of integrity. The impact of strategic objectives on organizational integrity is the subject of the following chapter.

Integrity and achieving objectives

This chapter examines the pressures on businesses to behave unethically when aiming to achieve different levels of objective.

At the survival level businesses may be expected to behave with only scant regard for ethical niceties. Directors of businesses which are threatened with extinction often take heroic personal risks, behaving illegally, fraudulently and without regard for the whole truth, with the aim of steering the business through its crisis so that all stakeholders might benefit.

At the intermediate levels on the objectives hierarchy, satisfying stakeholders and pleasing customers, the pressures to act unethically are not so pressing. Nevertheless, businesses should not allow themselves to be side-tracked into wasteful investments in 'good works' if their top level strategic objectives are not being achieved.

The strategic level objective is essentially concerned with beating competitors. Even businesses which seek to avoid competition and achieve their strategic self-actualization by building a better mousetrap, will not long avoid competitors if they are successful. Beating competitors would be regarded by business ethicists as essentially unethical. Both competitive aims and the means of their achievement can lead organizations perilously close to the unethical if not the illegal. Competitors are different in kind from all other stakeholders and the difference needs to be recognized and understood.

The chapter looks at interactions with each category of stakeholder and provides numerous examples. These are not ethical dilemmas raising the question 'Is it ethical?', but real situations for which the organizational integrity model provides tangible guidance.

Introduction

Ethical performance and judgements can only be understood in their context. Here we are concerned with the strategic perspective of business and make use of the summary suggested in Figure 4.1, the hierarchy of business objectives. Not only does this suggest the business aims, which it should be remembered do not normally include any explicitly ethical initiatives, but it also indicates the various stakeholders with which the business has transactions. The transactions could be of a one-off, amoral, profit-maximizing nature or, alternatively, part of an ongoing Gauthierian strategic relationship which depends on each party believing the other has internalized the principle of trust. Figure 5.1 highlights these interactions and the agencies with which they are conducted. It is crucial to recognize the level in the hierarchy on which the business is focused, if its level of integrity is to be understood.

A business whose survival is threatened may be expected to behave in a quite different fashion from a business that is securely focused on achieving its strategic intent, whatever that is. In this respect a business is no different from any other biological or social system. Constraints that are fully operative under normal stable conditions, including all ethical constraints, are completely relaxed when continued survival is threatened.

At the intermediate levels of the hierarchy, normal ethical standards—whatever they are—might be expected to prevail. However, at the top, strategic level, different rules apply. The focus at this level is essentially to be better than competitors; to provide the customer with better value than

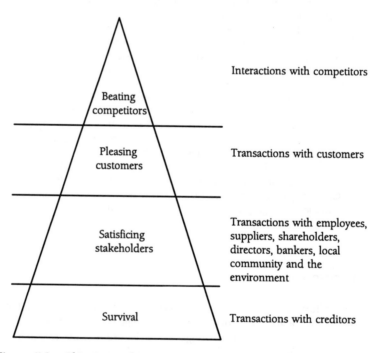

Figure 5.1 *Objectives and transactions.*

competitors in ways that the customer thinks important. This is the normal meaning of beating competitors. Where competitors try to provide value by exactly the same means there is head to head competition and then the intention to beat competitors may lead ultimately to their destruction. According to universalist philosophy this would in principle be unethical, while for utilitarians it would also be unethical if successful. This is why, for most normative moral philosophers, business is a fundamentally unethical pursuit to which they have little to contribute. They completely fail to achieve what Kohlberg identified as necessary: an understanding of the actor's perspective.

The following sections briefly examine the various transaction categories and provide examples of each.

Survival

When survival is threatened, the niceties of ethics inevitably take second place. This is hardly new or surprising. A vixen will try to avoid confrontation with a pursuer until she is cornered and her life is threatened. Then she will turn and fight wildly without constraint to her last breath. This is a common phenomenon with many biological, social and political systems.

Gauthier emphasized exactly this situation in his model of the two cooperating farmers. If one farmer retires the whole cooperative agreement collapses. It is not significant that retirement was the cause of the discontinuity, it could have been any cause. The important point about the impending retirement was that it was predictable and therefore affected the collaboration. If only the retiring farmer was aware of his forthcoming retirement, then he would be able to exploit the situation by taking advantage of his neighbour and then not cooperating when his turn came. If both farmers were aware of it, then the arrangement would collapse altogether.

In the case of threats to the survival of a business the level of knowledge is also important. The threatened business may try to carry on as before in order to preserve the fiction of its continuity so that confidence is not damaged. However, at some stage, like the cornered vixen, the business is likely to take whatever action is necessary to preserve or prolong its existence. When the business with which it is cooperating—for example, a creditor—also learns that the business is about to collapse, it will probably change its mode of behaviour. The creditor may change immediately from being a trustworthy collaborator to being a suspicious opponent out to secure the best possible terms of terminating the partnership. Nor in most cases would it be significant how long the previous cooperative arrangement had been in place. Loyalty and sentiment are likely to play little part in a bankruptcy.

The change in behaviour occurs when survival is threatened, not just when the due process of winding-up is under way. It is this change in behaviour that is likely to place ethical considerations to one side. When Gauthier's farmer is going bust and his only chance of survival is to double-cross his friend, then perhaps he will do it. Perhaps he will do it even though they have known each other and collaborated for a life time. In the case of a business it would be prudent to assume that this would be the case.

If a business continues to trade although it is insolvent, its directors are guilty of fraud. It may be perfectly possible to weather the liquidity crisis and recover to more normal trading, but the directors who take a business through such a crisis take a considerable risk. If there is a 60 per cent chance of becoming bankrupt and a 40 per cent chance of surviving, what should the directors do? If the company fails, everyone suffers; if it survives, everyone wins. In many cases the difference between success and failure in these situations is simply a matter of confidence. Like a Chancellor before devaluation, company directors are bound in these situations to preserve the fiction that everything is OK. If they were to breathe even a word about cash problems it would be a self-fulfilling prophecy, causing the company's failure. Moreover, as one director described how his business went bankrupt–'slowly to start with and then bloody fast'–directors do not have too much time at the critical stages to think through their reasoned responses to the situation. Kant would have hated it.

The directors in such a situation have to behave in a way that they know could subsequently be interpreted as continuing to trade when insolvent, i.e. fraud. Is the manager who carries on and takes that risk–after all he or she is the prime sufferer if it fails–to be condemned as unethical or applauded for being courageous?

There is, however, a brighter side to threatened extinction. Management is liberated to take the sort of action which, in any other circumstances, would be unthinkable. There are many well-known examples of this phenomenon. One of the most publicized situations was Michael Edwardes' British Leyland. BL was the creation of politicians and at its birth the company enjoyed around 44 per cent of the UK car market. Its early managers were expected to make a success of it, even though professionals in the industry recognized the impossibility of the task. By the time Edwardes took over, the company's survival was in question and a much more aggressive management style became sustainable. Action which was imperative, but which had nevertheless previously been rejected by the unions, became actionable, simply because the alternative was recognized as being closure. Significant parts of the company were in fact closed and it was generally recognized that management would put thousands more employees out of work, without compunction, if the survival of the company itself was placed in jeopardy. Edwardes recognized the new freedom he had in his time at BL in the title of his book, *Back from the Brink* (Edwardes, 1982). Had the company not been at the brink of extinction, his freedom to act would have been much more restricted.

The freedoms that are opened up when a company's survival is threatened include a great relaxation of ethical standards. Kohlberg looked at several parallel personal situations; for example, a postconventional analysis of whether or not someone should steal a drug to save his wife:

> *It is the husband's duty to save the wife. The fact that her life is in danger transcends every other standard you might use to judge his action. Life is more important than property.*
>
> *Suppose it were a friend, not his wife.*
>
> *I don't think that would be much different from a moral point of view. It's still a human being in danger.*
>
> *Suppose it were a stranger.*
>
> *To be consistent, yes, from a moral standpoint.*
>
> (Colby and Kohlberg, 1987, p. 21)

Thus, even at the more sophisticated postconventional level—the moral perspective where the individual understands why something is right or wrong rather than simply what is right or wrong—the threat to life transcends normal rules. So it is with businesses and the people who run them.

Kohlberg's analysis is, of course, concerned with the moral development of individuals over time, and particularly as they progress from childhood to adulthood. The application of this approach to a social organization may well be questioned, but such application has precedents. For example, the application of Kelly's repertory grid (Kelly, 1955), based on his theory of personal constructs which was developed from longitudinal research of the psychological development of individuals, has been widely applied in social research design and data analysis. The use of Kohlberg's theory is similarly justified, especially as the application is restricted to analogy and metaphor, which are used to provide insights, rather than a full in-depth application.

One of the more obvious differences between Kohlberg's application and the present use of his model is highlighted in this consideration of business survival. Kohlberg's postconventional subject quoted above has explained the reasons why ethical considerations are overturned when life is threatened. Business does not provide postconventional explanations. The business perspective does not go beyond the conventional level of moral development, so that postconventional explanation is not available. Nevertheless, considerations of survival certainly dominate the ethics of normal business. Perhaps the best Kohlbergian analogy would be to suggest that business, as a social institution rather than a maturing individual, is capable of renewal and regression and when its survival is threatened the moral perspective regresses back to the preconventional level.

As a reminder of the preconventional level, recall that the response to the question 'Why shouldn't you steal from a store?' was:

> *It's not good to steal from the store. It's against the law. Someone could see you and call the police.*   (Colby and Kohlberg, 1987, p. 17)

This is the level of ethical consideration that is to be anticipated in a situation where survival is threatened. The gloves are off. Any action to preserve the business is open to consideration. The only constraint is the law, the likelihood of being caught and the probable punishment. Survival is one reason why business cannot be run according to the rules of moral philosophy.

Satisfying stakeholders

If the lowest level objective, survival, is prepotent, then the business may be expected to behave as though its moral perspective is preconventional. But at higher levels in the hierarchy, such as satisfying stakeholders, the business might be expected to behave at the conventional level. This has already been briefly examined, but at this point it is worth elaborating a little on the definition.

Kohlberg explicitly considers the issue of trust, which is such an important component in Gauthier's cooperative model. At the conventional level, trustworthiness is something one expects of others in society. One of Kohlberg's subjects, at age 17, expressed this as follows:

> *Why should a promise be kept, anyway?*

> **Friendship is based on trust. If you can't trust a person, there's little grounds to deal with him. You should try to be as reliable as possible because people remember you by this. You're more respected if you can be depended upon.**
>
> (Colby and Kohlberg, 1987, p. 21)

At this conventional level, the subject views trust both as a truster and as someone who could break a trust. He sees that individuals need to be trustworthy, not only to secure respect and to maintain social relationships with others, but also because, as members of society, they expect trust of others in general.

Seven years later, the same subject provided a postconventional explanation. At this level he did not automatically assume he was in a society in which people need the friendship and respect of other individuals. Instead he considered why any society, or social relationship, presupposes trust, and why he, if he was to contract into society, must be trustworthy:

> I think human relationships in general are based on trust, on believing in other individuals. If you have no way of believing in someone else, you can't deal with anyone else and it becomes every man for himself. Everything you do in a day's time is related to somebody else and if you can't deal on a fair basis, you have chaos.   (Ibid.)

These expressions identify the moral perspective to be expected of people in business actively engaged in forging the collaborations and alliances and operating the teams and networks which are an essential aspect of the contemporary business organization. They also identify the chaotic result if everyone in business adopted a short-term profit-maximizing perspective. Axelrod's tit-for-tat games strategy (see page 43) suggests that trust is built up through 'clarity, niceness, provocability and forgivingness'. If these four are evident then trust can be both established and robust (i.e. survive some failures). It is important that the characteristics are evident. Moreover, establishing credibility in the strategic sense means that you are expected to keep promises and make good on all threats, i.e. be predictable.

In *The Maltese Falcon* Gutman gives Sam Spade an envelope containing $10 000, and Spade points out they had been talking about more money than that. Gutman agreed,

> ... but we were talking then. This is actual money, genuine coin of the realm. With a dollar of this, you can buy ten dollars of talk.
>   (Quoted in Dixit and Nalebuff, 1991, p. 142)

Credibility is crucial. Unless trustworthiness is credible it will have no strategic effect, i.e. it will not enable firms to engage in mutually advantageous collaborations. Firms have therefore to be very careful not to take actions that damage credibility.

The following sections provide a few examples of stakeholder satisfying interactions and show how relevant ethical issues might be understood and resolved.

Employees

Firms are involved in a tremendous variety of transactions with their employees, some once only, others continuously. They arise in the following areas: selection and recruitment, induction, health and safety, training and development, remuneration, working conditions, job content, supervision, management and motivation, discipline and grievances, holidays and working arrangements (i.e. hours and place of working, flexitime, etc.), achievement and recognition, promotion, equal opportunities and an endless list of factors that might conveniently be lumped together in the catch-all term 'culture'—items that may crucially affect the climate and attitude of people at work.

Most of the above are worthy of books in their own right and there is little point in examining each in detail here. They each contribute to the employee's psychological contract with the employer, and they all interact. A dishonest transaction between an employer and employee in one area is inevitably going to influence the relationship as a whole and affect how transactions are undertaken in other areas. Having once been treated dishonestly, the party to the transaction, whether it is the employee or the employer, will be wary about any recurrence. The principle of trust that may have been painstakingly established, will have been quickly destroyed or damaged and will take a great deal of concerted effort to rebuild.

Rather than discuss each aspect of such transactions in detail, two alternative approaches to employee relationships are evidenced. The paraphrase from Waterhouse's piece on Robert Maxwell (see Box 5.1) indicates the bullying style of management that is still common.

Box 5.1: Atrocity tales from Maxwellia

Maxwell is, of course, now well known as having been a crook, a bully and a big-head. He regularly reduced new secretaries to tears. Told that Soviet tanks were rolling into Lithuania, he rubbished the idea: 'nonsense ... Gorbachev wouldn't do anything without ringing me first.' But more than all this he was an absolute nuisance to those working for him. According to Waterhouse (1992) 'he interfered, or tried to interfere, with every stage of his newspapers' production, from the make-up to the news content'.

Moreover he frequently invented 'scoops', and insisted his staff wrote them up. He even tried to get them selling encyclopaedias to the American troops when they were risking their lives reporting the Gulf war. With Scuds flying through the headlines, the *Mirror*'s newsdesk had to postpone until after the final edition their nightly task of combing the newspapers for every reference to Maxwell or his companies and faxing the clippings to wherever he happened to be. Informed of this slight delay, Maxwell said, 'F**** the war. I want my faxes.'

He couldn't bear to have his judgement questioned and would rant at his executives, slamming the phone down if they should query anything he said.

Greenslade told how Maxwell wanted the *Daily Mirror* to carry a money-off promotion offer for bottles of vitamin pills which were supposed to improve children's IQ—a stupid venture for any newspaper. Needless to say Maxwell was involved with the firm concerned, and equally needless to say, he got his way.

As he was wont to say, 'Remember, I own the stadium; you are just the manager.'

(Waterhouse, 1992)

Directors and chief executives are in a position where they can behave as though they 'own the stadium', rather than merely manage it, and this all too often has an unhinging effect on them. Such a situation was described in the opening chapter in the story of S.T.P. Ltd. It does not require a crooked megalomaniac like Maxwell to convince themselves they own the stadium—capitalist business is built up on such assumptions and realities.

The alternative approach is evidenced in various accounts of the Levi Strauss business (see Box 5.2 for examples). While the word 'empowering' has been rather overworked, it nevertheless best describes the Haas approach. Even though Haas is a latter-day member of the original owning family, the style of employee–employer transactions that his management has developed does not appear to be paternalistic. It is a calculated relationship—the sharing of profits from employee suggestions is quantified and shared on what appears to be a 'fair' basis, but is not operative until certain other criteria have been met. These transactions are agreed in detail and implemented according to the detailed agreement. They are very much calculated. The calculations are up front and open, as required in their aspirations statement.

Box 5.2   Aspirations at Levi Strauss

Levi Strauss has always been known for combining strong commercial success with a commitment to social values and to its workforce. During the recession of the 1980s the company went through a sea change and under the leadership of CEO Robert Haas (great-great-grand-nephew of the founder) Levi Strauss has reinvented itself. Haas flattened the organization, cut a third of the workforce and invested heavily in new technology, marketing and new product development. The result, achieved with no little difficulty, was that this big, mature business is now hugely flexible and innovative, profitable and growing.

In an interview reported in *Harvard Business Review* under the title 'Values make the company' (Howard, 1990) Haas claimed that at Levi Strauss, the company's most important asset was not, as might be expected, its people, but its people's aspirations. A major initiative for Haas during his first few years was the development of the Levi

Strauss aspirations statement. According to Haas it is the Aspiration Statement that really brings things to life.

The statement starts with the following declaration:

We all want a company that our people are proud of and committed to, where all employees have an opportunity to contribute, learn, grow, and advance based on merit, not politics or background. We want our people to feel respected, treated fairly, listened to, and involved. Above all, we want satisfaction from accomplishments and friendships, balanced personal and professional lives, and to have fun in our endeavours.

The Aspiration Statement goes on to identify the type of leadership that is necessary to make the aspirations a reality. In particular it identifies:

Leadership that exemplifies directness, openness to influence, commitment to the success of others, willingness to acknowledge our own contributions to problems, personal accountability, team-work, and trust. Not only must we model these behaviours but we must coach others to adopt them.

Haas keeps reminding Levi's people: 'You don't work for Levi's, you work for yourselves; you just happen to work at Levi's.' The admonition is part of his struggle to put the needs of individuals on the same level as those of the organization.

Waterman (1994) examined the Levi Strauss approach in further detail. He found that

people who said they used to be praised for being tough now consider themselves to be more effective if they let go some of their authority. And those who are gaining some authority seem to relish it. Before Levi's aspirations caught on, 'I would see my brain fuming into chewing-gum,' said Marji Meade, a sewing-machine operator at Blue Ridge who specialised in affixing waistbands to jeans. Now she and others at her plant not only participate in decision-making, they also get added recognition for their efforts.

Besides the psychological pay-offs, Blue Ridge employees are rewarded financially under a gain-sharing programme. If they make a suggestion that saves the factory money—anything from recycling rubber bands to streamlining postal delivery—they take home half the profits added by the idea. (The only catch is that the plant must have met its production and quality targets before gain-sharing kicks in.) The programme adds about $600 a year to a typical Blue Ridge employee's take-home pay.

Gain-sharing is just one of many efforts under way at Levi's to applaud contributions from employees.

(Howard, 1990)

The transactions have what Axelrod referred to as 'clarity'—they are clear and simple. It would appear that Levi Strauss would not initiate cheating, i.e. the transactions also involve 'niceness'. They probably also involve 'provocability'—any cheating, by either participant, would not go unpunished. Moreover, the relationships almost certainly also involve 'forgivingness', i.e. an outbreak of cheating would not bring the relationship to an end, but after 'punishment', efforts would be made to resume transactions on the former basis. This calculated nature to the relationship is important. It is the foundation of the enlightened self-interest which enabled Gauthier's farmers to collaborate to their mutual advantage.

Over time, transactions that continue on this basis become relationships that are based on these certain values. Their foundation, however, is not some extraneous value system or philosophy, or even religion, no matter what the origination of the business; it is the dependence of both parties on their mutually advantageous transactions and thus their mutual interest in continuity.

Transactions with employees are therefore carried out on the basis of a contract which is both formal and informal. If either written or unwritten parts of the contract are broken the parties which contravene must, according to Axelrod's model, be punished, and be seen to be punished. Many contraventions are obvious and direct. In some areas, however, contravention is less explicit.

Aspects of 'equal opportunities' still lie in this twilight area. For instance, a report on the position of women in the IT industry (Virgo, 1991) suggests that there are still far fewer women in the industry than men (e.g. 3 per cent of DP managers) and even fewer in top jobs. They also get paid less than men and get promoted less often. This is despite the fact that in many respects IT is an industry for which women are apparently well suited. In aggregate it appears that there must be a fairly powerful prejudice against women in the industry, but it may be extremely difficult to identify particular instances, even from within the organizations (or even individuals) that exercise the prejudice.

Equal opportunities issues may arise only obliquely, not as a direct part of the employee-employer transaction, but as part of the interactions between fellow employees. These may be extremely difficult to manage, but nevertheless form an important part of the fabric of the employee-employer relationship, and the employer has to create a culture where equal opportunities abuses (relating to race, sex, disability or age) are not tolerable and not tolerated. Examples of punishment for such abuses are not widely reported. Presumably this is because the firms involved do not wish to bring themselves this odious publicity.

Nevertheless, if the relationships are to be conducted on the basis of trust, such punishments need to be carried out and seen to be so. Box 5.3

demonstrates the importance Goldman Sachs accords abuses of trust in this rather ambiguous area. In order to preserve the principle of trust with its employees, the company fired three valuable employees who abused the principle in the area of sexual harassment, risking, though seeking to minimize, the adverse publicity that inevitably ensued.

In all these various interactions with employees, business need to maintain a consistency of integrity. Mistrust arising as a result of some shortfall in one area, will affect the level of trust accorded transactions in other areas. Firms need therefore to behave as though they have internalized the principle of trust as a value affecting all their transactions and relationships with employees. This means being vigilant in all the areas

---

Box 5.3 Sexual exchange costs foreign money dealers their Goldman Sachs jobs

Three highly paid foreign exchange dealers at the London offices of the top American investment bank Goldman Sachs have been forced to leave the firm after allegations of sexual harassment by a secretary.

The scandal will be especially embarrassing for Goldmans, which prides itself on its integrity and high moral tone.

The bank hit the headlines recently when it emerged that more than 100 staff in its London office would become dollar millionaires with one senior partner rumoured to have received $25m—after bonuses for a bumper year.

A secretary asked one of the dealers, who earns up to £1m a year, how she could advance her career. The three traders allegedly responded with a series of crude comments. Goldmans confirmed yesterday that three foreign exchange dealers had resigned. It would, however, neither confirm nor deny details of the case, and emphasised its standing policy of not discussing staff affairs in public.

Sources close to the firm pointed out that the bank had a strong tradition of fully investigating all staff complaints and dealing with them in a strong manner. It is understood that no further action is being taken by the secretary concerned.

The scandal was the buzz of wine bars around the bank's Fleet Street offices in central London last night, but employees were told not to talk about the affair.

Goldmans made its name as a meritocracy, relying on 12-hour days and total dedication from staff rather than the traditional City dependence on the old school tie. Getting a job is notoriously difficult. Once in, recruits are paid comparatively modestly by City standards but rewards rise rapidly if they show ability.

(Willcock, 1994)

where employee transactions are active and ensuring that any actions by people acting on behalf of the business, or by other employees, that might affect the credibility of the business' trustworthiness are punished and seen to be punished.

Suppliers

The traditional way of looking at suppliers is that of the economist, typified by Porter (1979), and focusing on an assessment of their bargaining power. The buyer–supplier transaction is seen as one which itself produces an economic surplus that will be divided between the two parties according to their bargaining strength. This is essentially the short-term profit-maximizing model.

The transaction becomes more complex when viewed as a continuing relationship over a strategic timescale. Businesses need to forge links with suppliers who can support long-term as well as short-term objectives. Marks & Spencer, for example, has some suppliers who date back over a hundred years. No M&S supplier makes a quick killing out of the high street chain, but they earn enough to ensure continued capital investment to maintain top quality and productivity.

However, long-term relationships are based on much more than long-term viability. Whether one is considering the supplier of raw materials, of technology or of knowledge and information, the buyer needs to be assured of the supplier's standing in several different aspects. Reliability and predictability are crucial parts of this relationship. The supplier must be trusted to deliver the detailed specification, quality, price and delivery schedule agreed. The buyer must be trusted to accept delivery as agreed and to pay on the basis agreed.

This is a calculated relationship. The terms of the supply agreements will all be written down. Adherence to those terms needs to be monitored and any deviation from the terms needs to be punished—the terms of punishment may be written into the agreement. The satisfactory performance of such transactions will result in the cementing of a strategic relationship which may develop in surprising ways. For example, the supplier of technology may agree to supply, run and test prototype/development equipment and plant in its customer's facilities, with a mutual benefit in terms of innovation and new product development.

There is also an increasing pressure on ensuring that the suppliers perform in ways that are seen, by the customers, as being ethical. The example quoted in Box 5.4 is typical of many new arrangements arising from the increasing awareness and sensitivity of the general public. Suppliers with connections with the old racist regime in South Africa needed to be treated with extreme care. Student action at British

---

Box 5.4   Clark's spurn sperm whale oil

It is significant that the only time anyone can remember Daniel Clark giving a direct order was when the integrity of the company was at stake. The issue was whether the company would renounce the use of leather cured with sperm whale oil. The initial reaction from the company, when it was asked by conservationist groups for such an undertaking, was that it had no control over its suppliers. The pressure from the conservationists grew and there was even talk of organising a boycott of Clark's shoes.

At this point Daniel Clark stepped in and issued an edict. Not only would the company adopt an immediate policy of buying only leather cured without sperm whale oil, but it would invest in expensive spectroscopic analysis and testing equipment to check that supplies conformed to the new specifications. A few suppliers demurred, but Clark's is such a major customer that most readily agreed. Six months later Clark's was able to report that at least 98 per cent of its supplies were free of sperm whale oil. Typical of its Quaker background, the company would not claim 100 per cent, on the grounds that it had not checked every single bale of leather to come into its warehouse.

(Goldsmith and Clutterbuck, 1985)

---

universities forced Barclays to reconsider its policy towards its South African business. Levi Strauss issued global sourcing guidelines setting out the terms on which suppliers would be engaged and excluding any operating in countries with 'oppressive regimes'.

Premier Brands has launched a fair trade initiative sourcing Ty-phoo tea only from plantations which satisfy them in terms of social and environmental criteria, and placing the 'Caring for tea and our tea pickers' logo on all Ty-phoo packaging.

Grand Met phased out the use of CFCs in freezing vegetables because of public concern over the role of CFCs in global warming.

Public concern over ethical issues is being responded to directly by several firms in ways not strictly related to their prime business. For example, Timberland, the shoe manufacturer, ran an advertising campaign against racism. In the US Timberland collaborated with a charity called City Year which was campaigning for the public to help regenerate the inner cities. Timberland's press advertisements publicized Timberland's stance on racism as well as City Year's inner city project. Whether or not this is a viable business initiative, or is in effect a charitable donation by Timberland, will depend on the public's response. If people demand that firms behave in this way, i.e. they are prepared to pay for it, then firms will surely supply that demand.

Shareholders

Under the capitalist system, shareholders owned the business and therefore had largely unrestricted freedom to do with it what they liked. Directors were appointed to implement the wishes of shareholders and acted on behalf, and in the best interests, of shareholders. The objective of directors was widely held to be to maximize the wealth of shareholders. Those days have now gone.

Today, we are in a 'post-capitalist society' and the grand old man has eloquently pointed out that shareholders are now very largely the pension funds (Drucker, 1993) that are managed on behalf of their members (i.e. employees). The pension funds by and large do not seek to act as owners, but as participants in the capitalist system, with the freedom to invest their members' funds wherever it would be most advantageous, but at the same time recognizing their members' interests in long-term security. This group of shareholders therefore do not behave as short-term profit maximizers, but seek a longer term relationship with the companies whose shares they own.

The pension funds and other financial institutions are, however, only one class of shareholder. There are at least two others which businesses need to consider. First, there are individual shareholders. Their interests may be similar to those of the pensions funds, or they may well seek a quick profit and be prepared to act on an extremely short-term view. Some firms try to identify the wishes and intentions of their shareholders, but without much success. Private shareholders are not readily classifiable as a coherent group and it is not therefore feasible to relate to them coherently.

The third group of shareholders are the acquisitive opportunists. These are other firms, financial conglomerates swimming around the business pool hoping to pick up something for nothing. These are highly fluid: shareholders today, gone tomorrow. Their motivation is entirely self-interested and short term. If short-term profit maximizing has any relevance today it is to these firms. A long-term relationship with such shareholders has no meaning.

It is therefore difficult to conduct relations with shareholders in any meaningful sense. Their expectations and demands are extremely disparate and may change quite rapidly. It is unknown whether they are friends or enemies of the firm. Their long-term interests may lie in the firm prospering, or they may lie in attacking the firm, killing it and, like a hungry vulture, picking over the entrails.

The best way of establishing any systematic relationship is to regard shareholders essentially as customers, or potential customers, for the firm's shares. But rather than trying to please the shareholders, the aim is to satisfy them, and the measure of their satisfaction is the share price. It is not the aim to maximize the share price, but to maintain it at a level that preserves the firm's continued autonomy, and makes it feasible when necessary to raise either debt or equity finance. Anything more than this is wasteful.

The means by which the share price is managed and through which the firm conducts its relationship with its shareholders is first and foremost through its financial results and, second, through its regular reporting, financial and otherwise. Reporting either directly or through the press provides the firm with an opportunity to inform stakeholders about strategic issues so that they know what the firm is about and may be able to interpret its financial results against that strategic backdrop. Thus a firm may engender in its shareholders a loyalty (i.e. a short-term financially irrational support) for a course of action that may produce short-term problems but long-term success. Pilkington achieved this when it successfully fended off BTR's unwelcome opportunistic takeover bid.

Thus, business–shareholder transactions are also calculating. The business does not waste more than is necessary on satisfying the shareholder, but it does at the same time try to increase the understanding of shareholders about what the business is trying to achieve. Trust can be a crucial part of this relationship. If the business management has developed trust, then its shares will be valued that bit higher, all else being equal. Moreover, the firm will attract the right shareholders who understand the role the business will play in their particular portfolio, whether it is capital growth or dividend yield, low risk or high. From time to time credibility of trust is forfeited: a board will break promises, fall down on profit forecasts, etc., and if their credibility is finally eroded they will in the end be forced to go.

The professionals at calculating the business–shareholder relationship are those businesses that are built on their stockmarket operations rather than on their ability to make and sell products or services. These are the financial conglomerates such as Slater Walker, Jessel Securities, Hanson Trust and countless others. Most of them have long since gone to the wall, but the species survives.

Ironically, they treat their external shareholders not simply as parties to a calculated transaction and relationship, but as adversaries, to be 'bamboozled' or at least told less than the whole truth (see, for example, Box 5.5). These firms are exceptions from the current discussion since their aim is not the creation of wealth but its redistribution, their sociomoral perspective is firmly set at the preconventional level of development rather than the conventional, and they are largely engaged in short-term profit maximizing rather than anything more substantial and long lasting.

Sir James Goldsmith, one of the arch exponents of such financial engagements, pointed out that the diversified conglomerates created as a result of such financial motivations rarely outlive the original entrepreneur by very long. The list of such conglomerates, and their whizz-kid creators,

Box 5.5   Pre-acquisition provisions bamboozle shareholders

Companies like Hanson, BTR and Williams use pre-acquisition provisions 'to ensure that the costs of integrating acquisitions—from redundancies and head office closures to Christies' commission on selling the directors' paintings—are not allowed to detract from the future performance of the enlarged group. For take-over specialists, such provisions can offer a real boost to the bottom line. The biggest and best at the game—Hanson *et al.*—are expert at exploiting the rules, or lack of them. But they are also one of the biggest remaining black holes of British-accounting. The provisions can be used to smooth out dips in earnings for years after the take-over, bamboozling shareholders and analysts who can find it impossible to measure accurately the performance of the Company and the success—or otherwise—of the take-over.

Take Coats Viyella. In 1991 it bought Tootal, the thread maker, and provided £80m for rationalisation and reorganisation of the company. That represented more than six times the £12.9m pre-tax profit Tootal made in the year before it was acquired. Coats used £31m of the provisions in the first year and a further £22m in 1992. Even if Coats had disclosed Tootal's contribution to profits in 1991, investors would have found it impossible to tell how much was due to improved trading, and how much to the release of provisions. . . . The small print in its accounts reveals a lucrative spin-off from acquisition account-ing—clearing up its own business. More than half the provisions—£42.8m—related to planned reorganisation of Coats's own factories. Charging that against its own profits would have made a severe dent in the £111.4m pre-tax it made in 1991.

Coats's treatment was perfectly legal. Other companies have also used pre-acquisition provisions to shelter the cost of restructuring their own businesses. TI Group—which provided £87m following the acquisition of Dowty—has even gone back and adjusted its estimates in subsequent years.

Hanson, however, is justly recognised as the master of the art. In last year's accounts, it provided £1.3bn against Beazer, the building and aggregates group it acquired at the end of 1990. The previous year it provided £105m against Cavenham, while in 1990 it established a record breaking £1.67bn reserve against Peabody, the coal mining business, largely for future claims for black lung disease among miners. In September 1992, its accumulated provisions of £4.8bn were £500m larger than its shareholders' funds.

(Connon, 1994)

is extremely long, but few have survived much more than a decade, Hanson being an exception; but even in that case a succession from the first generation management is extremely problematic, and recent noises suggesting that they are trying to create an industrial logic for the group that might then focus back on those core businesses has been greeted with dismay by the City cognoscenti.

Directors

Directors operate in locus of the legal business entity and they therefore have a statutory responsibility to behave in its best interests at all times. The best interests of the business may be difficult to interpret. It is certainly much less clear than, for example, acting in the best interests of the shareholders. The business comprises various stakeholders, including employees, customers, and suppliers as well as the owners. Assessing whether a director has or has not acted in the best interests of the business is therefore often quite difficult. Both the business and, more particularly, its best interests, are open to interpretation. Second guessing a director's decision to assess whether he or she acted appropriately, without the benefit of hindsight, is notoriously difficult. Consequently, there are few examples of directors being found guilty of acting against the best interests of the business. The only exception to this is the case where there is a conflict of interest, i.e. where the personal interests of the director and the best interests of the business, appear to be in direct conflict. Where this is the case, the record of directors is not edifying.

Directors control the till. They have more or less complete dictatorial power within their company to do as they please. They have ample opportunities for dishonesty that will not be detected. Even if their actions are known by their peers, they are unlikely to be stopped. Consequently, company directorship is an exceedingly attractive field of endeavour to the straightforwardly crooked. Few crooks make it into the big time of company directorships, but those that do make it big, like Maxwell. Most have to put up with small-time crime in small-time companies.

The vast majority of company directors are not crooks, but just ordinary human beings with ordinary human frailty. This is where the record may be unedifying. Given the opportunity of paying themselves a 4 per cent rise, or a 40 per cent rise, most directors would go for 40 per cent. They might even go for 40 per cent, while trying to hold everyone else's rise to less than 4 per cent. They might even go for 40 per cent while trying to eliminate the jobs of substantial numbers of their employees. NatWest took this approach (see Box 5.6) and they are probably not the most self-serving, exploitative board of directors in the country. But justification for their pay-outs is difficult to sustain.

Box 5.6   NatWest chiefs get huge rises as staff are cut

Directors of National Westminster Bank have received bumper pay rises at a time when the bank is trying to freeze employee pay and cut more staff than any of its rivals. Main board directors were awarded increases of up to 40 per cent on 1st April and received generous share option packages last year.

The Banking Insurance and Finance Union (BIFU) has taken the bank to the Advisory Conciliation and Arbitration Service (ACAS) to try and get a 4 per cent across-the-board pay rise. The bank favours performance-related pay, which would mean some staff receiving nothing. NatWest also plans to cut 4,200 of its 91,400 staff this year.

Dr John Owen, chief executive of NatWest Markets, the stockbroking business, saw his pay climb around 40 per cent from £215,000 to £300,000. John Melbourn, a deputy group chief executive, also got 40 per cent more. But his rise from £207,000 to £290,000 accompanied his promotion from chief executive, group risk. Derek Wanless, the group chief executive, is on the highest basic salary. His pay has risen from £267,000 to £350,000. Last year's highest paid director, Richard Goeltz, group chief financial officer, got a rise in basic pay from £200,000 to £250,000. He was paid a total of £554,238 in 1993, including a performance-related bonus of £72,739 and £242,170 to cover the costs of moving from New York to London.

These pay rises follow substantial share options issued in September 1993. Mr Wanless was granted options to buy 114,115 shares at 503p between September 1996 and August 2003. National Westminster's shares closed at 442p on Friday.

A BIFU spokesman, who also attacked top pay at Barclays, said: 'There are double standards at NatWest, with increasing rewards for a few at the top and a difficult life for those at the bottom.

'We are talking about a very small world that is concerned only with the markets and the shareholders. It shows scant regard for staff and customers.' NatWest declined to comment.

(Bruce, 1994)

The justification for directors' bonuses is usually made on the back of productivity increases, as though the increases came about as a result of the skill and effort of the recipients. In point of fact most productivity increases are achieved through the availability and application of new technology, for which few directors have any responsibility or even real knowledge. They benefit from the new technology in just the same way as did members of the pre-Wapping print union; the only difference being that whereas those unions had to fight to negotiate their inequitable gains, directors just put their hands in the till.

Even without gains in productivity directors have still paid themselves handsome increases. A 1990 *Guardian* survey showed that the pay of Midland Bank's highest paid director rose by 500 per cent while the bank was in the red; Barclays' highest paid director rose by more than 215 per cent while earnings had fallen by 30 per cent; at Enterprise Oil the highest paid director was given a rise of 120 per cent while earnings per share fell by 30 per cent.

Directors' pay is largely out of control. Burton Group proposed a share option scheme that could have been worth £8m to Sir Ralph Halpern, then UK's highest paid executive with a salary of over £1m p.a. Sir Anthony Tennant, after five years at Guinness, collected a 25 per cent rise to £777 000 p.a. plus an annual pension of up to £500 000 despite the company's 12 per cent drop in profits. There is a trend to extremely high salaries irrespective of company performance. This was confirmed in a 1993 survey by Stefan Szymanski of London Business School:

> During the boom there was a definite relationship between rapidly increasing profits and rises in board pay. During the recession, however, this relationship broke down. Profits fell, but earnings stayed the same or kept on rising. (Martin, 1993)

The same applies to pay-offs as well as to pay. Sir Ralph Halpern received about £2m from Burton together with a £456 000 pension for life, plus various bonuses that were revealed subsequently. Peter Scott was paid around £2m when he left Aegis. Chrispen Davies was paid a two-year £670 000 compensation package by Guinness when he resigned after 15 months as MD of United Distillers. Robert Horton was paid £1.53m on his departure as chairman and chief executive of BP. The list is extremely long. Directors have the opportunity to take more than is justified by any conceivable criterion, and, being normally frail human beings, many of them take.

The question that needs to be answered in the present context is whether such 'taking' alters the perception of would-be collaborators about the trustworthiness of the individuals or the businesses concerned. The answer is not completely clear. One might assume that such 'taking' has no positive impact on the credibility of trust, but whether it adversely affects trust is less certain. In aggregate such gross abuses no doubt contribute to the general level of cynicism about business and business people among the population at large. There is also at least a probability that 'taking' has a negative effect.

The existence and level of this directorial abuse also presents a considerable opportunity. To be seen to be fair and equitable in all such dealings will attract some recognition and enhance the credibility of trust out of all proportion to the reality.

Community

Interactions between the company and its local community have for some time been largely restricted to those roles it undertakes with members of the community as employees, customers, suppliers, etc. Apart from these the business may have to take special care with its business operations so that they do not have uncompensated adverse impacts on the local community, e.g. noise pollution, traffic nuisance, etc.

In earlier times the business played a much more important role in the community. Many of the old Quaker companies, for example, built 'model villages' to accommodate their employees. Companies which dominated their locality not only built housing and shops, but also provided schools and churches. Companies laid on social events such as children's parties and Easter parades as well as providing sports and leisure and other social facilities. The companies supported their own football and cricket teams and their own brass bands. Some even provided hospitals.

Companies no longer have these roles, and despite the growing reluctance of governments to tax and pay for all these undertakings, companies are unlikely to resume. Companies are no longer mass employers and, with few exceptions, no longer dominate their local communities.

Nevertheless, there is considerable interest in some quarters in encouraging business to engage more with its local community. For example, 'Business in the Community' is a UK umbrella organization with over 500 corporate members, aimed at helping create partnerships between business, government and local communities to improve the economic, physical and social environment. This initiative is based on extremely worthwhile ideals and may well result in a significant increase in a business's community involvement. However, viewed in the context of the hierarchy of objectives adopted here, these community activities, whatever form they take, are irrelevant. In themselves, they may be laudable, but they only serve to confuse business strategy and get in the way of the business focusing on its strategic objective. Transactions with the community are at the intermediate satisfying level of the hierarchy and trying to do more than satisfy merely serves to distract and prevent concentration.

The modern role of the business in community—beyond carefully targeted investment or sponsorship—should probably be restricted to ensuring that any adverse effects of the business are minimized and compensated. If a company's interactions with its local community are seen to have adverse or pollutive (very broadly defined) effects, this may well impact on the way other stakeholders perceive the business as a potential collaborator. This effect may then be multiplied by any attempts to avoid compensation or to deny the pollutive effects. Such denial or backsliding, if recognized as such, will certainly be perceived by potential collaborators as indicative of untrustworthiness.

Companies no longer have the community responsibilities that were undertaken by their Victorian forebears. Minimizing and compensating for any adverse (pollutive) impacts are the main concerns for management regarding their business–community interactions. Beyond this, the main responsibility of business management is to ensure success in business terms, so that they maintain a contribution to local prosperity.

Environment

A business does not interact with the environment in quite the same way as it does with other stakeholders. The environment is not a stakeholder. The environment itself is rather passive, there to be exploited as far as regulations and the law will permit. The law and the increasingly active environmental pressure groups are there to protect the environment. It might well be argued that as long as their requirements are *satisfied*, then surely businesses will have done enough.

The environment might be regarded as a proxy for the best interests of future generations and it is these stakeholders with whom the business is really interacting when it impacts on the environment. A business that has long-term aspirations needs to be aware of its impacts on future generations. It needs to conduct itself in a way that is not only regarded as generally ethical by today's standards of awareness and understanding, but by the standards that will be applied by future generations.

The asbestos companies, for example, in the past conducted their businesses in ways that would be totally unacceptable today. They poisoned generations of employees, their families and local communities, as well as distributing potentially lethal material for multifarious applications throughout the world. People today are suffering because of the 'sins' of the asbestos companies half a century ago. It is still not known when the last repercussions of this particular form of environmental pollution will have been finally worked through. The behaviour of the asbestos companies has been assessed with all the benefits of hindsight and most of them have been destroyed as a result. Turner & Newall, a notable survivor, has long known about the adverse effects of asbestos. It instituted the research on which health and safety standards were subsequently based. It invested heavily in both research and in safer methods of working (e.g. wet-weaving processes, better extraction, working conditions and practices, etc.). This does not exonerate the company from criticism. It continued to produce asbestos-based products when we now acknowledge it was unsafe to do so. It promoted asbestos as a life-saving material and, with hindsight, stands accused of being a cynical, exploitative profit maximizer. It argued vociferously over compensating its victims. T&N was exceptional in that industry in the care it took to find out the facts and the actions it took when it began to understand the facts. Nevertheless, it is judged not by contemporary standards, but from the perspective of today's knowledge and understanding.

In interacting with the environment, long-term businesses must therefore take into account the knowledge that future generations will have of their environmental impacts. They must accept responsibility for being expert on their environmental interactions and behave in a way that future generations will find acceptable, otherwise they will not survive those future generations. T&N survived, but many asbestos companies failed.

In thinking through the response of future generations it is important to recognize that environmental issues is another area in which there is a growing awareness, and it is becoming fashionable to suggest that business should take a more proactive stance. But the interactions a business has with its environment are not an end in themselves. The business needs to ensure that its environmental impacts are sustainable in the long-term future, but it does not need to take a missionary stance with regard to the environment.

Satisfying these future stakeholders through environmental interactions is therefore one of careful balance. With hindsight, even quite well-intentioned actions might look cynically exploitative (as in the case of asbestos) and therefore a bad risk for any potential long-term collaborator. How much less acceptable is the cynically exploitative, whether it is the Japanese gifting pesticide to Cambodia (see Box 5.7), western tobacco firms selling high tar cigarettes to unsophisticated third world markets, or western firms exploiting less rigorous environmental regulation in developing economies.

There is also a positive side to interactions with the environment. First, genuine, new opportunities are created by the need to sustain the environment. The areas of potential are extremely wide as the few examples listed below indicate:

■ Energy saving, e.g. Pilkington's new glass 30 per cent better insulator.

■ Recycling materials, whether it is the recyclable BMW, or the more mundane business of rebuilding and replenishing cartridges for laser printers, represents a huge potential market.

■ Cleaning up processes, e.g. the Corex process for reducing iron ore directly to hot metal, developed by the state-owned Voest-Alpine group of Austria, produces substantially fewer emissions than traditional methods and is viable on smaller scale production.

Box 5.7   Poisoned chalice

The brown plant-hopper, an insect pest which eats Asia's staple rice crops, is playing a leading role in a drama about the future of Cambodian agriculture, but it is not the true villain of the piece. If environmentalists and scientists are to be believed, the villain is the Japanese government.

Japan's decision to supply Cambodia with free pesticides has provoked sharp criticism from environmental pressure groups and from officials of respected bodies such as the International Rice Research Institute and the Food and Agriculture Organisation.

Cambodia, after more than two decades of war, has no legislation or controls on the use of pesticides. Nor do farmers or agriculture ministry officials have much experience in handling chemicals.

The Japanese government is therefore suspected of donating the pesticides not to help Cambodian farmers but to help the Japanese chemical industry secure a new market for its products. These suspicions are fuelled by the knowledge that Japan may eventually be forced by world trade negotiations to open its rice market to foreign suppliers. Japanese farmers account for only 2.5 per cent of world rice production, but they are heavy buyers of pesticides.

(Mallet, 1993)

■ Creating and selling to the environmentally aware, e.g. The Body Shop which publishes the 'green book' which balances an objective if incomplete account of The Body Shop's activities and their effects with corporate propaganda in an attempt to push corporate accountability for the environment a stage further.

These interactions with the environment might become more than simple satisfying objectives and represent the strategic focus of the business. This has, to a considerable extent, happened at The Body Shop. The fact that The Body Shop makes and sells cosmetics is not incidental, but the environmental aspect is of crucial importance and is certainly the factor that differentiates The Body Shop from its main competitors.

For most businesses, however, environmental interactions will remain at the satisfying level in the hierarchy and the aim will be to conduct such interactions in a way that will suggest to future stakeholders that the business is trustworthy and suitable for long-term collaborations.

Pleasing customers

At the intermediate levels in the objectives hierarchy, a business would be expected to behave at Kohlberg's conventional level. This applies to both satisfying stakeholders and pleasing customers. From the perspective of a moral philosopher, the business of pleasing customers is a little more problematic than satisfying the other stakeholders. If you deliberately set out to please a customer, there is implicit in your strategy an unstated intention to compete.

Competition is a difficult concept for business ethicists, implying as it does an attempt to inflict some kind of defeat on a third party or parties. For the present, however, we shall set competitive issues on one side and simply consider the interactions a business has with its customers.

The opening of any customer–supplier relationship will generally be through some form of marketing initiative. These are categorized as the set of variables that are controllable by marketing managers and include promotion, product, price and distribution—the four Ps or marketing mix. Here we shall look at these, but in a slightly idiosyncratic way, following the chronology of a typical customer interaction. The first step is typically some form of promotion, whether it is an advertisement or PR release, a sales promotion or even contact with a personal salesperson. The second part of a customer interaction will be through the product itself, which is defined here as a set of attributes, one of which is the price of the product. The third part of the transaction—which may or may not be crucially important, depending on the product—is its distribution. Then, finally, there is an after sales contact, which may be very important to the repeat of the transaction and its eventual development into an ongoing relationship.

Promotion

This first contact is likely to set the tone of the whole relationship whether it is in the form of advertising, personal selling, public relations or sales promotion. The aims of promotion may be to inform, to persuade, or to alter the underlying affections and perceptions of the audience. Whatever the promotional activity and whatever its aims, it will always be vital to create and maintain an image of trustworthiness and credibility. If the audience disbelieves the message, its communication will be counter-productive.

Advertising, public relations and personal selling all fairly obviously have the power to create whatever image the promoter desires. There are notoriously deceptive examples of each: the advertisement claiming for its product magical powers to reduce the weight of the purchaser; the public relations 'story' being a thinly veiled advertisement; the second-hand car salesperson claiming one careful owner and extremely low mileage. Some may be deceived, but probably few. The implicit message of such promotional initiatives is that the promoter is not to be trusted. While the reality and the image are in conflict, the resulting perception is likely to be exactly the opposite of what was intended.

The same applies equally, though less obviously, to sales promotions. Consider the famous Hoover blunder referred to in Box 5.8. The problem here was not one of intended deceit, but rather one of incompetence, followed initially by a less than full-hearted admission and openness. Even though Hoover pumped £28m more than intended into the scheme just to maintain its reputation for trustworthiness, its image was severely dented.

Whether it is advertising, selling, PR or sales promotion that first introduced the customer to the promoter and seller of the product, these are the means of creating first impressions. The initial expectations of trustworthiness and credibility are established, to be reinforced or reversed by the product or service itself and the subsequent relationship.

Box 5.8 Promotion to cost Hoover £28m more than planned

Hoover admitted yesterday that its ill-fated free flights offer had cost £48m, more than double the £20m it put aside a year ago to cover the cost of the promotion.

A spokesman for Maytag, Hoover's US parent, said there might be further provisions but would not quantify them. However, Richard Rankin, co-chairman of the task force set up to sort out the fiasco, pledged that when the promotion ended on 30 April, everyone who had complied with the terms and conditions of the offer would have been made an offer of free flights.

The disclosure in Maytag's full year figures of the final cost confirmed expectations that a £20m provision in last year's first-quarter figures would prove inadequate.

Hoover said 220 000 people had either flown or been booked on flights as a result of an unexpectedly popular promotion that offered two free flights to anyone who spent more than £100 on a Hoover product.

The offer became a farce after thousands bought appliances solely to take advantage of the promotion. Hoover had to create a team of 250 staff overnight to cope with the deluge of applicants.

The scheme became a case study in how not to run a promotion after a torrent of bad publicity followed complaints from hundreds of customers that they were not being offered flights to which they were entitled.

(Stevenson and Cooper, 1994)

Product

The most important transaction with the customer is through the product itself. The degree to which it satisfies customer expectations will be the most powerful and lasting communication of all. So, what is a product? It is clearly more than just the physical object. An expensive bottle of wine is not usually purchased simply to satisfy a thirst; an automobile is not bought solely as a means of transportation. Products are loaded, both physically and psychologically, with many extras that may be important determinants of sales success. Marketing literature is replete with descriptions of the many and various components that comprise the modern conception of a product.

One widely held view sees the product as having several layers: the core benefit or service, the formal or expected product and the outer, augmented product layer which includes such things as warranty, service support and so on (e.g. Kotler, 1984). This onion-like model implies that the product can be unpeeled to reveal hidden depths. The analogy only partially stands up to scrutiny.

The various attributes of a product are not necessarily related in any predictable fashion, onion-like or otherwise. There are many and various attributes that could be categorized, for convenience, as physical, implied and psychological, as shown in Figure 5.2.

What matters about this complex product is the customer's perceptions of its various attributes. Producing the best mouse trap is of no avail if it is not perceived as such by potential customers. The customers' perception of the product is an amalgam of their perception of the various product attributes, *any* of which may be critical in adding up to a concept of value which is a combination of price and quality. The concept of quality is not simply unidimensional, but complex. Moreover, its definition clearly depends on the type of product or service being delivered. For example, in

Physical attributes	Implied attributes	Psychological attributes
Price	Distribution	Corporate image
Quality	Delivery	Brand image
Performance	Reliability	Product image
Design	Warranty	Need image
Packaging	After sales support	
	Advertising	
	Service	

Figure 5.2 *Product attributes.*

the case of food products, distribution is clearly critical, whereas in the case of RAM chips, failure rates and reliability are more important to the customer.

Garvin suggested eight characteristics of quality, any of which might be crucial in particular circumstances (Garvin, 1987):

1. Primary performance

2. Secondary features

3. Reliability

4. Conformance

5. Durability

6. Serviceability

7. Aesthetics

8. Perceived quality

Primary performance refers to the product or service's primary operating characteristics, and Garvin noted that these were usually capable of objective measurement. In the case of cars, for example, performance would include such measures as speed, acceleration, noise levels, etc. Or, in the case of fast food or airlines, performance may be mainly a matter of prompt service.

Secondary features are also usually amenable to objective measurement. They are the extras that may differentiate an otherwise standard product. The following are examples of secondary features:

■ Customer selection of detailed product specification, e.g. General Motors dealers provide computer terminals which allow customers to select the features they want and the specified car is delivered within 7 days.

■ Free drinks on an aeroplane.

■ 'Clever' remote controls for a hi-fi set.

■ Flexibility and a wide variety of options in personal investment plans.

Reliability refers to the probability of a product breaking down in use. Clearly this is the key characteristic of many industrial and, increasingly, consumer durable products. Improved standards of reliability achieved in one sector, notably in electronics, appear to have a knock on effect in other sectors. Customers are now generally less tolerant of poor product reliability than previously.

Conformance refers to the achievement of product specifications—for example, dimensions within agreed tolerances. Again this is most usually critical in industrial products, particularly where products are to be assembled with other products of similarly defined specifications.

Durability is the expected product life and may be determined either by technical or economic factors. For example, the expected life of cars has increased significantly over the past decade because the rising cost of petrol and general economic stringency has reduced average annual mileages. Durability is a characteristic which differed widely between brands—Garvin gives examples of washing machines that have expected lives of from 5.8 to 18 years, and tumble dryers from 6 to 17 years, for makes of differing quality.

Serviceability refers to the ease, speed, competence and courtesy with which service is provided (i.e. products delivered, queries answered, repairs achieved, etc.). Clearly this characteristic is in some respects less amenable to objective measurement. Actual machine down-times resulting from breakdown may be open to accurate measurement, but the competence and courtesy of the service engineer are clearly subjective measures, likely to be influenced by individual circumstances. Subjectivity highlights the importance of customer complaint handling and in particular of obtaining the maximum amount of information about customer perceptions as a result of these transactions.

Aesthetics, the look, feel, sound, taste or smell of a product is clearly a subjective measure, which again means deliberate and calculated steps being taken to achieve any measure of consumer perceptions.

Perceived quality refers to consumers' perceptions of quality which may or may not be the same as reality. A firm may have established a reputation for quality which naturally attaches to any product the company offers. The corporate or brand image affects the way potential customers will perceive the product even before its introduction. Clearly this is a powerful factor which may make the difference between success and failure with the introduction of a new product.

These eight dimensions of quality to a great extent accord with the product attributes of Figure 5.2. The main omission is the price attribute. However, Garvin's dimensions of quality strike much deeper into the organization than do the marketer's product attributes, affecting the way each individual in the organization does his or her job. The marketer's product attributes may, in organizational terms, be quite superficial even though they may be important aspects of the product or service itself. For example, packaging may contribute substantially to a customer's perception of the product, but the impact of packaging on individuals in the organization may be minimal.

A ten-attribute product, based on Garvin's eight dimensions of quality and including also the essential attribute of price, plus a tenth attribute labelled as 'Ingredient X', is proposed here as the vehicle for pleasing the customers. 'Ingredient X' is not simply a selling proposition (unique or otherwise), or a marketing gimmick of some kind, but an extra attribute which arises directly from the core competences of the producer and is intended to provide customer satisfaction above expectations.

Canon's infinitely scaleable fonts on its low-cost laser printer when it was first offered was an added ingredient which gave it an extra competitive advantage over its main rivals. Similarly, Honda's four-wheel steering is another 'Ingredient X' example. In the case of service sector businesses, 'Ingredient X' may well relate to special elements of superior service that differentiate the business from its competitors. 'Ingredient X' is not simply a marginal additional factor in differentiation, it is a remarkable added attribute which takes the customer by surprise. It is a fundamental attribute, stemming directly from the firm's core competences and is therefore not easy for competitors to replicate. Clearly it will not be possible for every business to develop a product or service with a real 'Ingredient X', but for those that do, it may be the most important attribute of all.

These ten attributes are the components of value which the firm delivers to please its customer. No firm can successfully pursue all ten attributes; being leader simultaneously in all ten is hardly possible. Being the price leader may well preclude leadership on any other attribute, and several of the others may well conflict. Management's aim must be to provide a balance of attributes which accords with the requirements of customers. This is the business of pleasing customers and is clearly a far more demanding task than simply satisfying them. The integrity of the ten-attribute product is crucial.

Distribution

Delivery and distribution channels can play an important part in confirming the image that has been created by promotion and by the product itself. An inappropriate distribution channel might severely dent the impact of the image so far created and standard marketing texts are comprehensive in addressing this issue. However, there is an aspect of distribution that is particularly important to the current examination.

In Porter's competitive strategy video (Porter, 1988) he provides a fairly detailed case study on Skil Corporation, the American power tool manufacturer. Skil had around 7 per cent of the US market against Black & Decker's 44 per cent, had no particular competitive strengths against Black & Decker and no very strong strategic focus. After extremely moderate financial performance they were taken over by Emerson Electric in 1979.

Emerson standardized and improved Skil's product range, cut back and re-equipped its manufacturing facilities and introduced TQM, JIT, Kaizen and the whole raft of modern management approaches. However, the key to their subsequent strategic success was their distribution strategy. They stopped selling to mass merchandisers and discounters and told their specialist retailers they would no longer have to compete with Skil products for sale at cut prices. Black & Decker, who depended on the discounters for their volume, were unable to follow suit. As a consequence, Skil were able to demand and get special support from their chosen distributors, special displays, in store promotion and product support. The strategy was a great success. The distributors and Skil had formally reached a relationship of strategic importance to both. Their agreement to collaborate was of great mutual benefit. Gauthier would be proud. Skil chose their distributors with great care, the credibility of their trustworthiness being a prime factor. The distributors were also careful. At first they frankly disbelieved that Skil would refuse to deal with the mass merchandisers. Only as the strategy was implemented, and they found that Skil kept its word, were they finally hooked into the relationship. And it worked for both parties.

Distribution is often important and can be paramount.

After sales

The after sales relationship that a business has with its customers varies according to the product. A fast-moving consumer good will require detailed control of the often repeated transactions, order processing, delivery and payment. Reliability and predictability in these various parts of the transaction can be vital, especially with more firms requiring just-in-time service. One-off major purchases need attention to quite different characteristics. For example, the advertising of Porsche cars has had to focus on past purchasers, not simply to maintain customer loyalty but also to eliminate the phenomenon marketers refer to as *cognitive dissonance*, the uncomfortable feeling that spending around £70 000 on a means of getting from A to B was not smart.

One important issue in all sales is the handling of payment. Insensitive credit control can undo all that has been achieved through promotion, the product and its distribution (see Box 5.9).

Marketing research can be another ongoing after sales contact. This demonstrates a continuing interest in the customers and their needs and desires and in improving the way those needs and desires are satisfied and even pleased. Lost customers can be a highly productive source of invaluable customer intelligence.

Box 5.9   Creditors send in the bunnies

Companies suffering from late payment of debts have probably fantasised often about doing unspeakable things to tardy payers. An entrepreneur in Germany, Burckhard Hell, a former waiter, has set up an agency that puts pink rabbits on the case.

According to a French news magazine, *Nouvel Observateur*, the agency sends someone dressed in a pink velour rabbit costume and Ray-Bans to trail the target debtor. This ostentatious display is meant to embarrass them into coughing up. Upon capitulation, the agent hands the victim a card bearing the phone number of a creditor.

It works like a charm. The agency says that two-thirds of debtors pay up straight away, though one hardened Scrooge put up with a rabbit trailing him for three days. Several others have called the police—but there is no law against dressing up as a pink bunny.

(Cope, 1994)

General

Pleasing customers is not just an ill-defined holier-than-thou intention. It involves all of the subparts of the customer transactions outlined above. If each aspect is effectively managed they will all serve to reinforce the customer's initial perceptions. If any particular aspect is not focused effectively on pleasing the customer, it will tend to undercut the intended image and customer perceptions and severely reduce the level of trust that the business is able to establish.

Beating competitors

The strategic objective was identified in Figure 4.1 as 'being unique, beating competitors, being best at something'. This is the objective on which every business should ideally be focused. Making profits, creating shareholder wealth, even pleasing customers, are only means to the end of beating competitors. The way to beat competitors is to establish and exploit a distinctive competence.

Every viable business has some 'distinctive competence', something at which it is peculiarly effective. It may not be absolutely unique and the firm may not be the best in the world, but at least, in some aspect, it must be better than the competitors that also serve its markets. If it were not so, the firm would go out of business.

For the distinctive competence to be of any strategic value it must be embodied in the product the customer buys. For example, a firm may be peculiarly effective in R&D, but if the fruits of its research are not incorporated in the firm's product this competence will avail it nothing. Similarly, the distinctive competence might relate to some aspect of cost, but if that strength is not embodied in the product either in the form of reduced price or increased quality, etc., it will have no strategic impact.

If the distinctive competence accords with the customer need and is embodied in the product, it creates a leadership position. The idea that 'economic results are only earned by leadership, not by mere competence' has been a central Drucker concept over the years (Drucker, 1964). While he is sometimes accused of making things seem too simple, his concept of leadership is in fact much more subtle than some of the later contributions, such as Boston's.

Leadership, for Drucker, did not mean that a business had to have the dominant share of the market, or that it had to be first in every product line, or the most technologically advanced. Leadership had merely to relate to 'something of value to the customer'. It might be in service, or distribution, or some quite narrow aspect of the product; it might even relate to the firm's 'ability to convert ideas into saleable products'.

Potentially, then, a leadership position attaching to anything that the customer values provides the business with economic results. With no leadership position, even if the firm has the major share of the market, the business will at best be 'marginal'. Porter suggested ways in which leadership could be achieved, and though Porter's approach has been regularly criticized since it was first published in 1979, it has established a prominence in strategic management literature and so far, despite the contributions of Hamel, Prahalad, Quinn, Mintzberg and others, Porter's original model has not been substantially improved. Moreover, it has the great virtue of simplicity.

Competitive strategies

The main weakness in Porter's model is that it is based on a flaw. Porter takes the simple economics idea that the only way to maximize profit is either to maximize price or minimize cost (see Figure 5.3). He thus defines the two strategies, cost leadership and differentiation, for doing this. The strict meaning of 'differentiation' is 'premium price' strategy, because differentiating the product in a way that does not earn a premium price will not serve to maximize profit, which is what Porter intends his strategies should achieve. But Porter acknowledges that profit is not an adequate measure of strategy. He quotes the example of Skil Corporation where it took Emerson five or more years to establish the new strategy, during which time Skil's financial performance remained poor. By 1986, all pieces

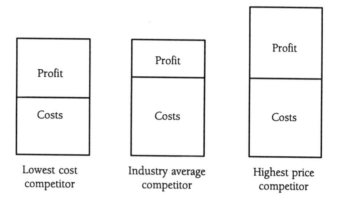

Figure 5.3 *Profitability and competitive strategies.*

of the new strategy were in place, but profitability would have suggested that the company was in decline, rather than about to succeed. Strategic health and performance need to be measured by something other than profit, and yet Porter establishes his strategic model on the basis of the simplest profit-maximizing assumptions.

Figure 5.3 suggests that competitive advantage can be gained by beating competitors or avoiding them. Beating competitors means achieving lower costs than they so that they can be confronted head on. In this way, with an undifferentiated product commanding a standard market price, a firm is able to achieve the highest rates of profit in its industry. Avoiding competitors is achieved by differentiating the product from that of competitors and achieving a premium price which enables the higher margins to be earned that will lead to long-term prosperity.

Both of these strategies can be applied either across a broad front, or by focusing on a limited segment of the market rather than the market as a whole. Cost leadership and differentiation, focused and unfocused, according to Porter's analysis, are mutually exclusive and represent the only competitive strategy options available. Any attempt to pursue more than one such strategy only leads to the firm being 'stuck in the middle', i.e. without any coherent strategy, lacking direction and with no prospect of concentration and consistency, unable to focus on the top strategic objective.

Cost leadership is a term that has come to mean many different things. A firm that is accounting dominated and constantly emphasizes efficiency is frequently referred to as having adopted a cost leadership strategy. This is not necessarily correct. One of management's jobs, no matter what the business strategy, is to try to operate efficiently, but this does not imply they are necessarily seeking to be cost leaders.

The strategy of cost leadership applies to a business that attempts to become the lowest cost producer in an industry. If competing products are more or less undifferentiated and therefore sell at a standard market price, the competitor with the lowest costs will earn the highest profits. However, in any industry there can only be one cost leader. All other competitors following a cost leadership strategy cannot by definition succeed. The degree to which their costs exceed those of the cost leader is some measure of their vulnerability. In the event of direct price competition the would-be cost leaders who came second best will almost inevitably be forced to reduce market share or stand making losses, and in the extreme may be driven out of the industry altogether. Following a cost leadership strategy without success frequently leads managements to redouble their efforts to reduce costs. Their focus on cost reduction and efficiency, at the expense of all other factors, may become totally dominant and an end in itself.

A cost leadership strategy is widely followed by firms in Britain and America in the interests of short-term profits, often with disastrous results. In an award-winning article, Wickham Skinner (1986) wrote about what he called the productivity paradox:

> the efforts to improve productivity actually drive competitive success further out of reach. This is because cost leadership is a syndrome, a mindset, which stunts strategic vision and inhibits innovation. Breaking loose from ... the mindset is not easy. It requires a change in culture, in habits, instincts and ways of thinking and reasoning.

This phenomenon had been previously identified in two articles in the *Harvard Business Review* (Hayes and Abernathy, 1980 and Hayes and Garvin, 1982). It was noted that American industry was starting to lose ground to Japanese and European competitors.

> In the past, American managers earned world-wide respect for their carefully planned yet highly aggressive action across three different time frames:

> **Short term**—using existing assets as efficiently as possible.

> **Medium term**—replacing labour and other scarce resources with capital equipment.

> **Long term**—developing new products and processes that open new markets or restructure old ones.
>
> (Hayes and Abernathy, 1980)

While American managers were credited with continuing to achieve with short-term actions, they were no longer effective in the medium- and long-term requirements. Hayes and Abernathy illustrated the point with a number of quotations from American managers:

> *To undertake such (medium and long term) commitments is hardly in the interests of a manager who is concerned with his or her next quarterly earnings reports.*

> *We understand how to market, we know the technology, and production problems are not extreme. Why risk money on new businesses when good profitable low risk opportunities are on every side?*

The short-term cost focus inhibits investment in new plant and new technology which in due course results in firms losing the ability to compete effectively. In the face of price competition such firms inevitably lose both in terms of profit and market share. Consequently,

> *morale sags, performance suffers, and employees—generally the best ones— begin to leave. Faced with these circumstances, top management often concludes that a division or product line is unsalvageable and purposely continues the process of disinvestment.* (Hayes and Garvin, 1982).

Once started, this disinvestment spiral is extremely difficult to reverse. Thus, at the very least, a strategy of cost leadership may be regarded as extremely dangerous. In practice the actions taken by would-be cost leaders often prove counterproductive.

While there is little empirical evidence of successful implementations of cost leadership strategies, there is a great deal of support for the strategy of differentiation—that is, providing a product or service that is in some way differentiated from competitive products. For example, Hall (1980) investigated 64 American companies and found that businesses that followed differentiation strategies performed much better than the rest. All the high performers in Hall's sample,

> *used careful strategic analysis to guide their investments, avoiding simplistic adherence to doctrinaire approaches towards strategy formulation which come from naive application of tools like: share/growth matrices ... experience curves and PIMS.*

The basis of the differentiation does not appear to matter. It may be to do with the product, its quality or with customer service. It may also be combined with aspects of cost leadership as, for example, Philip Morris were found to combine

> *lowest cost, fully automated cigarette manufacturing with high cost focused branding and promotion to gain industry profit leadership without the benefit of either largest unit volume or segment market share.*

To be strategically valid the point of differentiation must be one for which there is a need, i.e. customers perceive it as being worth a premium price. Differentiation for its own sake has no strategic value whatsoever. If it is not worth a premium then the product will only command a basic, general market price and the business, unless it is the cost leader, will be unable to earn an economic return.

This point is worth emphasizing since there have been some misconceptions about the nature of differentiation in the context of competitive strategy. Some have suggested that the idea is simply to maximize the differentiation from competitors. Thus, the product might be differentiated by virtue of the degree of automation involved in its production. The leader in such a form of differentiation may consider therefore that further investment in automation will serve to reinforce and strengthen the differentiation strategy. However, the critical point is whether the customer perceives and values the differentiation, not whether or not the degree of differentiation from competitors is maximized.

The most successful differentiation strategies are those where the point of differentiation perceived and valued by customers, coincides with the organization's distinctive competence. This may be some skill or knowledge, often embodied in some unique or patented plant or process. It could also be in some organizational characteristic which, for example, enables the organization to deliver a product of uniquely high quality. Distinctive competence is the key to effective competition in specific market areas or niches.

Ethics and winning

The aim of competitive strategy is quite simply to achieve a leadership position or competitive advantage, so that the firm can proceed to beat its competitors. It may do this directly if it has achieved a cost leadership position, or indirectly through differentiation. If a leadership position is successfully achieved, it will attract the competition—as the CEO of Skil reported when their strategy started to be implemented: 'we have been discovered'. Thus, even with a differentiation strategy, it will not prove possible to avoid competitors for long. In the end, every successful business, whether or not it competes head on from the outset, will find itself in direct competition. No matter how reluctant, it will inevitably have to deal with the problem of competition and it will not want to lose. Nor will its suppliers, employees, or shareholders want it to lose. Nor will its managers' wives, husbands and offspring want it to lose.

According to the philosophers, however, winning is unethical, never mind deliberately setting out to beat a competitor. Thus, in this, the strategic purpose of business, moral philosophy has little contribution to make to ethics in business. This is amply demonstrated by considering Sainsbury's approach to competitive strategy as outlined in Box 5.10.

Sainsbury, a famously ethical business, adopts a quite ruthless competitive stance, extracting the most from its very considerable

Box 5.10   The real thing put to the test

Coco-Cola is good for you; Coca-Cola is the real thing; Coke is it. This is the three-in-one creed of the Coca-Cola Corporation of Atlanta, Georgia, producer and promoter of the fizzy nerve tonic invented by Dr John Styth Pemberton, a pharmacist, in 1886 and guardian of '7X', its secret recipe.

The British have taken to the sticky, caffeine-laced pop like dogs to aniseed balls. Coca-Cola was the top-selling grocery brand in the UK last year, with sales of £247m. This represented 60 per cent of the retail cola market, well ahead of Pepsi with over 20 per cent and supermarket brands with less than 10 per cent.

Coca-Cola did not get where it is today without a phenomenal and relentless expenditure on advertising, most of it to keep rivals at bay. It has been extraordinarily successful, so much so that Coke—in the 195 countries that constitute its empire—is synonymous with cola. According to Coca-Cola, the brand is known by 94 per cent of the world's population, making it more popular than Jesus *and* John Lennon.

This might worry Pepsi, Coke's century-old rival—but it is clearly water off the back of J Sainsbury. Last week, as every newspaper blurted across its front page, the British supermarket giant launched its own brand, cut-price cola. Classic Cola caused a stir because it is to be sold in red and white cans that bear a close resemblance to Coke's cans. And just like Coke, Sainsbury is offering classic, diet and caffeine-free alternatives.

Coca-Cola is worried chiefly because Sainsbury's Classic Cola is being produced by the cut-price Cott Corporation of Canada. Cott's cut-price cola has pushed Coke into third place in the Canadian market in just five years and forced its famous rival to close half of its 16 Canadian bottling plants. ...

'Copy-cat' design—similar but not identical—once the speciality of Japanese manufacturers, is now part and parcel of the British supermarket business. This inevitably infuriates manufacturers who spend millions of pounds on the research, development, marketing and advertising of new brands.

'The issue here is one of intellectual property rights', says Alan Marshall, national manager of Unilever UK, which makes many of the product lines sold in Sainsbury supermarkets. 'It doesn't help anyone to have this polarised clash between retailers and manufacturers. We are not against ownbrands; all we ask Sainsbury and the super-markets is they design their own labels'.

... Coca-Cola ... while 'not willing to make enemies with Sainsbury's', according to a spokesman, it is investing millions in a campaign to promote and protect its image. Bogle, Bartle & Hegarty the ad agency ... is working hard for Coke.

So, too, are Tim Bell of Lowe Bell, the strategic marketing

consultants, Brunswick the public relations agency, Goldman Sachs the investment bank and, most important of all, Clifford Chance, Coca-Cola's solicitors.

Clifford Chance is taking a long hard look at the UK Trademarks Bill, currently worming its way through Parliament. The Bill is an attempt to bring British laws on unfair competition into line with those of other EU countries. It aims to make it easier for manufacturers to register trade marks as well as specific shapes, words and logos on their packaging. Manufacturers say that the bill does not go far enough to protect trademarks.

The British Producers and Brand Owners Group—which includes Mars, Nestlé, Procter & Gamble, Grand Metropolitan, Allied-Lyons and Unilever—has pushed for an amendment to the Bill that will protect manufacturers from copy-cat designs.

(Glancey, 1994)

bargaining power as a mass retail outlet. Sainsbury apparently has little regard for the fact that Coca-Cola (and the others) have invested huge amounts in defining and establishing their distinctive brands. Perhaps FMCG brands are no longer as valuable as they used to be, because their distinctiveness is no longer so sustainable. In Coca-Cola's case it would appear that Cott's have satisfactorily copied the flavour (despite the hype around the '7X' secret recipe) and achieved consistent quality. So the brand is only worth the image, i.e. the psychological attributes which the Coca-Cola millions have established in the name (see Box 5.11).

Post-war improvements in quality that have become available generally across markets and for most products and services have undermined the real value of brands. They remain as a marketing tool, but no longer as a distinctive assurance of quality, reliability and service. In this sense the Sainsbury initiative is merely another small step along the way to the elimination of differentiation as a viable competitive strategy for FMCG.

It is uncertain how Sainsbury might react if one of the new breed of retail discounters entered the market with a name such as J. Sailsbury and a general logo and colour scheme reminiscent of their own. The moral philosopher would ask the question 'Is it ethical?' A more pertinent question would be, 'Is this the sort of partner with which you would wish to engage in a long-term collaboration?' Sainsbury remains the essentially ethical business it has always been. It is extremely concerned with delivering value to its customers, and at the same time does not shrink from beating its competitors if it can, even if those competitors are also its suppliers. Sainsbury's position is quite clear, though it appears to operate at the preconventional integrity level in dealing with its competitors, rather than the conventional level. As long as its perspective is understood, there is no reason to suspect Sainsbury would be in any way unreliable as a

---

Box 5.11   Cola challenge

As a contribution to the debate over whether J Sainsbury could challenge The Real Thing, the *Independent* conducted its own 'Cola Challenge'. Twenty children aged 11 to 15 who were standing by a bus stop in central London on their way home from school were recruited for a pavement tasting.

Coca-Cola, Pepsi Cola and the new Classic Cola each gained 30 per cent of votes. Five per cent admitted to not being able to tell the difference, while a further 5 per cent plumped for a variety called Geebee, exclusive to Kwik Save.

Many of the boys had strong views against Sainsbury's cola. Thomas O'Neill, 15, said: 'If you drink Sainsbury's, people think "cheap cola, cheap person". If you drink Coke it's credit.' Ugar Tuc, 15, said: 'It's crap because it's got Sainsbury's on it. It's just a duplicate and the Classic bit's the worst of all.'

(Williams, 1994)

---

collaborator. But if you were the owner of an internationally known brand, you could equally expect them to undercut your prices while maintaining or improving on your quality with a copy-cat product.

The question might arise, when considering how to beat a competitor, whether it would be right to drive it out of business. For moral philosophers this may be a deeply unethical proposition. They might question whether there could be any circumstances in which such a course of action—a sort of social murder—could be justified.

For those that adopt the enlightened self-interest approach this possibility causes no dilemma. The only reason for not driving a competitor out of business if the opportunity is available, is one of self-interest. A competitive market is one where the participants are deliberately and systematically trying to beat each other for their own advantage, if necessary to the death. A competitive market frequently prevents or punishes the would-be monopolist and it may be the most sensible strategy to allow a competitor to preserve its independence. Nevertheless, such a strategy has its dangers. A weak competitor that only exists on sufferance can help breed a dangerous degree of complacency that may result in the whole market becoming vulnerable.

Whether or not a competitor is driven out of business, the key issue remains one of how to behave in such a way that the credibility of your trustworthiness is enhanced rather than diminished by your actions. It is by no means clear that tolerating a weak competitor is the strategy most likely to achieve this aim. If you cannot be trusted to operate as an effective competitor, could you be trusted in a crucially important strategic alliance?

The imperative of beating competitors is the second fundamental reason why moral philosophy, even if it provided any answers, could contribute very little to ethics in business.

Competitive collaboration

While no successful business ever forgets that its competitors are fundamentally its enemies whose interests are diametrically opposed to its own, they nevertheless present unique opportunities for strategically effective and highly profitable collaboration. Collaborating competitors

- can and do fix prices at which they can survive and prosper;

- can and do carve up markets and agree where and when they will compete and, more importantly, where and when they will not compete;

- can and do exchange 'confidential' information about prices, price increases, discounts and special tenders, about customers and about other competitors;

- can and do agree the specifications of generic products in their industry;

- can and do agree variations that they will adopt in order to provide some differentiation.

In some industries these arrangements are more effective than in others. In some industries they are more common than in others. In most industries such collaborations are potentially valuable strategies. And in all industries they might possibly be illegal. The vagueness on legality arises because these are not simple black and white issues. There are degrees of competitive collaboration, from the formal exchange of product information at a regular meeting of an industry research association, to a secretive conspiracy to fix prices.

The question, as always, is not 'Is it ethical?' but 'Would it enhance or inhibit chances of being invited into mutually advantageous collaborations?' and 'Would it increase or diminish the credibility of our trustworthiness?'

In this world of global markets, technological collaborations and strategic alliances competitors also get together for the most positive of reasons, for example, to take forward an industry's technology when separately the costs could never be justified. The case of Kodak and Canon described in Box 5.12 well illustrates such an arrangement.

Box 5.12 Competitors click in for a better profile

Kodak and Canon are both household names in photography. By adapting their know-how, both have also entered the photocopier business. It seems odd, then, that they should have launched a strategic alliance. But not as odd as all that. In the automobile industry such relationships are rife. For instance, the leading US companies have joined forces to develop an electric car, while some firms—like Rover and Honda in the UK—have started to cooperate with the Japanese 'enemy'. Similarly, Apple has linked with Sony to take on Microsoft in the market for integrating business equipment with computer systems.

The justification is that nobody has all the answers when technology is developing all the time. It is becoming increasingly hard for one company to bear the costs of research and development and marketing and sales, and then deliver an ever-more sophisticated product at the right price. As a result, businesses are identifying their own core strengths and those of their competitors and seeking alliances.

Although the partnership route is not without its difficulties, more and more companies seem to prefer it to going alone. As Mike Mansell, Kodak's manager for the UK office-imaging business, says: 'There is little sense in investing huge amounts of capital in areas outside your core expertise if a good complementary fit with a business partner can be identified.'

Mr Mansell feels such a fit should allow the partners to achieve both a stronger business position and a maximum return on capital investment. But he cautions against putting all your eggs in one basket, pointing out that Kodak has a number of arrangements with such companies as IBM, Lotus, Olivetti and Unisys. Nevertheless, at a time when the parent company, Eastman Kodak, has announced another round of job cuts, the link with Canon is seen as an important potential boost to profitability. In the UK, the company's office-imaging arm has consistently produced double-figure growth. But for this to continue in a sector still dominated by Rank Xerox, it needs to transform a strong market position into 'an extremely powerful' one. Hence the tie-up with Canon.

Although this may appear to be a case of two direct competitors getting into bed with each other, the companies have identified a number of distinguishing characteristics that they feel make them a well-suited couple. For instance, Kodak believes its basic strengths are design and development allied to customer service and support, while Canon's are manufacturing and distribution. And although both are strong on marketing, they have different sales channels, with Kodak selling direct and Canon via dealers. Finally, the products are complementary in that Canon deals with the low- to medium-volume end while Kodak serves the upper reaches.

Moreover, the two companies have had an informal relationship since the late 1980s, under which they market each other's products in their own territories. This suggests, says Mr Mansell, that they recognised the benefits of alliances earlier than most.

Doubters might feel that such cosy arrangements would make the companies softer than if they were conducting all-out war with each other. But Mr Mansell is adamant that they are still rivals in many ways. 'We don't want to compete on project development. But if you've got two salesmen going for the same customer, keen competition helps there. You lose a lot of the energy of an alliance if you don't compete.'

Perhaps the strongest fear is that a friendly alliance can become an unfriendly takeover. It is for this reason that those seeking to enter such arrangements do so from positions of strength; it is not a way of patching over problems. 'Canon could eat us. If they do, we deserve to be eaten,' says Mr Mansell.

(Trapp, 1993)

What collaborating competitors must never forget is that they are fundamentally adversaries and that though their potential partners may appear to operate generally at the conventional level of moral development, behaving in ways that are generally regarded as ethical, in competitor transactions they are likely to adopt a preconventional stance, behaving ethically only because they would probably be caught and punished for their actions.

Conclusion

This chapter has served several purposes. First, it has described and exampled the way businesses may be expected to behave in their various different transactions with various stakeholders and at different levels on the hierarchy of objectives.

It is only in transactions with stakeholders that the firm's ethical values become apparent and operative. Abstract ethics have no relevance to social organizations.

At the level of survival, businesses may be expected to adopt different standards of behaviour than when they are better established and aiming at the intermediate level satisfying objectives (see Figure 5.4). When survival is threatened firms will behave as though they were at the preconventional level of moral development, constrained only by the prospect of being apprehended and the certainty that, if they were, the individuals responsible would be punished.

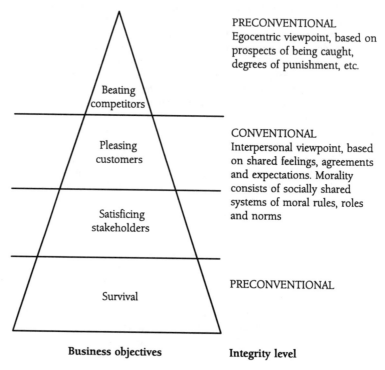

Business objectives   **Integrity level**

Figure 5.4 *Objectives and levels of integrity.*

At the intermediate level of objectives firms may be expected to behave as though they were at the conventional level of moral development, i.e. they behave in ways that are generally considered ethical.

When firms are focused on their top strategic level objective of beating competitors they may again be expected to behave at the preconventional level. Their behaviour regarding competitors will thus be different from their behaviour with regard to any other of the firm's stakeholders.

In identifying these various transactions as the vehicle for expressing a firm's ethical standing, it is clear that ethics can be defined more simply as integrity in relationships. Having seen examples of how integrity impacts on the business's ability to engage in mutually advantageous collaborations, we are able to recognize that integrity in business is a calculation rather than a passion or value.

As Axelrod suggested, integrity in relationships must have clarity, niceness, provocability and forgivingness. Potential strategic partners must be able to understand the basis on which they both will collaborate; they must be able to believe in each other's trustworthiness; they must each keep their promises and punish cheating; and if it is to be long lasting they must not 'hold grudges'—i.e. if a lapse in cooperation has been punished, the normal collaborative partnership is resumed.

As well as illustrating these various points, the examples and discussion in this chapter have also served to examine further the sociomoral perspective of business, so that the progressively emerging model can be understood more readily.

A culture of integrity

The initial aim of this book was to identify an alternative to the currently orthodox approach to business ethics because that approach has failed to be relevant to business. The alternative, enlightened self-interest perspective was adopted, but rather than leaving it as an ill-defined expression of generally good intent, a more rigorous attempt has been made to relate the project closely to the realities of a strategic business.

A model of organizational integrity which takes account of the strategic business perspective has been defined. Its relevance to different stakeholder relationships in different circumstances has been examined and examples have been provided.

However, before applying the model to any particular business it is necessary to make a small number of linking assumptions. These are the subject-matter of this chapter.

The linking assumptions relate to whether integrity needs to be real or merely perceived; whether integrity is a fundamental characteristic or a style that can be adopted by management to fit particular circumstances; whether integrity should be based on a system of values or whether it would be more effective simply as the result of economic calculation. These are critical elements in the application of the integrity approach. They suggest that managements need continually to be considering questions such as 'What if the truth were known about this?', 'What if all stakeholders knew about it?', 'What if all stakeholders knew the whole truth about this?', 'What would be the effect on our perceived trustworthiness if all stakeholders knew the whole truth?'

In addition, some potentially confusing issues are also clarified: the question of transcultural integrity, the question of ethical status in different business organizations; and the increasingly fashionable question of corporate philanthropy.

The assumptions and clarifications made explicit in this chapter are critical to the practical application of organizational integrity examined in the closing chapter.

Introduction

Most of the pieces are now in place to complete the definition of the organizational integrity approach to business ethics. The flow diagram shown in Figure 6.1 shows the main stages in developing the approach. Its foundation is, as far as possible, value free. From the start no judgements have been made about the morality of business as currently practised. No suggestion has been made that the ethical standards of business, or business managers, should be improved. Instead it has been recognized that business is an ethically ambiguous enterprise. When a business is first set up the entrepreneur is professionally advised to minimize tax payments

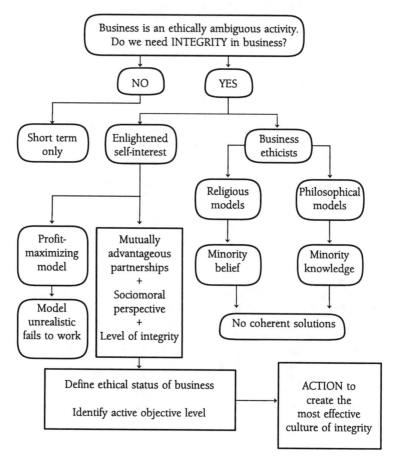

Figure 6.1 *Approaches to integrity in business.*

and maximize the pre-tax 'take' from the business. To do otherwise, i.e. to pay more tax than is necessary, would simply be wasteful; as would paying suppliers more than is necessary or earlier than necessary, providing the customer with more value than required, or paying employees more than enough to retain their active cooperation. In all these ways, business deliberately pushes at the boundaries of what would widely be regarded as ethically acceptable behaviour. It is of no concern to the business that the surplus taxes it might choose to pay could be put to the greater good of the greatest number.

In becoming an effective competitor, the simple rule that 'all is fair ...' seems to apply—the avowed intent is to beat competitors. Similarly, when a business is itself being beaten and its continued existence is threatened, it is likely to act in ways that might normally be regarded as unethical.

In the face of all these very real pressures, it is futile to expect that managements will behave in certain ways because of a belief in a Superior Being or because of the philosophical teachings from an earlier age. Neither God nor Kant has had to run a modern business.

So, setting these various value systems on one side, it needs to be asked: 'Do we need business to be ethical?' The answer is: 'It all depends.' It depends, largely, on who is answering the question. From whose point of view should it be judged whether business should be required to behave ethically? From the point of view of the local community, a business would be required to behave in a socially responsible way, adding to, rather than detracting from, the community. From the point of view of suppliers, the business would be required to complete its various transactions in the spirit of their agreement, paying the agreed amount for the goods, within the agreed timescale and accepting the product in good faith, etc. Looking at the interactions between a business and its ecological setting, it is clear that business should be required not to pollute the environment. In short, it is clear that, from the point of view of each of the stakeholders with which the business transacts, it would be important that the business carries out those transactions in an ethical manner. However, the business itself might not see it like that. It is therefore important, as Kohlberg's model suggests, to look at the problem from the perspective of the business itself.

The perspective of the business is essentially one of self-interest. However, there are degrees of self-interest. A business which seeks only to achieve a quick killing, and then cease, will find it most rewarding to ignore ethical considerations completely. Society must find effective means of dealing with such organizations: they are not of concern here. Other businesses share a perspective of *enlightened* self-interest, enlightened in the sense that the business seeks to enjoy a longer lasting prosperity. Some might argue that the profit-maximizing model is one of enlightened self-interest in that if everyone maximized profits, then social welfare would also be maximized as a result of the optimized allocation of resources. However, the assumptions of perfect competition are wholly unrealistic and the model simply does not work in practice. The model of enlightened self-interest of concern here is the simple one suggested by Gauthier: one of mutually advantageous interdependence, where those businesses that are excluded from such collaborations, alliances and partnerships will inevitably lose competitive strength.

The relevance, at this particular time, of a model of interdependence has already been emphasized and many examples of strategic alliances and technological collaborations have been given. Moreover, the newer, flexible, network- and team-based organizational forms which are so vital to businesses as processors of knowledge, rather than material, make acceptability as a partner just as important inside the organization as it is externally.

The enlightened self-interest perspective therefore suggests that management must demonstrate a level of integrity that will make them generally acceptable as partners and collaborators. They need to be perceived as having reached Kohlberg's conventional level—i.e. they do not need to be perceived as god-like in their virtue, but they do need to be perceived as trustworthy, as having internalized the principle of trust, as keeping to agreements and fully meeting expectations. How does a business ensure that it is so perceived?

Answering this question is the primary concern of this and the following chapter. The approach is one of deliberate calculation. In order to participate in worthwhile partnerships the organization needs to be perceived in a certain way and it is management's job to see that it is so perceived by the various stakeholders with which it transacts. This is very different from the idea of a value-driven organization that has ideals and passion, etc. In addressing stakeholder perceptions there need be no emotion, no passion, nothing woolly or emotive. Calculating stakeholder perceptions should prove more robust than reliance on the passionately held convictions of key individuals. Moreover, such calculations accommodate survival issues, whereas convictions are likely to crumble when the organization is faced with extinction.

This chapter makes some basic arguments that are important to the enlightened self-interest approach to integrity. These are not revealed truths, but are deliberately set out as arguments on which the reader can form his or her own view. They are basic issues that underlie the question of how a business ensures it is perceived as trustworthy.

Perception or reality

Perceptions determine behaviour. Perceptions as to potential partners' trustworthiness critically affect whether or not they will be invited to join in collaborations and alliances. It is the image that is perceived, not necessarily the reality. 'Sincerity is everything–if you can fake that, you've got it made!'

Images are what Kotler (1991) calls 'sticky', i.e. they persist and take a long time to change. A famous restaurant might have deteriorated and yet continues for some time in the public mind to be highly regarded. This is because once people have a certain image of an object they perceive further data selectively, accepting confirmatory data and rejecting new data which does not confirm their previous image. It will therefore take considerable time and expense to change an image.

If a business manager is perceived as untrustworthy, no matter that he or she is in fact absolutely 100 per cent honest and reliable, a potential partner will act on the perception. The reality is only important in as much as it affects the image, but in practice this turns out to be crucial. Closing image gaps, i.e. the variance between the reality and the perceived image, is a notoriously slow and expensive process. Closing a gap is the process of changing an inaccurate perception to coincide with the reality. Deliberately opening such a gap to create a false image would be even slower and more expensive and extremely difficult to sustain. The truth would inevitably become apparent from time to time and, in the end, would tend to overwhelm the false image being created, so that in the end selective perceptions would work to reinforce the dominant image. It should also be noted that the larger the image gap the more expensive it will be to open and the less likely it would be to be sustained.

The fact that these processes are 'sticky', i.e. slow to change and expensive to manipulate, suggests that in practice any attempt to create an image that differed significantly from the reality would be slow, expensive and unlikely to be sustainable. In the end the 'truth will out'.

Thus managements need to be concerned with the reality of integrity in their organizations, not simply with window dressing to build a false image of trustworthiness. Credibility is crucial. Unless trustworthiness is credible it will have no strategic effect, i.e. it will not enable firms to engage in mutually advantageous collaborations. Firms have therefore to be very careful not to take actions that damage credibility. The potential impact of actions and decisions on the firm's image should therefore be assessed on the assumption that the 'truth will out'. Thus management need continually to be considering 'What if the truth were known about this?'

Characteristic or style

In assuming that integrity can be calculated rather than being a passionately held conviction, it might also follow that it could be adopted as a 'style' of management rather than necessarily being a fundamental characteristic of the organization's culture. As a style it might be adopted in calculated fashion to reinforce the perceptions of stakeholders. Since there are so many different stakeholders, it might therefore be feasible to adopt one style for some stakeholders and perhaps a different style for others. Thus the organization might benefit from the fruits of being perceived as trustworthy with one group of stakeholders, but be saved from the expense of preserving the same trustworthy image with other less critical stakeholders.

Does perception of the organization's integrity with regard to one set of stakeholders affect other stakeholders' perceptions of the organization's trustworthiness? Is it possible, for example, to enjoy the fruits of high integrity with the customers and mercilessly exploit your employees? What would be the impact on The Body Shop, for example, if it was known that Anita Roddick, far from being a beautiful, energetic, inspirational idealist, was actually a dishonest, exploitative employer? It might be unimaginable, but there have been many less stark examples of such discontinuity. Guinness, long established, reputed for the integrity of its product, for a spell became synonymous with something quite different. Even today, in some circles, Guinness means financial fraud. The destruction of perceptions down to the lowest common denominator for a period destroyed the image of the dark beer with the white head. The image is now recovered but the full cost will never be known. Had the business not been so soundly based it might well not have survived, as was the case with Distillers themselves, or Perrier.

Can a company adopt and promote one level of integrity in one area, but not in others? The answer is necessarily circumstantial. There are examples both ways. At the very least it would be an extremely high-risk strategy. Perhaps the best answer is to suggest that, in the short run, a business might succeed with such a tactic, but not in the long run.

In the strategic time frame, businesses have to try to perform to the same conventional level with all stakeholders. Lack of integrity with one set of stakeholders will be perceived by other stakeholders as being evidence of a general lack of integrity. Integrity is a searching commodity, leaking from one relationship to another. Moreover, this leakiness is very much facilitated by the increasing intrusiveness of the media and openness of communications. For example, it is presumed that the directors of Independent Insurance would have preferred, even though nothing illegal is suggested, that the information disclosed in Box 6.1 would not have been published by the press. Information that might previously have been confidential to one set of stakeholders is today increasingly known by all other stakeholders and the question which managements must be concerned with is 'What if all stakeholders knew about it?'

Box 6.1 Directors' companies paid £360 000 by pension group

Independent Insurance and its pension scheme last year paid more than £367 000 to companies connected with three of the insurer's directors (writes Paul Durman). This was in addition to salary and pension payments, which last year totalled nearly £1.1m for the Independent board. Michael Bright, Independent's chief executive, was paid £382 000, including a £109 000 pension contribution, an increase from £333 000 in 1992. The insurer's first accounts since it was listed last November showed it paid £130 992 to Lambert Smith Hampton, a firm of property consultants where Mr Bright is a director. Both Mr Bright and Independent have shares in Lambert Smith.

Robert McCracken, an Independent director, said the insurers' business relationship with Lambert Smith began 'way before we had a shareholding'. He said Independent's expansion meant it was frequently in need of property advice.

Another £129 000 was paid to Whiteford and Foden, a firm of actuaries and pension administrators whose directors include Anne Clarke, wife of Alan Clarke, an Independent director. The firm advises Independent's pension scheme, which paid £59 766 of the total fees.

Independent paid £106 803 to Noble & Company, a merchant bank boutique headed by Sir Iain Noble, one of Independent's non-executive directors. The company provided advice on Independent's flotation.

Independent made a pre-tax profit of £15.8m last year on net premium income of £105.4m.

(Durman, 1994)

If this argument is accepted then integrity should be regarded as an organizational characteristic rather than a style that can be calculated to fit particular circumstances. As an organizational characteristic it will be applied equally to all the organization's transactions with its various stakeholders.

Calculation or value

On page 131 it was suggested that management should be concerned with the question 'What if the truth were known about this?' In the previous section it was suggested that management should be concerned with the question 'What if all stakeholders knew about it?' Putting these two questions together suggests that, in order to ensure that their business is perceived as being trustworthy, management must be concerned with 'What if all stakeholders knew the whole truth about this?'

This chapter started with the assertion that integrity has to be calculated, rather than a passionately held value. It is calculated in the sense that it is the perception of a firm's trustworthiness that affects its stakeholders' behaviour rather than the reality. Moreover, Axelrod's requirements of clarity, niceness, provocability and forgivingness, which seem to support the Gauthier model adopted here, are all clearly calculations.

It has been argued that if a perceived image is to be long lasting it must be supported by the reality—a false image is unlikely to be upheld. It has also been argued that integrity must be maintained consistently at the same level for all stakeholders—otherwise the perception will most probably fall to the level of the lowest common denominator, i.e. integrity is a basic characteristic not a style that can simply be adopted as and when appropriate.

Thus by calculation, rather than by using some extraneous value system, we have reached the point where it is tenable to suggest that a business which adopts the strategic perspective needs to behave with real integrity at all times and to all stakeholders. Thus we come to the position, suggested by Gauthier, that the principle of trust, i.e. integrity, needs to be internalized. In the case of an organization rather than an individual, integrity needs to be internalized by the organization's members.

This is the position no doubt reached by the successful chief executives interviewed by Goldsmith and Clutterbuck, who embraced integrity as an essential part of their culture.

This was clearly not window dressing. Each company was convinced that without absolute integrity the business simply could not operate.
                                        (Goldsmith and Clutterbuck, 1985, p. 123).

Integrity as an aspect of a company's culture is all pervasive.

Corporate integrity is vital to effective management. Peters and Waterman found that one of the eight characteristics of their excellent companies was 'hands on, value driven'. Much derided since, this characteristic has been identified as particularly relevant to the newer forms of loosely structured business where the value-driven organization outperforms tightly controlled, rigidly structured organizations using its shared values and strategic vision as a common perspective (Leitko and Szczerbacki, 1987).

An often quoted example of this was the IBM mainframe customer service engineer of old who was persuaded to perform beyond what one might regard as the normal call of duty because of basic belief in the high integrity of the business—even that it was in some way working for the greater good of society. This belief, or value, was deliberately instilled during the new employee's induction programme and carefully reinforced from then on. The methods have been described by Pascale (1985) and are uncomfortably close to a socialization process. Such methods would be wholly counterproductive if the organization was not soundly based on a culture of truth and integrity in which the employee could believe.

With no integrity, communications would, according to Barnard (1948), be perverted and secretive; individuals would be unable to make wholehearted commitment to the organization; and the formulation and implementation of strategy would become much less effective. As Barnard suggested, without integrity it would be extremely difficult to complete the executive tasks:

- Maintenance of organizational communication

- Securing of essential services from individuals

- Formulation of purpose and objectives.

Thus, integrity, even though it has here been approached essentially as a calculation, appears to be best regarded as an essential part of the organization's culture—in short, a value. The constancy and consistency required to ensure that the firm's integrity is truly perceived by stakeholders are only likely to be achieved if it is absorbed deep in the organization's culture. This will not be done if integrity is regarded simply as a matter of managerial decision.

Transcultural integrity

Each organization's culture is unique, like an individual's character or personality, but is influenced by the national, geographic, religious, social and economic characteristics in which it is located. What is true of organizations in the United States is not necessarily true of organizations in China, India or Egypt. What individuals perceive as important varies from country to country. Customs and practices in different countries vary so much that a compliment in one country might well be construed as a calculated insult in another. Language, body language, even assumptions about personal space, all highlight the different ways of doing things that humans have developed in different circumstances. Even life itself is valued differently, as Bophal's victims would testify following the Indian government's agreement of Union Carbide's compensation scheme.

These differences, which include many issues of ethics and integrity, are to varying degrees understood and taken into account by the modern multinational corporation. Box 6.2 outlines a notorious but typical example.

Box 6.2:   The Lockheed bribery case

The Lockheed Aircraft Corporation paid $3.8 million to various governmental officials and representatives of the prime minister in Japan to ensure the purchase of 20 TriStar passenger planes. Carl Kotchian, President of Lockheed, was directly responsible for the negotiations that led to the sale.

At the time, Lockheed were losing sales and had a deteriorating competitive position. Despite having a basically good product in the Tristar, they had failed over the previous two years to obtain orders from Alitalia, Lufthansa, and Sabena in Europe, and a large foreign order was vital to bring sales above break-even. No doubt Kotchian was worried about Lockheed's future—the loss of the $430m Nippon order would mean loss of R&D momentum as well as large-scale redundancies. This was the background to Kotchian's decision.

Kotchian did not speak Japanese and had to rely on advice and representations from a Japanese trading company that had been retained specially to act as Lockheed's agent. Kotchian would know about the interlocking structure of Japanese business firms and governmental agencies, but would certainly not be fully prepared for the intricate manoeuvring which this combination of group decision making and interlocking organizational structures generate and which he himself described as 'Byzantine'in their complexity.

Negotiations extended over 70 days. Being a foreigner, and acting as a salesman, Kotchian was excluded from the decision process. Lockheed's agents could meet with the prime minister at his private home, for breakfast, but the president of Lockheed could only meet with the technical and functional representatives of the airlines, who might advise but could not decide upon the purchase. While he waited in a Tokyo hotel room, he was exposed to hurried meetings, intentional delays, midnight telephone calls and continual intimations that the decision was at hand.

The demand for 'pledges' was made and Lockheed's agents simply assumed the required payments would be made—they explained to Kotchian that payments would be required to ensure the sale of 20 planes to Nippon, in Japan. This, as we now are more fully aware, was custom and practice of doing business in Japan at that time. Kotchian, being concerned about Lockheed's competitive position, would most probably assume that other aircraft suppliers would make similar 'pledges'.

The demands of Japanese officials for very substantial amounts of money were presented in a matter-of-fact manner by high government officials, with the endorsement and approval of Lockheed's own agents. Kotchian agreed to pay the bribes and, with hindsight in this notorious case, can be clearly seen to have made a fundamental mistake. When in Rome, a multinational cannot simply do as the Romans do, but neither can it ignore what the Romans do.

(Based on an account in Hosmer, 1987)

The repercussions for Lockheed, and of course for Mr Kotchian, were fairly profound. The question is: how are we to accommodate for the fact that what is regarded as perfectly normal in, say, Asia is generally regarded as wholly unacceptable in the Anglo-Saxon world? And vice versa?

There are no simple answers. Management must make a judgement. But what do they judge? Business ethicists might suggest that they should judge whether the action, for example, bribery, is in principle right or wrong. Or they might suggest that management consider whether the action increases, or diminishes, the general good. If judging the matter on principle, it might be very difficult to know where to draw the line. Some quite trivial act of courtesy, or expression of support or esteem (whether or not it is inscribed with 'don't let the buggers grind you down!'), might be regarded as a bribe. If judging the matter in terms of its consequences, it might also be highly complex. In the case of Lockheed, for example, it is not quite clear if anyone loses, while Lockheed's employees stand to gain. Business ethicists offer no definitive answers.

Neither is the enlightened self-interest model definitive, but it does highlight a crucial question for management. 'What would be the effect on our perceived trustworthiness if all stakeholders knew the whole truth?' Had Lockheed asked this question before committing itself to paying the bribes, it might have recognized the need for an alternative course of action. Even recognizing that Lockheed was operating at Kohlberg's preconventional level and might therefore be expected to act as it did as long as it believed it would not be detected, the real question should still have saved it from itself.

That question about *all* stakeholders suggests that management need to consider stakeholders in all the markets in which they operate, not simply their home base, nor even the particular market in which the action or decision is going to be operative. Quite clearly they need to consider both. This implies that the company must adhere to courses of action that will not damage its perceived trustworthiness in any markets, or cultures, in which it operates. The organization must thus raise its performance to a level that would be regarded as consistent with the required level of integrity in every served market.

This may sound extremely onerous, but in practice it is becoming less problematic. As products, markets, technologies and industries are becoming more global, so too are business practices and standards of integrity. Differences are actually becoming less pronounced and an understanding of those differences is becoming more universal. It remains a matter for management judgement, but the judgements are becoming both less significant and easier to make.

Ethical status

Integrity is a dimension, or discontinuum, rather than a single-point characteristic. At the conventional level, firms maintain standards of integrity that are generally regarded as sufficient to be trusted in partnership. The preconventional level suggests behaviour that would normally exclude a business from partnership, but which in competitive or survival circumstances can be regarded as comprehensible and to some extent predictable.

This analysis is entirely general and makes no distinction between businesses or organizations. Yet it is clear that different businesses require to achieve different levels of integrity. The simple dichotomy between businesses that are out to make a quick killing and those that have a strategic perspective is too broad. There are different categories of business having a strategic perspective. Some simply regard the achievement of a minimum level of integrity as necessary in order to make themselves acceptable to others. They regard integrity as what Herzberg would have referred to as a hygiene factor (Herzberg et al., 1959). Others look at corporate integrity in a more positive light, as a corporate strength to be utilized for the strategic gain of the firm. These firms recognize ethical standing as, again using Herzberg's terminology, a motivator.

The hygiene factor approach defines a level of ethical standing below which the performance of internal stakeholders would be badly affected and external stakeholders dissatisfied. Thus it needs to be maintained at the level at which it would not to be the source of dissatisfaction for existing stakeholders and at which the firm would not be excluded from partnerships, i.e. it suggests a minimum perceived level of integrity to be achieved. For such firms, over-achieving in terms of integrity would simply be wasteful. For firms using integrity as a motivator, however, the approach is quite different. For these firms, corporate integrity is recognized as a priceless strategic asset, which while not a balance sheet item, is there to be exploited like any other asset. Even within these 'motivator' firms there are different categories, having different perspectives on ethical status.

It is important that managements know their own particular organization's perspective and decide the ethical status they need to achieve. Organizations can be categorized as falling into one of four levels, as depicted in Figure 6.2 and described below:

- *Ethically negative.* In some industries firms are not expected to operate with integrity. Legality is a sufficient criterion. The general public would not be surprised if firms involved in these activities were not also engaged in illegal operations. Examples might include junk bond operators, pornography shops, etc.

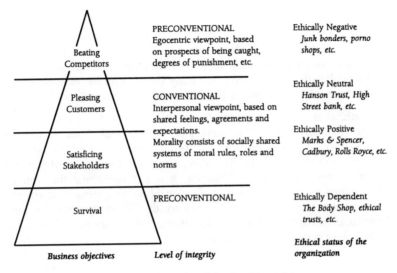

Business objectives	Level of integrity	Ethical status of the organization
Beating Competitors	PRECONVENTIONAL Egocentric viewpoint, based on prospects of being caught, degrees of punishment, etc.	Ethically Negative *Junk bonders, porno shops, etc.*
Pleasing Customers	CONVENTIONAL Interpersonal viewpoint, based on shared feelings, agreements and expectations. Morality consists of socially shared systems of moral rules, roles and norms	Ethically Neutral *Hanson Trust, High Street bank, etc.* Ethically Positive *Marks & Spencer, Cadbury, Rolls Royce, etc.*
Satisficing Stakeholders		
Survival	PRECONVENTIONAL	Ethically Dependent *The Body Shop, ethical trusts, etc.*

Figure 6.2 *Objectives, perspectives and levels of integrity*

- *Ethically neutral.* Many industries or firms are expected to behave without any particular regard for integrity. Their products may be used by the general public and yet the firms that manufacture or sell them are recognized separately from their products. Financial conglomerates are typical of this level. They might own the shares in many businesses which supply products well known to the public, yet the subsidiary businesses themselves would only be expected to behave in line with the parent's own standards of integrity, which are most widely recognized as being opportunistic and self-interested, without too much enlightenment. The high street banks are also now widely perceived as being at this level, especially with regard to their transactions with customers, though this might be a more temporary phenomenon.

- *Ethically positive.* Some firms are, for various reasons, recognized as being positively oriented to integrity. Marks & Spencer embody the very best traditions in retail giving value for money, reliability and quality. They represent a firm that might be expected to completely fulfil Axelrod's requirements of clarity, niceness, provocability and forgivingness. Other examples are firms such as Levi Strauss (see Box 5.2), the many inheritors of Quaker and other religious traditions, such as Cadbury and Rowntree, and the many firms whose competitive strength is built on product quality, typified by Rolls Royce plc. In addition, firms in 'life and death' industries, e.g. pharmaceuticals, also need to have a positive orientation to integrity. If they do not their strategic future is threatened (e.g. Distillers after its thalidomide débâcle).

■ *Ethically dependent.* Some businesses base their competitive strength on a dependence on integrity. Their particular ethical approach is their source of differentiation. A number of investment trusts have been so focused and have generally outperformed competitors with no particular ethical orientation. The Body Shop is a further example of a business which deliberately makes itself ethically dependent.

The ethical status of a business, i.e. the level at which it is oriented, is a matter of management judgement and should result from an explicit management decision process, just as does business strategy itself. In practice, it may well emerge, like strategy, as a result of continued trial and error, or even by accident. However, it is not something that can be determined as a result of the application of some systematic diagnosis. Management needs to decide the level that is appropriate for their particular business and then to follow through the implications in terms of subsequent actions outlined in Chapter 7.

Corporate philanthropy

The decision as to the appropriate level of integrity is calculated according to the needs of the business. It is important to make the distinction here between the idea of an ethically dependent business, such as Body Shop, and a business that has adopted the concept of corporate philanthropy. The Body Shop has a distinctive ethical stance which is at the heart of its true strategic objectives. It beats its competitors because of its particular brand of integrity. Corporate philanthropy is different from this.

Corporate philanthropy is one way in which firms demonstrate their social responsibility. In a world of increasing social injustice, both within and between different groupings and where governments are failing to deal with the underlying causes of such injustice, it is widely argued that the wealth creating sector must play a bigger role in such causes as urban poverty, education and health. Firms are encouraged to act as corporate citizens having a broad view of their own self-interest which they should seek to align with the greater good of society at large. However, the strategic direction of a business is of crucial importance to its long-term prosperity and the dangers of letting concern for social responsibility interfere with a clear strategic focus have already been highlighted in Chapter 4. Too great an emphasis on social responsibility puts the real strategic purpose of the business at risk by muddying its direction. Corporate philanthropy, if given an inappropriate emphasis, risks doing exactly the same.

Nevertheless, corporate philanthropy does provide genuine benefits, both for the recipient and the philanthropist. Part of the attraction of Levi

Strauss, for example, lies in its Aids awareness initiatives which are perceived as worth while by all stakeholders, not least employees who can feel they are involved with an organization that is taking actions to make the world a better place.

Corporate philanthropy has often been regarded simply as a way of disposing of surplus funds. Recognized as more attractive than investing in what Cyert and March (1963) referred to as managerial slack (i.e. perks, bonuses and status symbols), philanthropy used to be deliberately steered away from the firm's core business. Thus, bankers gave to the arts and manufacturers gave to sick children, though few firms, even with a formally established foundation, focused their giving in any systematic way. While such investments appear not to relate to the purpose of the business, they are sufficiently subordinate that they are hardly likely to obscure the firm's strategic focus.

However, the approach has shortcomings that were realized with the 1989 Exxon Valdez oil spill. Exxon had established the much admired Exxon Education Foundation, deliberately separated from Exxon's business and policies. The foundation could instead have focused on supporting environmental leaders and pressure groups. Had it done so, Exxon's handling of the oil spill crisis could have been much better informed and the likely public relations effect much less damaging. Smith (1994) contrasted Exxon's approach with that of its competitor, Arco, who focused its funding strategically on supporting and forming alliances specifically with environmental groups. This strategic approach to corporate philanthropy was most clearly articulated by the AT&T Foundation. AT&T brought in Reynold Levy, an outsider, to head up the foundation specifically to avoid it becoming a fiefdom of the CEO and focusing on his pet projects. In his first report to the AT&T board, Levy insisted that,

> the foundation, which had its own endowed funds, should not be 'a thing apart' from business. Rather, foundation initiatives should be tied to business functions. Philanthropic initiatives should help advance business interests through strategic alliances with the marketing, government affairs, research and development, and human resources functions. In return, Levy stressed that those business units should support philanthropic activities with all their resources, from management know-how and technological expertise to employee volunteers, thus producing initiatives that would benefit the community as much as possible. Furthermore, Levy argued, such a giving program would heighten the company's responsiveness to its social environment and help executives make decisions that would draw on the experience of the non-profit world.
> The key to success would be the empowerment of the **philanthropy**

professionals who would run the foundation. They would have the opportunity to make their case with top managers and to have a seat at the table in corporate strategy sessions. They would serve not only as the company's ambassadors but also as its eyes and ears. Levy argued that the foundation staff should be 'Janus-faced' one face serving the community, the other serving AT&T's business units.

(Smith, 1944, p. 108)

Such strategically focused corporate philanthropy, on the face of it, looks attractive. It is designed specifically to reinforce the strategic focus of the business, rather than detract from it. Moreover it also serves to raise the perceived integrity of the philanthropic firm in the eyes of the stakeholders who are aware of its actions.

It is clear that a business whose survival is threatened would be unable to make such investments. Moreover, a business that is not yet satisfying its various stakeholders, and not pleasing its customers, would surely have more pressing calls on its finances than to invest in philanthropic projects, strategic or otherwise. Even a company that has achieved all its lower level objectives should still be firmly focused on its strategic aim of beating its competitors. Investments in corporate philanthropy should therefore only be made when they are strictly aimed at achieving this strategic objective. As such, they are not distinctive by their philanthropy, but by their strategic nature, and their control should not be left to *philanthropy professionals* but to strategic management. Smith's concept of philanthropy professionals having 'a seat at the table in corporate strategy sessions', though perhaps fashionable, is likely to lead the business to losing its strategic focus. The debate between philanthropy professionals and strategic management is pointless. Where they agree, there is no need for the empowerment and debate; where they are in disagreement, it is strategic management's view that must prevail if the business is to stay focused.

However, there is more to corporate philanthropy than this. Broad levels of ethical status—negative, neutral, positive and dependent—have been briefly examined. Managements must ask themselves which level is right for their business. Their answer is likely to depend on the expected costs and benefits involved. The main benefits are that the higher a firm's perceived level, the more acceptable it is likely to be found as a potential partner in mutually advantageous transactions. From this point of view there is hardly any downside. Potential partners have their own integrity levels and though they would not generally be happy to transact with partners who they regarded as less trustworthy than themselves, they would be perfectly content to transact with firms they perceived as more trustworthy than themselves. In this sense the higher the perceived integrity level of a firm, the better.

Thus, if a firm is perceived as being at the neutral level, there would be a clear benefit in raising those perceptions to the positive level. Corporate philanthropy can serve to achieve this end. At the same time, if the philanthropic programme is strategically focused, it will not conflict in any way with the firm's strategic direction. Such philanthropy will be perceived as another additional and attractive attribute of the firm's product.

Given two perfectly reliable suppliers of essentially similar, or undifferentiated, products, most people would choose to trade with the firm that adopts a high-profile corporate philanthropy programme in preference to the firm that is perceived as being at the neutral level of integrity. Even Tom Peters has paused, in mid 'sweat and shout', to support this view:

> I am a capitalist through and through. I champion the rights of business to do nothing more than make damn good products, serve their customers well, train the hell out of their workers and, hopefully, create new jobs that pay well. But I will champion even more vigorously those that take the bottom line as a starting point; who worry about Aids, Rwanda, etc.– and then do something. (Peters, 1994b)

Corporate philanthropy can play an important part in creating the most effective culture of integrity, but it must be approached analytically, with clear aims in mind. The business that lets its *philanthropy professionals* lead it into action on Aids or Rwanda risks losing its strategic focus. The business that sees a strategic opportunity that can be assisted by focused corporate philanthropy is much more likely to enjoy long-term success.

Conclusion

Integrity has been examined from different business perspectives in order to see how different organizations, in different circumstances, are likely to relate to integrity, and how the different approaches to integrity are related to different levels of long-term business success. No single clear ethical standard has emerged from this process.

On the one hand, it is the perception of a firm's integrity that determines the behaviour of potential partners, but if the perception is too different from reality it is unlikely to be long lasting. Thus the reality of a firm's integrity is what really matters.

It is perfectly possible for a firm to operate with high integrity towards one set of stakeholders and be much less ethical with others. Integrity might thus be like a management style that could be decided on and adopted to fit particular circumstances. However, perceptions of integrity determine behaviour, and if the firm behaves unethically towards one set of stakeholders it would be perceived as generally unethical by all stakeholders aware of its unethical behaviour. This perception would then determine stakeholder behaviour. The level of a firm's integrity must be adopted consistently across all its transactions, more as though it were a fundamental characteristic rather than a style.

Thus it has been acknowledged that, although the approach to integrity adopted here has deliberately set out to be one of calculation based on the firm's strategic self-interest, it is simpler to adopt integrity as an essential aspect of the firm's culture, so that it is, and is perceived by all stakeholders to be, both real and consistent.

The ethical status of business organizations has been recognized as a continuous variable measured on a continuum from negative to highly positive. Four broad regions on this continuum were identified—negative, neutral, positive and dependent. Examples of firms in each of these general areas have been provided, but there is no definitive mechanism for identifying a particular firm's position. This whole area is riddled with ambiguity and uncertainty and even Kant cannot help. However, managers are increasingly used to handling ambiguity, and will be familiar with the problems inherent in this analysis of integrity.

It has been concluded that there are considerable benefits in being, and being perceived to be, at a high level of corporate integrity. From the point of view of Gauthier's model of mutually advantageous collaborations and partnerships, the higher the level the better.

Despite all the caveats and limitations that must be placed on generalized statements, a final conclusion can be drawn. Successful organizations are right to place considerable importance on behaving with high integrity in all transactions with all their stakeholders. This is not new. In order to achieve this organizations should deliberately establish a high-integrity culture which is recognized by all stakeholders, both inside and outside the organization. This, again, is not new.

This investigation of an alternative business ethic has sought to be analytical, calculative and as value free as possible. The conclusions, however, are that the most effective way of building enlightened self-interest into an organization is to deliberately inculcate a system of corporate values into all stakeholders. The value-free starting point is important. It needs to be recognized that this is not a flabby or sentimental approach to ethics, but a deliberately hard-nosed business approach. And the route taken to reach this conclusion is also important. Because of these, it is possible to identify the actions necessary to achieve this high-integrity culture as a result of dispassionate analysis, rather than as the imperatives of fervently held, but possibly idiosyncratic, systems of personal morality.

Action on integrity

This final chapter suggests how organizations might set about the task of creating a high-integrity culture.

The most important aspect of a high-integrity culture is openness. Where there is not openness there is usually something to hide. 'Openness and ethics go together'.

Recent initiatives on corporate governance are intended to assist this process of establishing openness in organizations. These universal approaches can, however, only assist the process. The main responsibility lies with corporate management who take responsibility for their own organizations.

To make integrity explicit, management need to focus on specifying, assessing, reporting and 'improving' standards of integrity in all the organization's relationships.

If an organization's integrity is to be truly perceived by stakeholders it must be communicated to them. If employees are to fulfil their roles in achieving the organization's integrity they need to receive specific training.

Integrity starts at the top, and needs to be reinforced continually by example: an appropriate top management role model, the public punishment of transgressors and the public reward of achievers.

Introduction

Leading business ethicist DeGeorge prefaces his book on *Competing with Integrity in International Business* by highlighting various themes that underly his approach. The first, and perhaps most crucial, of these is that the business can be no more ethical than the persons who run it. This is a basic tenet of most business ethicists and has long been part of the orthodox wisdom:

What matters most is where we stand as individual managers and how we behave when faced with decisions which combine ethical and commercial judgments. (Cadbury, 1987)

This approach to business ethics is personal, the intention being to inform, educate and indoctrinate so that the ethical standards of the individual recipients are raised and the business organizations in which they operate are therefore also 'improved'. In this context, an individual such as Robert Maxwell would presumably be regarded as an interesting challenge.

The organizational integrity approach, on the other hand, recognizes that business organizations have an existence above and beyond the individuals who run them. Businesses develop long-lasting cultures which may or may not coincide with the values and beliefs of individual managers.

Cadbury's Quaker origins, for example, still permeate the company. Nevertheless, Cadbury has almost certainly employed senior people whose personal standards were far less ethical than those of the company that employed them. In order to survive and prosper in that culture such individuals would have to behave at the Cadbury's level of integrity. If instead they had tried to lower Cadbury's standards to their own there would almost certainly have been a disputation resulting most probably in the rejection of the individual concerned.

The reverse is also true—despite the high ethical standards of some individuals they do not necessarily impose their standards on the organization. A non-business example is described in Box 7.1 which highlights the very strong cultural pressures that can persist long after they are demonstrably inappropriate. DeGeorge's opening assertion seems to deny the power, even the existence, of organizational cultures in which standards of organizational integrity are embedded.

Since their approach is personal, DeGeorge and the business ethicists want managers with 'moral imagination and courage'—the Sugiharas of this world. In reality, people in business are much the same as people in any other walk of life: not perfect, riddled with inconsistencies and ambiguities, with the potential for both huge achievement and ignominious failure. For every Sugihara there is likely to be at least one Maxwell. But businesses do not depend on Sugiharas or Maxwells. They depend on energetic entrepreneurs who get their satisfaction from building a successful long-term business, who enjoy their working life and like their people to have fun at work. Moral imagination and courage are not necessarily part of their repertoire.

Rather than seeking to convert the Maxwells into Sugiharas, the organizational integrity approach seeks to create organizations that are seen as trustworthy, and attractive as potential allies and partners. The enlightened self-interest approach to integrity in business therefore starts out from a basically different premise from that of the business ethicists. It starts from a position that is as far as possible free from extraneous values and defines a course of action aimed at making the business behave so that it is perceived as having high integrity. The outcome of this attempt is to

Box 7.1 'Still no Oscar for Sugihara's list'

Chiune Sugihara was 40 years old and serving as Japan's consul-general in Lithuania when the Jews from Poland arrived. It was the summer of 1940, the Nazis were on the rampage in Europe, Jews were being rounded up, and the only escape route was across the Soviet Union to Japan and then to the United States. But first they needed a visa.

Japan did not go to war until its attack on Pearl Harbor in December 1941, but already its military government was leaning towards an alliance with Germany. When the terrified Jews queued up at Sugihara's residence and begged for transit visas, the Japanese consul was faced with a dilemma. Three times he cabled Tokyo asking for permission to issue visas, and each time he was refused. But he knew the Jews faced internment and likely death if they returned to Poland.

Sugihara decided to defy instructions and issue hand-written visas: in 28 days he processed 1600 permits which allowed some 6000 Jews passage through Japan. More people were applying, but then the Foreign Ministry in Tokyo ordered Sugihara to move to Berlin. Sugihara had already saved more than four times as many people as Oskar Schindler—celebrated in Stephen Spielberg's film. And he had not made a single yen or pfennig, unlike the industrialist Schindler.

When Sugihara returned to Tokyo after the war, he was fired by the Foreign Ministry. The humanitarian concerns were never entered into: he had disobeyed orders. Although he received the Yad Vashem Prize for Righteous Gentiles from Israel in 1985, he died in 1986 without receiving any official recognition from Japan.

It was not until 1991, when a top diplomat was preparing Japan's first official visit to newly-independent Lithuania, that the case of Sugihara came up again. He was still the most famous Japanese figure in Lithuania, and protocol demanded some gesture on Japan's part. After much high-level bickering, a Foreign Ministry official was dispatched to visit Sugihara's family, and although no apology was issued, the official expressed his 'regrets' that Sugihara had been cold-shouldered by the Japanese Establishment for five decades. The prime minister at the time, Kiichi Miyazawa, mentioned Sugihara in a speech in the Diet (parliament), but also refrained from issuing any apology. ...

In the popular imagination, Japan in the 1930s was caught up in a battle for supremacy with the West. This was a racial confrontation between whites and the only Asian nation capable of resisting them. Japan had no choice but to go to war. If tens of thousands of civilians in Nanking had to be sacrificed to consolidate Japanese advances in China, that was just part of war. And wars are inhuman and full of atrocities. But everyone was following orders.

> The issue of moral accountability again gets pushed aside, overridden by uncontrollable historical forces, racial prejudices, 'national destiny' and the power of fate. They are irresistible, that is, to all but a few individuals like Chiune Sugihara.
>
> (McCarthy, 1994)

recognize that the simplest way is to establish an organizational culture that has high integrity embedded in it, so that all individuals in the business, no matter what their personal standards, are encouraged to behave in accord with the values of the organization. Rather than seek to convert the Maxwells into Sugiharas, the organizational integrity approach seeks to build conditions where Maxwells would be less likely to prosper and Sugiharas more likely to be rewarded.

This chapter examines the essential characteristics of a high-integrity culture and identifies some actions managements can take to develop their organization's culture. The outlines of management action are largely based on the survey of firms in the FT SE 100 index described in Appendix I. The three main broad findings of this survey were:

- that the vast majority of major/successful businesses (i.e. from the FT SE 100) are not particularly interested in investing in good works that are unrelated to their business activities (i.e. in altruism)—business success is their prime motivation;

- that they are, nevertheless, very much concerned with integrity and ethical issues and regard being ethical as crucial to business success;

- that while this concern appears to be genuine and the majority of firms express it formally as a code of behaviour or at least refer formally to such ethical issues in other documents, only a minority of firms take positive action to ensure that the required standards of integrity are maintained in practice in all their dealings.

Several firms in the survey recognized the need to take action, for example, to assess how well they performed against their published code of conduct, but had not decided what action should be taken. There was a reluctance to embark on a course of monitoring and reporting not because they were fearful of what they might find, but because they feared they might be setting up a whole new bureaucracy that would only serve to reduce focus on the prime business objectives.

The actions outlined later in this chapter have all been undertaken by firms in the survey sample. They are not suggested as the final solution, but they clearly work in particular circumstances and the manager's job is to recognize the most appropriate initiatives for his or her organization, balancing the need for some element of formality on the one hand with the necessity to avoid adding to the bureaucratic jungle on the other.

A culture of openness

In an award-winning article on ethical managers, Sir Adrian Cadbury discusses the very real problem of bribe payments (Cadbury, 1987). Having considered the issue in the context of differing national cultures he proposes two simple tests of acceptablility:

1. *Is the payment on the face of the invoice?*

2. *Would it embarrass the recipient to have the gift mentioned in the company newspaper?*

He explains the value of these two simple tests as follows:

The logic behind these rules of thumb is that openness and ethics go together and that actions are unethical if they will not stand scrutiny. Openness in arriving at decisions reflects the same logic. It gives those with an interest in a particular decision the chance to make their views known and opens to argument the basis on which the decision is finally taken.

The sequence of questions that were raised in the previous chapter are based on very similar concerns:

■ 'What if the truth were known about this?'

■ 'What if all stakeholders knew about it?'

■ 'What if all stakeholders knew the whole truth about this?'

■ 'What would be the effect on our perceived trustworthiness if all stakeholders knew the whole truth?'

Openness is overwhelmingly the most important characteristic of a high-integrity culture. In the opening chapter an incident was recounted (see Box 1.6) which satisfies Cadbury's first question, after a fashion, but singularly fails the second. Exposing the same incident to the series of questions above sheds further light on it, particularly the final question. What would be the effect on the firm's perceived trustworthiness as an employer if employees, for example, knew that the MD was stealing in that way? The answer to this question is rather more specific than the answer to the Cadbury questions and suggests some possible ways of dealing with the situation.

The incident referred to in Box 1.6 is taken a stage further in Box 7.2. The S.T.P. saga of Chapter 1 was based on a combination of true cases, and the actual events referred to in Box 7.2 are real and the consequences were also true. This is emphasized simply to highlight the position of whistleblowing. The aim in a high-integrity culture should be to ensure that there should never be any need for whistleblowing. The fact that people are placed in a situation where the only way they can get their grievances aired is through whistleblowing indicates a closed and repressive culture.

Whistleblowing is a notoriously dangerous activity. Support for whistleblowers is extremely difficult to find. Even where there is support it usually fails to stay the course. Donkin describes how Jim Smith blew the

---

Box 7.2: Whistleblowing at S.T.P.

Having established a modus operandi with Gerald Smith, his chief accountant, Charles Kirtchin took advantage of the situation, his relatively minor abuses quickly increasing in scale and frequency. Over an eighteen-month period he had an extension to his house, his country cottage re-roofed and central heating installed, purchased a new bathroom suite, kitchen equipment and a hi-fi plus an exotic Chinese carpet. In addition he had two vintage motor cycles restored to concourse condition, plus holidays in Greece and America for himself and his wife. Smith, feeling extremely unhappy but powerless, arranged for all these items to paid by the company and coded according to Kirtchin's instructions.

Staff in the company were well aware of these purchases and the personnel manager was anonymously given copies of all the above invoices and many more. He took them to his immediate boss, the manufacturing director, who considered his possible courses of action. None was without risk to his job, prospects and pension, not to mention Gerald Smith's also. Moreover, it was his family that concerned him, not simply his own position. The most obvious course of action—reporting the abuse to Kirtchin's immediate boss in the parent company—appeared also to be the most risky since Kirtchin and he seemed to be very close and might even be 'in it' together.

In the end he decided to raise the issue formally at a board meeting under Any Other Business. There were two non-executive parent company representatives on S.T.P.'s board, and they would presumably be forced to take notice. Before the board meeting, however, the manufacturing director was summarily fired and given a generous compensation package including two years salary plus his company car. The real reasons for this were never made clear, his departure being minuted as resulting from 'differences over manufacturing policy'.

whistle on his firm's excess profiteering on Ministry of Defence contracts. His allegations were highlighted by Parliament's Public Accounts Committee and following support by more than 300 MPs who signed an early day motion calling for his compensation, the Institute of Directors and his professional body the Chartered Institute of Management Accountants, he was finally vindicated. Nevertheless the result was that he became a corporate outcast, penniless, evicted from his home of 20 years, ostracized by companies that once courted his talents, ignored by a government that valued his help, and was all but forgotten by the professional bodies to which he once belonged (Donkin, 1994). Smith's case is typical of big time whistleblowers, but a similar fate awaits anyone who decides to blow the whistle publicly when the position cannot be rectified internally and in a relatively low key fashion. According to a survey of 87 whistleblowers in the US six years ago, some 17 per cent of them lost their homes, 8 per cent filed for bankruptcy, 15 per cent filed for divorce and 10 per cent attempted suicide.

Openness should ensure that whistleblowing is never necessary. The openness should be deliberately designed so that structures and processes are in place that the would-be whistleblower is encouraged to use, so that a 'grievance' is aired and appropriate action taken long before it becomes a substantial problem. Such an open culture would of course eliminate most of the practices that could become the subject of whistleblowing. If corporate integrity was explicit and noticeable, the only way a Maxwell could prosper would be by explicitly changing the rules and culture back to being secretive, closed and repressive—a process that is not easy to achieve.

Corporate governance

The phrase 'corporate governance' is short-hand for a raft of initiatives, some statutory, some voluntary, that are intended to help the process of openness in order to 'clean up' the private sector and inhibit fraud and corruption. The Cadbury initiative on corporate governance was a major attempt to achieve this.

The Cadbury code of best practice is included in Box 7.3. These recommendations are amplified by a series of notes intended to assist application to the particular business. The intention was to encourage, through a process of independent audit and review, the spread of the boardroom practices of the best run companies. The main thrust is to reduce the opportunities for abuse of personal power by company leaders, by setting certain specific limitations on it, by making its exercise more open and more subject to independent audit and review.

Adoption of the Cadbury code is not mandatory but it is required that all

Box 7.3   Cadbury report on corporate governance —Code of Best Practice

1. Board of directors

1.1 The board should meet regularly, retain full and effective control over the company and monitor the executive management.

1.2 There should be a clearly accepted division of responsibilities at the head of a company, which will ensure a balance of power and authority, such that no one individual has unfettered powers of decision. Where the chairman is also the chief executive, it is essential that there should be a strong and independent element on the board, with a recognized senior member.

1.3 The board should include non-executive directors of sufficient calibre and number for their views to carry significant weight in the board's decisions.

1.4 The board should have a formal schedule of matters specifically reserved to it for decision to ensure that the direction and control of the company is firmly in its hands.

1.5 There should be an agreed procedure for directors in the furtherance of their duties to take independent professional advice, if necessary, at the company's expense.

1.6 All directors should have access to the advice and services of the company secretary, who is responsible to the board for ensuring that board procedures are followed and that applicable rules and regulations are complied with. Any question of the removal of the company secretary should be a matter for the board as a whole.

2. Non-executive directors

2.1 Non-executive directors should bring an independent judgement to bear on issues of strategy, performance, resources, including key appointments, and standards of conduct.

2.2 The majority should be independent of management and free from any business or other relationship which could materially interfere with the exercise of their independent judgement, apart from their fees and shareholding. Their fees should reflect the time which they commit to the company.

2.3 Non-executive directors should be appointed for specified terms and reappointment should not be automatic.

2.4 Non-executive directors should be selected through a formal process and both this process and their appointment should be a matter for the board as a whole.

3. Executive directors

3.1 Directors' service contracts should not exceed three years without shareholders' approval. (Note 8)

3.2 There should be full and clear disclosure of directors' total emoluments and those of the chairman and highest-paid UK director, including pension contributions and stock options. Separate figures should be given for salary and performance related elements and the basis on which performance is measured should be explained.

3.3 Executive directors' pay should be subject to the recommendations of a remuneration committee made up wholly or mainly of non-executive directors.

4. Reporting and controls

4.1 It is the board's duty to present a balanced and understandable assessment of the company's position.

4.2 The board should ensure than an objective and professional relationship is maintained with the auditors.

4.3 The board should establish an audit committee of at least 3 non-executive directors with written terms of reference which deal clearly with its authority and duties.

4.4 The directors should explain their responsibility for preparing the accounts next to a statement by the auditors about their reporting responsibilities.

4.5 The directors should report on the effectiveness of the company's system of internal control.

4.6 The directors should report that the business is a going concern, with supporting assumptions or qualifications as necessary.

(Reproduced from the Final Report of the Committee on the Financial Aspects of Corporate Governance, published by Gee, South Quay Plaza, 183 Marsh Wall, London, E14 9FS.)

companies quoted on the London Stock Exchange should include a statement in their annual report identifying the extent to which Cadbury has been implemented.

Stiles and Taylor (1993) reviewed the extent of implementation among *The Times* top 100 UK companies. They focused on six of the key Cadbury recommendations (numbers in brackets after each refers to the number of companies *not* complying):

■ Separation of responsibilities of chairman and chief executive (20).

■ Disclosure of pay packages of chairman and highest paid UK director (66).

■ Appointment of at least three non-executive directors (1).

■ Appointment of audit committee composed of at least three non-executives (12).

- Appointment of remuneration committee composed of at least three non-executives (11).

- Appointment of nomination committee composed wholly of non-executives (88).

The code has been widely adopted: 73 of the top 100 companies had adopted four or more compliance factors, but implementation remains uneven. Moreover, as has often been pointed out, conformance is no guarantee of good behaviour. For example, British Airways complied with five of the six criteria, but nevertheless engaged in covert surveillance of Richard Branson, was forced to pay £3.5m damages for its 'dirty tricks' campaign, and offered a humiliating apology. Marks & Spencer, on the other hand, complies with only one of the six criteria, but has a unique reputation for both financial performance and high integrity.

As Box 7.4 suggests, the Cadbury code of practice remains controversial in some quarters and seems likely to be dragged into the political dog-fight between legislators and self-regulators.

The underlying philosophy behind Cadbury is clearly very much in tune with the present approach to establishing a culture of integrity, but the means of its achievement may be problematic. On the one hand, there will be firms which become adept at playing the superficial game, complying with the various criteria but at the same time not achieving the spirit of Cadbury. On the other hand, there will be many companies of high integrity which find the Cadbury process too bureaucratic and restrictive to follow to the letter.

A more flexible, contingent approach would probably be more appropriate where the detailed implementation is left open to interpretation by directors as seems most appropriate for their businesses. While the Cadbury recommendations were undoubtedly well intentioned, they seem destined not to achieve their intended aims because they will only be accepted in spirit by the already converted or superficially complied with by the unethical. Some of the issues Cadbury's code tackles, such as board composition, may need to be the subject of legislation if they are to be achieved.

The essence of Cadbury is openness protected by a form of independent audit and review, the independence being assumed to be inherent in the position of non-executive directors (NEDs). This is spelled out in paras 2.1 to 2.4 of the code, which are supported by explanatory notes. These notes suggest that it is up to the board to decide whether the definition of independence has been met, but that relevant interests of the NEDs should be disclosed in the Directors' Report; they also suggest that NEDs should not participate in share option schemes, should not be pensionable, and their letters of appointment should specify their duties, term of office, remuneration, etc. Nevertheless, as Box 7.5 indicates, they still face problems in the excecution of their duties.

Box 7.4 'Bosses lay into Cadbury rules'

Tim Melville-Ross, the new head of the Institute of Directors, is set to spearhead a noisy campaign against the recent rules on corporate governance. The campaign is the latest evidence of an angry backlash developing among Britain's leading company directors against the Cadbury Report which, they say, is choking business enterprise.

They believe many of the new measures, while costing business millions of pounds to implement, will not achieve their aim of preventing dishonest directors abusing their power over their companies.

If the rebellion continues to gather strength, an increasing number of companies will feel able to reject Cadbury in the corporate governance statements they are obliged to make in their annual reports. That could set back by years the attempt to reform the way companies are run in Britain.

Mr Melville-Ross, who is leaving his job as chief executive of Nationwide building society in August to head the IoD, said: 'The Cadbury report is too prescriptive, too limiting. We want to tell companies that they should not be frightened to say they are not following Cadbury and explain why.'

The IoD's attack is the most outspoken so far by any official body representing business interests. Although company directors have often grumbled about the plethora of new rules, few have complained publicly until now.

'The huge number of nonstatutory rules is making it difficult for directors to do the job of looking after the interests of their shareholders and directors,' said Rudolf Agnew, newly appointed chairman of Lasmo, the oil company fighting a bid from Enterprise Oil.

Sir Christopher Hogg, chairman of Courtaulds, Reuters and SmithKline Beecham, believes that it would be a mistake if British companies ever had to comply with regulations that had become as complex and bureaucratic as those of the Securities and Exchange Commission in the United States. Companies might cease to take risks and 'play the process'.

A large institutional investor said: 'Companies can spend all their time ticking the right boxes to show they've complied with the nittygritty of Cadbury, but it's rubbish really. It distracts from how well a company is actually doing. There is a danger of losing the big picture.'

Directors have so far held back from open criticism of the corporate governance rules, partly out of fear of sounding politically incorrect. They are also afraid that if they do not comply, their shareholders may wrongly conclude that they have something to hide.

However, many now fear that there is a danger of repeating the fiasco of City regulation in the 1980s. The broad principles of regulation embodied in the 1986 Financial Services Act commanded widespread support. But they were turned by the Securities and

Investments Board, led by Sir Kenneth Berrill, into thousands of detailed rules so onerous they had to be shortened and re-written three years later.

(Thomson, 1994)

Box 7.5 'Non-execs fail to learn the facts of company life'

Non-financial performance measures may be all the rage among management theorists, but they have apparently yet to reach non-executive directors, according to a survey by KPMG Peat Marwick, the accountants and consultants. The study, published last week, finds that while non-execs generally receive the necessary information on such traditional indicators as profit and loss, cash-flow statements and external auditors' reports, they tend to be short of data relating to newer performance measures, such as customer satisfaction, management ability and quality.

While more than half said these criteria were important in helping them do their jobs, two-thirds of the 235 non-executives questioned in the survey of the 1000 biggest companies in Britain did not receive details of customer satisfaction levels, 58 per cent were given no information on quality indicators and 52 per cent were not told about the results of management appraisals. Further, despite the current enthusiasm for benchmarking, 58 per cent were not told how their companies' performance compared with that of market leaders.

Gerry Acher, KPMG's head of audit and accounting, added that it was surprising that a large minority relied entirely on internal information. 'I urge them to use external sources to give a broad view of their companies,' he said.

The survey also finds evidence of patchy adoption of the Cadbury Committee call for non-executive directors to be appointed by a nomination committee rather than the chairman. Mr Acher said that with 51 per cent of those surveyed appointed in the old way, 'it will be interesting to see if, in the future, the chairman's influence wanes in this respect'.

At the same time, there is a clear indication that many non-executives face twin—and possibly conflicting—demands to give strategic advice and represent shareholder interests.

Mr Acher said: 'They appear comfortable with this dual role, but are clearly not getting sufficient information on some of the key strategy areas that one might expect'.

'There are areas where matters of strategic importance and the receipt of vital information need to be brought into line. The non-exec role should be to add shareholder value rather than just protect it.'

(Trapp, 1994)

The spirit of Cadbury is again clear and if companies wish to use genuinely independent NEDs Cadbury suggests useful ways to help this process. However, if directors choose the traditional route of mutual back-scratching on the old-boy network, they can also do so and still comply with the letter of Cadbury.

The fact that only a small minority of firms have adopted the nomination committee criterion in Cadbury suggests that companies are only moving slowly to the use of genuinely independent NEDs. Whichever route they take, the real independence of NEDs will remain problematic. NEDs will continue to be approved on appointment by the CEO and in practice will need to retain that approval, unless their independent status is protected by law.

For all its shortcomings the Cadbury recommendations provide one sort of example that can be followed with great effect if taken in the spirit of Cadbury.

Codes of practice

Despite their apparent limitations, codes of ethical practice are becoming increasingly popular among leading companies. A survey by the Insitute of Business Ethics indicated that in 1987, 18 per cent of leading companies had statements of business ethics. When the survey was repeated in 1991 this had grown to 29 per cent. A joint study by the Integrity Works consultancy and Ashridge Management College in 1993 suggested that 43 per cent of companies had codes of ethics. The 1994 survey of FT SE 100 index companies, outlined in Appendix I, suggests that 50 per cent now had written codes of practice, and a further 30 per cent had statements which included reference to such issues. Among those that did not, a significant number were working on developing a code.

Individual company codes of practice may be more effective than universal codes such as Cadbury or the Institute of Management's code of conduct and guide to professional management practice, because they can be related to industry-specific and company-specific issues. The universal codes are necessarily general and can become more or less meaningless. For example, the IM's code of conduct states:

> *At all times a member shall uphold the good standing and reputation of the profession of management; and while practising as a manager shall:*
>
> *a. Have due regard for and comply with relevant law.*
>
> *b. Not misuse or abuse power or position.*
>
> *c. Follow the Guides to Professional Management Practice, as approved by the Council.*

> d. *Have a duty to provide information on request to any committee or sub-committee of the Insitute established to investigate any alleged breach of this Code.*

The Council of the Institute, being the self-proclaimed fount of all wisdom on this topic, can only address the Institute's own members, so the codes approach is essentially personal. The members in turn may choose to accept or ignore the IM's code. Whether such a document would be of assistance to a member in conflict with his or her own organization is highly questionable. It seems most probable that such a code will have no practical effect.

Organizational codes, on the other hand, can serve two significant purposes:

- First, they can contribute to the establishment of an organization's culture and thereby impact on the way people in the organization behave.

- Second, they may identifiy items of business behaviour which are in some way measurable or monitorable and which might form the basis for audit and review of performance.

The most effective codes would serve both purposes equally, the least effective remain as simple statements of intent with no attempt being made to make further use of them.

Appendix II shows one way of developing a code of practice as advocated by the Institute of Business Ethics. This is included as a general check-list of areas and issues that might be covered in a code. Example statements related to ethical values by ICI and Shell are included in Appendix III. It is sometimes argued that such statements often amount to little more than window dressing, though this is clearly far from the intention with these two companies, both emphasizing the importance of implementation or application. If upheld in practice, such statements can be the foundation of a high-integrity culture. The key is implementation. As Cadbury pointed out:

> *The ethical standards of a company are judged by its actions, not by pious statements of intent put out in its name. This does not mean that those who head companies should not set down what they believe their companies stand for—hard though that is to do. The character of a company is a matter of importance to those in it, to those who do business with it, and to those who are considering joining it.* (Cadbury, 1987)

Developing a code which is going to be of practical use demands that it is pertinent to the distinctive features of the particular industry. For example, firms in an industry which involves a known health risk must pay particular attention to the way they control and monitor their performance in regard to that particular issue. Practically valuable codes should also focus on factors that differentiate the individual business from its competitors, as does, for example, The Body Shop. Practical usefulness also demands that the various statements of practice are as far as possible measurable, or capable of being monitored in some qualitative way.

Thus management's role in developing an effective code of ethical conduct is not simply to follow the guidance of the Institute of Business Ethics, or the examples of ICI, Shell and others, but to make their code strictly relevant to their own organization, and ensure that performance against it is effectively monitored.

Making integrity explicit

Management initiatives that can be taken to ensure that a business is perceived as being ethical fall broadly into three areas:

1. Being explicit about corporate integrity with all stakeholders. Making widely communicated statements about the standards of performance to be achieved.

2. Setting up the structures and processes by which ethical performance can be monitored and controlled.

3. Taking well-publicized actions to punish transgressors, and—wherever possible—publicly reward achievers.

The Nyrex experience referred to in Box 7.6 shows how one firm reacted, setting up ethics offices to make ethics explicit thereby removing the whistleblower culture, and establishing a code of business conduct and communicating it through company-wide training programmes.

Nyrex's initial approach of quietly sacking or disciplining culprits was inadequate. Subsequently the high profile given to ethical issues meant that disciplining would be similarly high profile and any sackings given the full symbolic weight needed to reinforce the required standards of behaviour.

The communications and training programme of General Dynamics (see Box 7.7) clearly had a similar impact in opening up the culture so that occasions for whistleblowing would be unlikely to arise because potential whistleblowers had the opportunity, even encouragement, to address issues through organized channels before they became significant problems. The introduction of their code and associated communications programme produced a high level of information exchange as well as some decisive actions to encourage the code's implementation. Interestingly General Dynamics also emphasize that their approach is not to 'improve' the moral fibre of their employees but to provide them with the guidance in how General Dynamics believes its business should be conducted.

Approaches to making ethics explicit in order to create and maintain a

---

Box 7.6 Nyrex's response to bad behaviour

In 1988 Nyrex discovered that a number of their executives were inviting senior representatives of their suppliers to sleazy parties in Florida. In the hope that it could be dealt with quietly, Nyrex treated the matter as an 'isolated incident' and either sacked or disciplined the culprits. But that was not the end of the story. The sleazy end of the New York press got hold of the story and all of a sudden Nyrex employees found themselves in the embarrassing situation of not knowing which colleagues were involved, or who they could really trust. In short Nyrex faced a crisis of confidence.

The company's subsequent response was thorough and decisive. It established an office of ethics at its headquarters, run by a senior executive with direct access to the chairman and responsible to the board's audit committee. Similar offices were established in each of its leading business units, with 'hotlines' for people to report misconduct. They also drew up a code of business conduct and then began company-wide training in business ethics.

Chairman Ferguson proclaimed his own law on ethics: '*The likelihood for unethical behaviour in an institution varies in direct proportion to the degree of imperialism shown by management.*' He also identified four main lessons from Nyrex's experience.

First, there is a large difference between 'compliance' with ethics codes and a genuine commitment to them.

Second, face-to-face communication is helpful in getting people to accept ethics codes. 'Counter the doubters and sceptics—and that's most people—by forcing them to engage in a sustained dialogue about how ethics affects their conduct.'

Third, make sure ethics is part of a continuing commitment, not just a 'programme of the month'.

Finally, leadership on ethics begins at the top. 'The role model that managers set for their employees, knowingly or otherwise, is the most important weapon in the ethics arsenal.'

(Based on Dickson, 1993a)

---

high-integrity culture are still developing. There is no one best way. The structures and processes that work best for one organization may be quite inappropriate for another. Respondents to the survey reported in Appendix I reported the following approaches:

1. Annual published review of the organization's ethical performance (20 per cent of respondents)

2. Establishment of a body with specific responsibility for assessing the organization's past ethical performance (50 per cent of respondents)

Box 7.7   Ethical action by General Dynamics

There is also a more practical problem: the difficulty of evaluating how effective codes of ethics have been in practice. For instance, General Dynamics, the US conglomerate, introduced a code in 1985 which it has distributed to its employees and covers topics such as receiving gifts from outsiders.

Between 1985 and 1991 the code and a related staff communication programme generated nearly 30 000 enquiries from staff, provoking 1419 sanctions such as reprimands and demotions. Some 165 employees have been sacked. But Mr Kent Druvvesteyn, vice-president for business ethics and equal employment opportunities, stresses that any attempt to quantify the economic gains derived from the company's code would be 'so difficult that it would be nonsensical'. He rejects the notion that there is any simple connection between General Dynamics' stance on business ethics and profitability, and he says the code does not attempt to instil basic moral values.

'We're not in the business of replacing missing virtues in our employees, but we owe it to them to tell them about slippery spots inherent in the business process,' he says. 'In a society with a web of rules and regulations, that makes good practical sense.' Detractors of ethics as a subject worth taking seriously in a corporate environment will probably need more convincing, but General Dynamics' pragmatism seems to be shared by a growing number of companies.

(Jack and Dixon, 1993)

---

3. Establishment of a body with specific responsibility for reporting on the organization's past ethical performance (35 per cent of respondents)

4. Establishment of a body with specific responsibility for improving the organization's ethical performance (25 per cent of respondents)

5. Setting measurable targets for ethical performance (18 per cent of respondents)

6. Annually assessing the organization's ethical performance (40 per cent of respondents, 30 per cent more frequently)

7. Parent board annually assessing the organization's ethical performance (40 per cent of respondents, 10 per cent more frequently)

8. Provision of business ethics training for new employees (20 per cent of respondents)

9. High profile dismissal of any employee breaking the code of ethical practice (45 per cent of respondents)

10. Recognition in some other formal way of the organization's ethical performance (15 per cent of respondents)

During subsequent interviews further detail was provided on how the bodies (i.e. individuals or groups) set about their tasks of assessing, reporting and 'improving' ethical performance. First, there appeared to be distinct differences in the terms of reference for such bodies. In some cases, terms of reference were laid down by top management (CEO or board). These differences, however, were in practice not so significant as, in most cases discussed, the terms of reference evolved as a result of a negotiation process. In all cases they were agreed between the body and top management. Terms of reference included what was to be monitored and how, and how it was to be reported. 'Improvement' in practice meant recommendations for management action. The negotiation of terms of reference was itself an important part of the process which both added credibility to the body and increased the knowledge of top management.

In addition to these approaches, a number of companies repeated the Nyrex claim that 'leadership in ethics begins at the top'. Two quotes from the survey indicate this strongly held view:

■ 'Leadership is key. Rules and regulations only go so far.'

■ 'Example from and leadership by top management is essential—without that "rules" and "codes" are useless.'

There were also several firms who, like General Dynamics, used formal communications programmes to get their message to different stake-holders.

■ 'The values of the organization must be communicated to help employees in shaping their behaviour.'

■ 'Our corporate communications programme informs customers and shareholders as well as employees about how well we are performing against our code of practice.'

Such programmes can successfully develop external stakeholder perceptions of the organization's integrity, while the training approach seems more appropriate for internal stakeholders. It was surprising that training is not more widely used among employees. Perhaps this is because business ethics education is perceived by practitioners as too theoretical and impractical. Business ethics training is clearly often seen as a contradiction in terms.

Industry and organization-specific training in organizational integrity, on the other hand, could be so designed as to be highly practical. Training employees on the way the organization does business, i.e. how it conducts relations with all its various stakeholders, can be entirely centred on the development of practical skills and competences.

There are thus a variety of approaches to making integrity explicit. Some firms are very concerned to avoid setting up any systems that might become bureaucratic and instead favour a minimized review and control process but a high profile, symbolically deterrent punishment of transgressors. One respondent suggested, no doubt tongue in cheek and aware of the paradox:

■ 'Chopping heads off for wrongdoing is the simplest and most effective way of making people behave ethically.'

Other organizations adopt a carefully planned system of audit and control, based on the establishment of business ethics committees or officers whose sole task is to monitor and review performance against the published code of practice, publish their assessments and recommend improvements. A few organizations have managed to define some aspects of ethical performance in strictly measurable terms and are consequently able to report performance in quantified terms.

A further possible approach that is currently receiving widespread attention, is for the accounting bodies to be proactive in developing a more balanced approach to their audit role—they should be well placed to conduct an independent and authoritative review. However,

> As things stand accounting rules and auditing practices continue to legitimise the appropriation of pension scheme surpluses. Directors continue to maximize the value of their share options and profit related pay by arbitrary choices and interpretation of accounting methods, all approved by auditors. Companies continue to dump toxic waste in rivers, yet their corporate audited reports remain silent on such issues. Corporate practices continue to create sweatshop conditions and low pay, resulting in poverty and deprivation for a large number of people, especially women. Published accounts described as 'true and fair' show directors salaries yet none shows the incidence of low pay. ... Whose truth and whose fairness to whom?   (Sikka et al., 1994)

Traditional auditing is currently in a state of flux. Having facilitated the infamy of names like BCCI, Edencorp, Polly Peck, Maxwell and others, auditors are now seeking to re-establish a reputation for truth and fairness and may well baulk at the responsibility of auditing ethical performance. Managements would do well not to expect too much from this quarter.

In summary, many management initiatives have been taken to achieve required standards of ethical performance. From these examples, it appears that a high-integrity culture might be achieved through the following:

- Establish bodies (individuals or teams) to have responsibility for monitoring, reporting and 'improving' the organization's integrity in its relations with all stakeholders. Consider a different body for each stakeholder category (e.g. a predominantly marketing body to be responsible for customers).

- Initiate these bodies in developing a code of practice covering integrity with stakeholders. The body itself to develop and agree its terms of reference with top management (CEO or board) to cover what should be in the code, what should be monitored and how, and how it should be reported.

- Make the code as industry-specific and organization-specific as possible, and include at least one objectively measurable criterion for each stakeholder category.

- Publish results at least annually.

- Have a formal top board minute to discuss integrity at least twice yearly. Different stakeholder categories can be discussed on separate occasions, thus increasing frequency but avoiding too broad a focus.

- Ensure that appropriate examples are provided for all stakeholders including an appropriate role model by top management, all transgressors being publicly punished and, wherever possible, achievers publicly rewarded.

- Develop a corporate integrity communications programme for external stakeholder groups.

- Develop a corporate integrity training programme for internal stakeholder groups.

The above indicates initiatives that various organizations have taken. The broad principles implied above appear to have wide validity, but the best approach for any particular organization can only be decided by its own management.

Conclusion

This book started from the view that moral philosophy does not apply to business. Beware the well-meaning 'do-gooder' who puts your business at a competitive disadvantage for purely personal religious reasons. Beware the business ethicists who would rather business did not exist—except that they earn their living from it—rather than see it act from self-interest to beat competitors or make a profit.

Business exists to create a surplus from which we all benefit. In order to make that surplus businesses need to be efficient and competitive. This necessarily leads them into conflict with many of the moral philosophers. Paradoxically, it also leads them to seek a reputation for trustworthiness and integrity. This book has sought to justify the quite solid theoretical basis for a model of organizational integrity and to suggest ways in which it can be of considerable practical value.

The main thrust of the approach can be summed up in the story of St George and the dragon. St George went forth and killed the dragon, which had been eating the neighbourhood's babies and doing even more unmentionable things to the local virgins. The utilitarian view of St George's action is that it was a highly ethical act because the consequences are a reduction in pain, an increase in happiness and, in general, his action has resulted in the greater good for the greatest number.

But that is not the whole story. The fact was that St George was a habitual drunkard and at the time of his famous deed he was so drunk he mistook the dragon for his mother-in-law, who he had intended to slay.

Kant and the universalists take the view that the intentional act of killing was unequivocally wrong and that St George was by no means a hero.

These are the two strands of moral philosophy most often applied to business ethics and they conflict, as they frequently do. They provide no answers. Moreover the Golden Rule ('do unto others as you would have done unto you') suggests that St George was wrong, while the categorical imperative ('would it be good if everyone did it?') suggests the opposite—the land would be cleared of flesh-eating dragons.

What would the alternative business ethic that has been presented in this book suggest? First, our present approach is concerned with a different question. The question is not so much 'Was St George right or wrong?', but 'Would you wish to enter a long-term collaborative venture with this person?' At least this question is relevant to the business situation and, moreover, it may be answerable.

If the person was St George, the hero, who fearlessly took his life in his hands to defend the local community against this terrible dragon threat, the answer would probably be 'Yes, we would like to collaborate with him'. On the other hand, if the person was St George, the coward, drunkard and would-be murderer, who could not tell the difference between his mother-in-law and a flesh-eating dragon, the answer would probably be 'No, thank you'.

So this approach asks the right question, but it does not provide, within itself, a definitive answer. The answer lies in the context of the particular decision or transaction. Which description more accurately describes St George?

We need to understand his sociomoral perspective (to use Kohlberg's terminology). Is his integrity a deeply held value, or a cynical calculation made for his own immediate benefit? Is it a fundamental characteristic or a style that he adopts as opportunity prompts? Is it the reality, or a misrepresentation of the truth? We recognize that if St George was really a habitual drunkard, he would have the utmost difficult hiding it from all the people all the time. The same is true with all false images.

The answers to these questions are likely to determine whether or not we shall wish to have dealings with St George and we would almost certainly wish to find the answers before we ever considered entering a long-term relationship or real interdependence.

If we were in St George's shoes we would wish to ensure that everyone recognized a true hero worthy of the very best alliances and partnerships. We would wish to be, and to be perceived to be, entirely trustworthy and of the highest integrity.

This is as far as the alternative business ethic goes. It is a modest step, but may be of help to those who have to grapple with the problem of corporate integrity and only have the tools of common sense and straightforward personal morality at their disposal.

Corporate integrity survey

Introduction

The survey, conducted during the first half of 1994, was the first part of an ongoing research carried out by the Keele Management Development Centre at Keele University. The purpose of the research is primarily to improve the practical value of management training in the area of business ethics.

The research programme comprised three distinct stages.

First, a pilot study was carried out to explore attitudes and the nature of management actions which participants considered feasible. The main survey questionnaire was developed and administered in various forms during the pilot study.

Second, the postal survey was conducted with companies in the 1993 FT SE 100 index.

Third, a series of semistructured interviews is being held with respondents to the survey. These are still continuing, and it is hoped to collect some time series data to gauge how attitudes and actions change over the medium to long term and how they adapt to changing conditions.

The pilot study

The pilot study initially focused on formal statements, codes of practice, etc., and mechanisms for setting standards of ethical behaviour and measuring ethical performance. By 'mechanism' is meant any procedure, individual or group, set up specifically for the purpose. For example, a regular board agenda item, an individual holding formal and specific responsibilities for reporting to the board, board or other committees or subcommittees on ethical issues, formal reports, etc.

Exploratory interviews were held in four companies to help design the questionnaire. This was then administered to 23 non-FT SE 100 companies by a variety of means: postal, telephone and some face to face. Replies were eventually obtained from 20 of these sources. In the responses received:

- 75 per cent put profitability ahead of corporate social responsibility

- 75 per cent saw corporate social responsibility as a constraint on, rather than an aim of, business

- 65 per cent said the 'good business is good business' argument is more persuasive than the 'good business benefits mankind' argument

- 30 per cent had either a written code of ethical practice or a section in their corporate mission statement specifically related to business ethics

- 25 per cent had developed specific mechanisms to monitor and control ethical performance

- none had taken specific action against people who contravened the code of practice.

Face-to-face interviews were then held with representatives of four of the responding organizations and telephone interviews with a further six. The interviews were partly of an exploratory nature regarding the research as well as being concerned with the specifics of attitudes and action in those particular companies. Regarding the research, the following responses were recorded:

- Only two of the interviewees expressed the view that their company would behave ethically for reasons that have been previously referred to as metaphysical, *irrespective of the company's situation*. This situational dependence was partly covered by the hierarchy of objectives—i.e. the business would be likely to be affected by the level of objectives on which it was focused: if survival were threatened then, in principle, 'anything goes'. In addition, it was pointed out that the business might behave differently in different national markets and also, as one interviewee added, as the climate changed, i.e. payment of suppliers might be delayed when interest rates are very high even if survival is not threatened, despite the position of the suppliers.

- Sixty per cent of interviewees regarded the establishment of their firm's trustworthiness as an important determinant of the way businesses might be expected to view ethics in business.

- Eighty per cent regarded considerations of moral philosophy or religion as irrelevant to business.

- It became clear that, *for business reasons*, different businesses accorded ethical performance a different degree of importance. These differences were highlighted by two interviewees who took very different approaches to most of the questions, one from a retail chemist who was clearly very aware of, and concerned about, ethical issues, whose business might be termed ethically dependent; the other from an engineering jobbing shop whose business might best be described as ethically neutral. Further consideration of this issue suggested the four possible categories of business:

1. *Ethically dependent*: those businesses whose ethical standing is a key aspect of their product offering—e.g. Start-rite, The Body Shop, etc.

2. *Ethically positive*: businesses whose ethical standing is important to the credibility of their offering but is not itself a key product attribute—e.g. Honda, Sainsbury, Hewlett Packard, etc.

3. *Ethically neutral*: those businesses whose ethical standing is less significant, though, it should be noted, obvious unethical performance will be disadvantageous—e.g. Ladbrokes, Hanson, etc.

4. *Ethically negative*: those businesses who are widely perceived as being in a business with negative ethical connotations and which may require specific management attention—e.g. BAT (tobacco), etc.

While it is not possible to draw any general conclusions from the pilot study there were a number of responses which indicate some attitudes and also actions which differed somewhat from prior expectations:

■ There was unanimous agreement that social responsibility was not a strategic aim of business, but a potentially powerful constraint.

■ There was a difference of view over what criteria might be used to assess whether behaviour was ethical or not. Both principle-based and consequentialist approaches were discussed without satisfaction. The nearest thing to consensus was over a criterion based on asking such questions as:

> 'If your customers knew, would they continue buying from you?'

> 'Would you be happy for all your employees to know?'

■ Three of the four interviewees agreed that it was important to give ethics a high profile, both as to the required behaviour/performance in the business and as to the consequences of falling below that performance. None of the businesses concerned had published a code of practice and there was some cynicism that these may be little more than expressions of pious hope. All agreed that codes of practice might play an important role in specifying behaviour and providing a basis for monitoring, if supported by other mechanisms (e.g. a senior manager or subcommittee charged with specific responsibilities).

■ One interviewee went further and suggested it was important to take symbolic action and demonstrate that ethical performance is important by being heavily punitive against transgressors. The dilatory and limited action taken by BA following the uncovering of their 'dirty tricks' campaign against Virgin Atlantic was highlighted as an opportunity missed.

The main survey

The survey focused on two basic issues.

■ First, to identify what motivates firms to take specific actions on ethical performance. Are they so motivated at all, and, if they are, are they motivated by the concerns of the business ethics movement—i.e. metaphysical issues drawn from moral philosophy or religion—or are they motivated by enlightened self-interest?

■ Second, to identify exactly actions firms take, rather than only what they say they do, to ensure that they achieve standards of ethical performance in their transactions (i.e. with employees, directors, customers, suppliers, shareholders, the local community, society at large and within the ecological environment).

The questionnaire (see Box AI.1) comprised a set of statements to which a semantic differential scaled response was required. Questions 1, 3, 5, 8, 10, 11, 13, 15, 17, 19, 21 and 23 are concerned with attitudes to ethics and integrity. The other numbered questions relate to management actions. The use of a seven-stage scaling system allows questions to be aggregated so that answers which indicate a positive attitude to integrity, for example, can be averaged to indicate an overall 'score'. Similarly with the questions relating to management action, 'scores' can be averaged to indicate how 'active' a firm is in ensuring that its integrity is upheld.

Of the 100 firms, 38 responded, 10 of which, for various reasons, did not complete the questionnaire. Some of these latter, nevertheless provided pertinent information which they felt more adequately reflected their approach to the issues raised. In terms of the questionnaire, therefore, there was a 28 per cent response rate. Clearly there is an extremely high risk of responses being biased towards firms interested in ethical issues and the results of the survey are not therefore claimed as being in any way representative. Nor are claims being made for their validity or reliability. They are merely indicative of the concerns and approach of 28 of the UK's leading firms.

The responses to the questions raised are indicated in Table AI.1.

Box AI.1: Integrity in Business Questionnaire

How true of your organization are the following statements? Please mark the appropriate number.

Completely True   Completely Untrue
1   2   3   4   5   6   7

1. We would be prepared to drive a competitor out of business if it was in our best long-term interests.
2. We have a written code of ethical practice or statement of ethical policy.
3. Our shareholders are more important than our employees.
4. We publish a résumé of our ethical performance in the annual report or other public format.
5. If it was clearly in the interests of the business to do something wrong, we would not even consider doing it.
6. An employee would be fired for behaving in a way that was clearly unethical.
7. There is an individual or group of individuals who have formal responsibility for reporting on the company's ethical performance.
8. We would never try to deceive a customer.
9. We set measurable targets for ethical performance.
10. We are ethical because ethical business is more profitable in the long term than unethical business.
11. We would never expect any of our employees to be dishonest during the course of their work.
12. We have appointed a body (individual or group of individuals) to assess the company's ethical performance.
13. The company's founder had high (religious or moral) ideals and this is still an important part of the company's culture.
14. We explicitly assess our company's ethical performance:
    Frequently / Half-Yearly / Annually / Occasionally / Never
15. The company exists to maximize shareholders' wealth.
16. Our parent board formally considers our company's ethical performance:
    Frequently / Half-Yearly / Annually / Occasionally / Never
17. Being a successful business is our most important social responsibility.
18. The company handbook indicates our general approach to ethical issues.
19. If our business activity damaged the environment we would wish to pay the costs of putting things right.
20. New employees are given some training in our approach to business ethics when they join the company.
21. Our main purpose is to maximize profits, as long as it is legal.

22. There is an individual or group of individuals who have formal responsibility for improving the company's ethical performance.
23. We believe the object of any business must ultimately be to benefit society.
24. The company's ethical performance is recognized in some formal way.
    - Any additional comments regarding your company's attitude to ethical issues:
    - Any additional comments on the actions taken in your company to ensure people behave ethically:

Table AI.1 Scored responses to each statement

Attitude questions	Mean scores	Action questions	Mean scores
1	4.1	2	2.2
3	3.8	4	5.1
5	6.9	6	2.2
8	1.8	7	2.8
10	1.8	9	4.8
11	1.3	12	3.7
13	4.6	14	4
15	5.5	16	5
17	2.1	18	2
19	2.3	20	2.9
21	5.7	22	3.3
23	2.8	24	4

NB: Questions 1, 3, 15 and 19 are reversed–i.e. 'completely true' scores 7.

The use of a seven-stage scaling system allows questions to be aggregated so that answers which indicate a positive attitude to integrity, for example, can be averaged to indicate an overall 'score'. Similarly, with the questions relating to management action, 'scores' can be averaged to indicate how 'active' a firm is in ensuring that its integrity is upheld. The meaning of these aggregated scores is highly problematic and imprecise and they are not claimed to be generalizations; they are only indicative. Nevertheless, they are not without interest.

Leaving aside, for the moment, the problematic nature of these 'scores', it is possible to envisage a simple matrix, as shown in Figure AI.1. This device appears useful in identifying different organizational types with differing attitudinal and action orientations. The point marked 'x' shows the mean position of respondents to the survey: a relatively positive attitude score but low on action.

The implications of these results and more qualitative information gathered in the research programme are discussed in the following section.

The interview programme

The interview programme is being conducted by semistructured interview among a subset of respondents to the first stage questionnaire and is still ongoing. The aim is to find out more qualitative detail about both the motivation of firms and the mechanisms used by different firms together with documentary evidence where possible, the main strengths and weaknesses of each approach, and the companies' assessments of their effectiveness.

The information so far collected is largely anecdotal. It has been referred to in a number of places in the main text, but is not yet adequate for a more definitive presentation.

Individual responses to the questionnaires have been considered in the context of the matrix shown in Figure AI.1. The mean score of all respondents suggested a positive attitude to integrity but not a commensurate level of action to achieve ethical performance. The individual responses, however, were distributed among all four quadrants. A commonsense interpretation of the four quadrants is suggested in

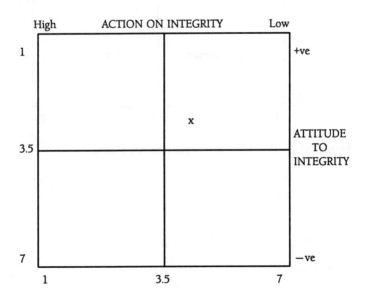

Figure AI.1 *The integrity matrix.*

Figure A1.2. It is emphasized that this is simply a commonsense interpretation, but several interviewees found the labels intuitively useful. This was seen as particularly relevant in terms of the organizations forging new relationships with customers, suppliers, technology suppliers, etc.

The development of long-lasting relationships, as opposed to doing business by short-term one-off profit-maximizing transactions, was recognized as one of the driving forces behind the desire of firms to behave ethically. For most responding organizations, being acceptable and accepted as a partner in some form of strategic alliance was seen as crucial, and being perceived as trustworthy was the essential prerequisite of such alliances.

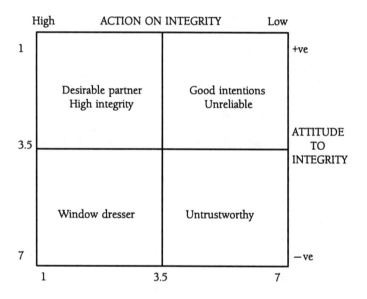

Figure AI.2 *Organizations on the integrity matrix.*

A model statement of ethical practice

The following model statement is extracted from *Company Philosophies and Codes of Business Ethics*, first published by the Institute of Business Ethics in 1988. It serves as a model that could help consideration of what is appropriate for a particular organization. Prior consideration should include not only the characteristics and requirements of the particular organization and its industry, but also the purpose of the code of practice, which is:

- to be used primarily as an image builder
- to develop a high-integrity organizational culture
- to be used as a basis for monitoring and controlling of ethical performance.

An effective code can be used for setting ethical standards and monitoring performance and in so doing can contribute greatly to the development of a high-integrity culture which will, in due course, achieve the benefits of a carefully constructed image.

A. Introduction

An analysis of a number of company statements and codes can provide a framework from which a company can develop its own individual statement or produce a code of ethics.

It is important that this is not left to an enthusiast on the board or delegated to the personnel manager but is seen as part of the responsibility of the whole board. Indeed, those companies which value their statements and make use of them in daily business life have involved the most senior officers in drawing up and publishing such documents. In some cases people throughout the company have been consulted.

Model business codes have existed for a number of years. The British Institute of Management's code and that of the Christian Association of Business Executives have been widely used. Some prefer to adopt one of the international codes; one oil company, for instance, has adopted the OECD Guidelines for International

Investment and Multinational Enterprise as its statement of business principles.

The following model draws upon a wide range of sources and may be helpful in preparing a statement which fits the particular organization's thinking about the issues involved.

B. Outline of a model statement of business principles

1. Preface or Introduction (signed by the chairman or CEO or both)

Start with a sentence on the purpose of the Statement—mention the values which are important to the top management in the conduct of the business such as integrity, efficiency, professionalism and responsibility.

Set out the role of the company in the community and end with a personal endorsement of the Statement and the expectation that the standard set out in it will be maintained by all involved in the organisation.

Date the Preface.

2. Key areas to include

(a) The object of the business

The service which is being provided—a group of products, or set of services, financial objectives and the business's role in society as the company sees it.

(b) Customer relations

The importance of customer satisfaction and good faith in all agreements. The priority given to customer needs, fair pricing and after-sales service.

(c) Shareholders or other providers of money

The protection of investment made in the company and proper 'return' on money lent. A commitment to effective communication with this group of people.

(d) Suppliers

Long-term co-operation. Prompt settling of bills. Joint actions to achieve quality and efficiency.

(e) Employees

How the business values employees. The company's policies on: recruitment, organisation, development and training, rewards, communication, work conditions, health and safety, industrial relations, equal employment opportunity, retirement, severance and redundancy.

(f) Society or the wider community

Compliance with the spirit of laws as well as the letter. The company's obligation to conform to environmental and safety standards. The involvement of the company and its staff in local affairs. The corporate policy on giving to education and charities. The leadership role of the business in maintaining high standards both within the organisation and in its dealings with others.

(g) Other matters

Relations with competitors, research and development policy and management responsibility. The ethical standards expected of employees. (This is best covered in a separate statement addressed primarily to employees.)

C. An outline of a code of business ethics

To be effective and understood by all employees, a specific code of business ethics should be relatively short and written in simple language. Ideally it should be concerned with problems experienced by employees and include something about procedures to be followed when confronted with an ethical dilemma at work. It should also make clear what will happen if the code is breached.

1. Introduction

A statement on the reason why the code has been produced and its status, e.g. that it applies to all employees and that any non-compliance will be considered a serious disciplinary matter.

2. *Conflicts of interest*

A clause covering possible conflicts of interest such as personal interest (or that of an immediate member of one's family) in an organisation with which the company does business, which could lead to perceptions of self-interested behaviour. This interest could include a directorship, employment of close family members or a significant shareholding. A directive that all such potential conflicts should be reported to the employee's immediate superior and recorded. A ban on share dealing as a result of information obtained in the course of work for the organisation.

3. *Giving and receiving of gifts*

Specific guidance on the giving or receiving of cash, goods, services, hospitality or bribes in any form. A statement that all offers made to employees of anything that might be construed as an inducement shall not be accepted. Company policy on the offering of gifts to others and the level of hospitality that it is acceptable to offer or receive. (Small 'goodwill gifts' exchanged at Christmas (diaries, etc.) are normally permitted.) Direction that any gifts offered or received should be reported to a superior and recorded. The fact that this applies equally to business with overseas customers and suppliers and should be subject to auditors' inspection. The fact that business entertainment should be on a reciprocal basis and on a scale consistent with the status of the employee in the organisation.

4. *Confidentiality*

A statement, where applicable, that information which is obtained in the course of work is the property of the company. The fact that it must not be disclosed to unauthorised persons and that this also applies when the employee is no longer working for the organisation. The steps to be taken to safeguard information which is of value to competitors or others.

5. *Environment*

Standards for the working environment of employees and the effect of business activity on local communities. A statement that the health and safety of employees and others involved with the business is of paramount importance and that staff are responsible for seeing that the products and operations not only comply with legal requirements but take into account the well-being of the general public, especially those living in the vicinity of manufacturing plants.

6. Equal employment opportunity

An undertaking that selection for a position in the company shall be based on suitability for the job and that there shall be no discrimination purely on grounds of race, religion, marital status, sex, colour, nationality, disability or ethnic or national origin. Similar undertakings on promotion and security of employment.

7. Other areas which might be covered

There are a number of other areas of company and employer activity which could be covered in such a code. These might include:

Political activities by individuals
Obligations under competition or anti-trust laws
'Moonlighting' by employees
Sexual harassment.

Example statements of ethical practice

ICI's statement on business ethics

Comments by the deputy chairman and chief executive

It always has been and continues to be our policy that the Group and its employees maintain the highest ethical standards in the conduct of the business. I believe it is timely and appropriate that we produce a statement on Business Ethics to demonstrate the importance which the Group attaches to this area. I would like to impress on every ICI employee that the Board expects full compliance with these policies.

(Signed Ronnie Hampel, deputy chairman and chief executive.)

Introduction

A business organisation can only command public confidence and respect by conducting its affairs with integrity. In all its activities ICI is committed to the highest standards of ethical conduct.

This statement is addressed to all people working in the ICI Group and applies to all activities in the Group. It is supplemented and amplified by Group and Company policies and guidelines on specific issues.

All employees are expected to comply with this statement of policy and to conduct their activities on behalf of the Group accordingly. If additional guidance is required employees should seek help from their managers.

Policy statement

It is essential that ICI maintains the highest ethical standards and thereby keep its reputation with, and ensure acceptability to, governments, regulatory bodies, communities and all those with whom the Group trades or has dealings. This requires all employees to maintain the highest standards of honesty, integrity and trustworthiness in the day-to-day performance of their duties and in any situation where the employee is representing ICI.

Group policies

ICI has promulgated various policies regarding the conduct of its business. For example, there are policies concerning compliance with safety, health and environmental standards and with regard to the employment of people. It is the responsibility of all employees to familiarise themselves with those policies and to comply with the spirit as well as the letter of each policy.

Compliance with laws

It is ICI policy that the Group and its employees must comply with the laws and ethical practices of any country in which it is doing business. The policy applies without exception. Particular areas which should be noted are competition laws, and safety, health and environmental laws. For both these areas annual assurances of compliance from all units and functions are required. It is the responsibility of all employees to ensure, by taking advice where appropriate, that they are fully aware of all relevant local laws.

Particular areas where individuals should take care include:

Insider dealing: it is ICI policy, and in certain countries a legal requirement carrying criminal sanctions, that employees in possession of confidential unpublished 'price sensitive information' must not make use of such information to deal in the securities of ICI or provide such information to third parties for that purpose. Similar considerations apply where confidential price sensitive information is used for dealing in securities of other companies. Employees must not use confidential information obtained through their employment for personal gain.

Group resources: the Group has valuable resources both in the form of tangible assets such as materials, equipment and cash; and intangible assets such as computer systems, trade secrets and confidential information. These resources should be used for no other purpose than for the proper advancement of the Group's business. They must not be used for unlawful purposes or for personal gain.

Security of information

Employees must observe the rules laid down in instructions concerning the classifying and handling of documents and electronic data. It is the responsibility of all employees to acquaint themselves with the applicable rules. Information generated within the Group is the property of ICI and should not, unless legally required, be disclosed outside the group without proper authority.

Conflicts of interest

Employees must avoid entering into any situations in which their personal or financial interests may conflict with those of the ICI Group. Employees dealing with customers, suppliers, contractors, competitors or any person doing, or seeking to do, business with ICI are to act in the best interests of the Group and must disregard any personal preference or advantage. Where any potential conflict of interest may arise, the employee should declare that interest and seek advice from senior management.

Examples of activities which should be avoided include:

■ borrowing from third parties with business relationships with ICI
■ ownership of an interest in such a third party, whether personally or by a close family member. While shareholdings in major public companies should not usually be a problem, interests in smaller public or private companies may cause a conflict of interest.

Business practices

Group funds should not be used in payments, direct or indirect, to government officials or employees of state organisations for unlawful or improper purposes. 'Payments' is intended to include money and gifts of other than nominal value and entertainment other than on a modest scale.

Gifts and entertainment may only be offered to any third party if they are consistent with customary business practice, modest in value and not in contravention of any applicable law. No such offer should be made if public disclosure of the fact would embarrass the Group or the employee.

No employee should seek or accept a personal gift or entertainment which might reasonably be believed to influence business transactions. Offers of entertainment must not be accepted unless the offer is within the bounds of accepted business hospitality. Unsolicited gifts which do not fall within acceptable limits should be returned or donated to a reputable charity.

Accounting standards

All accounts and records must be documented in a manner that clearly identifies and describes the true nature of business transactions, assets or liabilities, and properly and timely classifies and records entries in conformity with generally accepted accounting principles. No record, entry or document shall be false, distorted, misleading, misdirected, deliberately incomplete or suppressed. Group funds must not be held outside the Group's books of account.

Political contributions

The law applicable to political contributions varies from country to country. Political contributions are not made by the Group in the UK. Members of the Group outside the UK must in this respect comply with the laws of the countries in which they conduct business. Any lawful contributions they make should be approved under the procedures laid down by the board of the company concerned.

Transfer pricing

It is Group policy that business transactions between affiliated companies should be based on the arm's length principle. This means that a Group company entering into a transaction with another member of the Group should not allow the shareholding relationship to influence any aspect of that transaction. This principle extends not only to the sale price but to credit terms, provision of intellectual property or know-how, the provision of services, etc. If a third party would be charged for any such services, the affiliate should also be. The terms agreed between two member companies of the Group for goods or services must be defensible as those to which independent parties could be expected to agree. Those terms should normally be recorded in writing.

Equal opportunities

ICI values the individuality, diversity and creative potential that every man and woman brings to its business. All employees should be treated with equal respect and dignity, and should be provided with equality of opportunity to develop themselves and their careers.

Particular judgments about people for the purposes of recruitment, development and promotion should be made solely on the basis of a person's ability and potential in relation to the needs of the job, and should take no account of any matter not relevant to the performance of that job. Overall, success and advancement within ICI should depend solely on personal ability and work performance.

Sexual harassment

Conduct involving the harassment of any employee is unacceptable. In particular, sexual harassment will not be tolerated. Any person who believes they have been sexually harassed should report the incident and circumstances to their immediate manager or personnel manager who will arrange for it to be investigated impartially and confidentially.

Implementation

The examples given in this statement are not intended to be comprehensive and employees must endeavour to observe the principles which they embody. Failure to do so may result in disciplinary action against the employee.

The Group's reputation depends on effective implementation of policies and it is the responsibility of management to ensure that this statement and these policies and their application are communicated, understood and taken seriously by all employees. Management must secure the cooperation of employees and positively promote these policies by personal example, by clear guidance and by making advice available as appropriate.

Shell's statement of general business principles

Introduction

This document reaffirms the general business principles on which the conduct of the affairs of the Royal Dutch/Shell Group of Companies is predicated. They apply equally to corporate decision-making as to the individual behaviour expected of employees in conducting Shell business.

The Group is typified by decentralized, diversified and widespread operations, within which operating companies have wide freedom of action. However, the upholding of the Shell reputation is a common bond which can be maintained only by honesty and integrity in all activities. This reputation is a vital resource, the protection of which is of fundamental importance. A single failure, whether it be willful or due to misplaced zeal, or short term expediency, can have very serious effects on the Group as a whole.

The reputation depends on the existence and knowledge of clearly understood principles and responsibilities and on their observance in day to day practice in widely different environments. Individual operating companies may have their own statements to meet national situations based on these general business principles.

These principles have served Shell companies well for many years and will continue to do so in the future. It is the responsibility of management to ensure that their staff are aware of the principles on which their activities are based and that they comply with them.

Signed: *C.A.J. Herkströter*, Chairman of the Committee of Managing Directors of the Service Companies, July, 1994.

1. Objectives

The objectives of Shell companies are to engage efficiently, responsibly and profitably in the oil, gas, chemicals and other selected businesses, and to participate in the search for and development of other sources of energy. Shell companies seek a high standard of performance and aim to maintain a long term position in their respective competitive environments.

2. Responsibilities

Four areas of responsibility are recognized:

(a) To shareholders

To protect shareholders' investment and provide an acceptable return.

(b) To employees

To provide all employees with good and safe conditions of work, and good and competitive terms and conditions of service; to promote the development and best use of human talent and equal opportunity employment; and to encourage the involvement of employees in the planning and direction of their work, and in the application of these principles within their company. It is recognized that commercial success depends on the full commitment of all employees.

(c) To customers

To win and maintain customers' support by developing and providing products and services which offer value in terms of price, quality and safety, and which are supported by the requisite technological, environmental and commercial expertise.

(d) To society

To conduct business as responsible corporate members of society, observing applicable laws of the countries in which they operate and giving proper regard to health, safety and environmental standards.

These four areas of responsibility are seen as inseparable. Therefore, it is the duty of management continuously to assess the priorities and discharge its responsibilities as best it can on the basis of that assessment.

3. Economic principles

Profitability is essential to discharging these responsibilities and staying in business. It is a measure both of efficiency and of the ultimate value that people place on Shell products and services. It is essential to the proper allocation of corporate resources and necessary to support the continuing investment required to develop and produce future energy supplies to meet consumer needs. Without profits and a strong financial foundation it would not be possible to fulfil the responsibilities outlined above.

Shell companies work in a wide variety of social, political and economic environments over the nature of which they have little influence, but in general they believe that the interests of the community can be served most efficiently by a market economy.

Criteria for investment decisions are essentially economic but also take into account social and environmental considerations and an appraisal of the security of the investment.

4. Business integrity

Shell companies insist on honesty, integrity and fairness in all aspects of their business and expect the same in their relationships with their contractors and suppliers. The direct or indirect offer, payment, soliciting and acceptance of bribes in any form are unacceptable practices. All employees are required to avoid conflicts of interest between their private financial activities and their part in the conduct of company business. All transactions on behalf of a Shell company must be appropriately described in the accounts of the company in accordance with established procedures and be subject to audit.

5. Political activities

(a) Companies

Shell companies endeavour always to act commercially, operating within existing national laws in a socially responsible manner, abstaining from participation in party politics and interference in political matters. It is, however, their legitimate right and responsibility to speak out on matters that affect the interests of their employees, customers and shareholders, and on matters of general interest, where they have a contribution to make based on particular knowledge.

(b) Political payments

Shell companies do not make payments to political parties, organizations or their representatives.

(c) Employees

Where employees, in their capacity as citizens, wish to engage in activities in the community, including standing for election to public office, favourable consideration is given to their being enabled to do so where this is appropriate in the light of local circumstances.

6. Health, safety and the environment

It is the policy of Shell companies to conduct their activities in such a way as to take foremost account of the health and safety of their employees and of other persons, and to give proper regard to the conservation of the environment. Shell companies pursue a policy of continuous improvement in the measures taken to protect the health, safety and environment of those who may be affected by their activities.

Shell companies establish health, safety and environmental policies, programmes and practices and integrate them in a commercially sound manner into each business as an essential element of management.

7. The community

The most important contribution that companies can make to the social and material progress of the countries in which they operate is in performing their basic activities as efficiently as possible. In addition the need is recognized to take a constructive interest in societal matters which may not be directly related to the business. Opportunities for involvement–for example, through community, educational or donations programmes–will vary depending upon the size of the company concerned, the nature of the local society, and the scope for useful private initiatives.

8. Competition

Shell companies support free enterprise. They seek to compete fairly and ethically and within the framework of applicable competition laws; they will not prevent others from competing freely with them.

9. Communication

Shell companies recognize that in view of the importance of the activities in which they are engaged and their impact on national economies and individuals, there is a need for open communications. To this end, Shell companies have comprehensive corporate information programmes and provide full relevant information about their activities to legitimately interested parties, subject to any overriding considerations of business confidentiality and cost.

10. Joint ventures

Shell companies participating in joint ventures will promote the application of these principles in the management of the joint venture operation. The ability to do this effectively will be an important factor in the decision to enter into or remain in any joint venture.

References

Adams, R., Carruthers, J. and Hamil, S., *Changing Corporate Values*, Kogan Page, London, 1991.

Axelrod, R., *The Evolution of Cooperation*, Basic Books, New York, 1984.

Barnard, C.I., *Organisation and Management*, Harvard University Press, 1948.

Baumol, W.J., *Business Behaviour, Value and Growth*, Macmillan, New York, 1959.

Baumol, W.J., 'Entrepreneurship and a century of economic growth', *Journal of Business Venturing*, No 1, 1986.

Bentham, J., *Introduction to the Principles of Morals and Legislation*, 1789.

Bowen, D., 'Virtual power to the people as companies fade away', *The Independent on Sunday*, 27 March 1994.

Bruce, R., 'Natwest chiefs get huge rises as staff are cut', *The Independent on Sunday*, 24 April 1994.

Burke, T. and Hill, J., *Ethics, Environment and the Company*, Institute of Business Ethics, London, 1990.

Burke, T., Maddock, S. and Rose, A., *How Ethical is British Business?*, Research Working Paper Series 2, No. 1, Chap. 2, Faculty of Business, Management and Social Studies, University of Westminster, 1993.

Burns, T. and Stalker, G.M., *The Management of Innovation*, Tavistock Institute, London, 1961.

Cadbury, A., 'Ethical managers make their own rules', *Harvard Business Review*, September–October 1987.

Chorn, N.H., 'Organisations: a new paradigm', *Management Decision*, **29** (No. 4), 1992.

Clark, K.B., 'What strategy can do for technology', *Harvard Business Review*, November–December 1989.

Colby A. and Kohlberg L. *The Measurement of Moral Judgement—Vol. I*, Cambridge University Press, Cambridge, 1987.

Connon, H., 'Sweet deals may turn sour', *The Independent*, 1 April 1994.

Cope, N., 'Creditors send in the bunnies', *The Independent* 21 April 1994.

Croome, H., *Human Problems of Innovation*, Department of Scientific and Industrial Research pamphlet, Problems of Progress in Industry, 1960.

Cyert, R.M. and March, J.G., *A Behavioural Theory of the Firm*, Prentice Hall, Englewood Cliffs, 1963.

DeGeorge, R.T., *Business Ethics* (2nd edition), Macmillan, New York, 1986.

DeGeorge, R.T., 'Will success spoil business ethics' in *Business Ethics: the State of the Art* (ed. R. E. Freeman), Oxford University Press, New York, 1991.

DeGeorge, R.T., *Competing with Integrity in International Business*, Oxford University Press, New York, 1993.

Dickson, M., 'Baby Bell's bad behaviour', *Financial Times*, 14 May 1993a.

Dickson, T., 'The moral maze', *Financial Times*, 26 May 1993b.

Dixit, A. and Nalebuff, B., *Thinking Strategically: the Competitive Edge in Business, Politics and Everyday Life*, Norton, New York, 1991.

Donkin, R., 'Whistleblower's cautionary tale', *Financial Times*, 19 January 1994.

Drucker, P.F., *The Practice of Management*, Heinemann, London, 1955.

Drucker, P.F., *Managing for Results*, Harper & Row, New York, 1964.

Drucker, P.F., *Post-Capitalist Society*, Butterworth Heinemann, London, 1993.

Durman, P., 'Directors' companies paid £360,000 by pension group', *The Independent*, 21 April 1994.

Edwardes, M, *Back from the Brink*, Collins, London, 1982.

Emery, F.E. and Trist, E.L., 'The causal texture of organisational environments', *Human Relations*, **18**, 1965.

Garvin, D A, 'Competing on the eight dimensions of quality', *Harvard Business Review*, November–December 1987.

Gauthier, 'Morality and Markets: the implications for business', in *Market Morality and Company Size*, (eds B. Harvey, H. van Luijk and G. Corbetto), Kluwer, Dordrecht, 1991.

Glancey, J., 'The real thing put to the test', *The Independent on Sunday*, 24 April 1994.

Goldsmith, W. and Clutterbuck, D., *The Winning Streak*, Penguin, Harmondsworth, 1985.

Greenbury, R., Unpublished comments in response to Keele Management Development Centre's Organizational Integrity Survey, 1994.

Hall, W.K., 'Survival strategies in a hostile environment', *Harvard Business Review*, September–October 1980.

Hamel, G. and Prahalad, C.K., 'Strategic intent', *Harvard Business Review*, May–June 1989.

Handy, C.B., *Understanding Organisations*, Penguin, Harmondsworth, 1976.

Hayes, R.H. and Abernathy, W.J., 'Managing our way to economic decline', *Harvard Business Review*, May–June 1980.

Hayes, R.H. and Garvin, D., 'Managing as if tomorrow mattered', *Harvard Business Review*, May–June 1982.

Hellier, D., 'Signet pressed to restructure', *The Independent on Sunday*, 22 May 1994.

Henderson, D., Unpublished comments in response to Keele Management Development Centre's Organizational Integrity Survey, 1994.

Herzberg, F., Mausner, B. and Snyderman, B.B., *The Motivation to Work*, Wiley, New York, 1959.

Hitachi Ltd, 'Localising the multinational: globalisation holds the key', *Financial Times*, 17 September 1993.

Hogg, S, 'A dance to the music of economic time', *The Times*, 17 June 1986.

Hosmer, L.T., *The Ethics of Management*, Irwin, New York, 1987.

Hotten, R., 'Firms reveal they put profits before ethics', *Sunday Times*, 3 January 1993.

Howard, 'Values make the company: an interview with Robert Haas', *Harvard Business Review*, September–October 1990.

Institute of Business Ethics, *Company Philosophies and Codes of Business Ethics*, 1988.

Jack, A. and Dixon, H., 'What price a corporate halo', *Financial Times*, 17 September 1993.

Kelly, G.A., *The Psychology of Personal Constructs*, Norton, New York, 1955.

Kohlberg, L., 'Moral stages and Moralization: the Cognitive-development Approach', in *Moral Development and Behaviour: Theory, Research and Social Issues*, (ed. T. Lickona), Holt, Rinehart and Winston, New York, 1976.

Kohlberg, L. *Essays in Moral Development: Vol. II. The Psychology of Moral Development: Moral Stages: Their Nature and Validity*, Harper & Row, San Francisco, 1984.

Kotler. P., *Marketing Management, Analysis, Planning, Implementation and Control* (5th edition), Prentice Hall, Englewood Cliffs, 1984.

Kotler, P., *Marketing Management, Analysis, Planning, Implementation and Control*, (7th edition), Prentice Hall, Englewood Cliffs, 1991.

Lei, D., 'Offensive and defensive uses of alliances', *Long Range Planning*, **26** (No. 4), 32–41, 1993.

Leitko, T.A. and Szczerbacki, D., 'Why traditional OD strategies fail in professional bureaucracies', *Organizational Dynamics*, Winter, 1987.

Lorange, P., Roos, J. and Brønn, P.S., 'Building successful strategic alliances', *Long Range Planning*, **25** (No. 6) 10, 1992.

Lorenz, C., 'The good and the bad of bigness', *Financial Times*, 8 April 1994.

Mallet, V., 'Poisoned chalice', *Financial Times*, 24 March 1993.

Martin P., 'More than their job's worth', *Financial Times*, 15 May 1993.

Maslow, A., 'A theory of human motivation', *Psychological Review*, **50**, 1943.

McCarthy, T., 'Still no Oscar for Sugihara's list', *The Independent*, 16 May 1994

McGill, M.E., Slocum, J.W. Jr and Rei, D., 'Management practices in learning organisations', *Organizational Dynamics*, Summer, 1992.

Mill, J.S., 1861, quoted in Warnock, G., *Contemporary Moral Philosophy*, Macmillan, London, 1967.

Miller, W.F., 'Technology and global strategy', *Strategic Direction*, January 1990.

Modgil, S. and Modgil, C., (eds), *Lawrence Kohlberg: Consensus and Controversy*, The Falmer Press, Philadelphia, 1985.

Morgan, G., *Imaginization*, Sage, 1992.

Mueller, R. K., *Corporate Networking–Building Channels for Information and Influence*, The Free Press, New York, 1986.

Nash, L.L., *Good Intentions Aside: a Manager's Guide to Resolving Ethical Problems*, Harvard Business School Press, Boston, Massachusetts, 1990.

Ohmae, K., 'The global logic of strategic alliances', *Harvard Business Review*, March–April 143–54, 1989.

Pascale, R., 'The paradox of "corporate culture": reconciling ourselves to socialisation', *California Management Review*, **xxvii** (No. 2), 1985.

Pearce, J.A., 'The company mission as a strategic tool', *Sloan Management Review*, Spring, 1982.

Pearson, G.J., *The Strategic Discount*, Wiley, Chichester, 1985.

Pearson, G.J., *Strategic Thinking*, Prentice Hall, Hemel Hempstead, 1990.

Pearson, G.J., *The Competitive Organization*, McGraw-Hill, Maidenhead, 1992.

Pearson, G.J., Pearson, A.W. and Ball, D.F., 'Innovation in a mature industry: a case study of warp knitting in the UK', *Technovation*, **9**, 657–79, 1989.

Peters, T., 'Which way is up in a web?', *The Independent*, 20 March 1994a.

Peters, T., 'Ethical dry cleaning', *The Independent on Sunday*, 22 May 1994b.

Peters, T. and Waterman, R.H., *In Search of Excellence*, Harper & Row, New York, 1982.

Porter, M.E., 'How Competitive Forces Shape Strategy', *Harvard Business Review*, March–April, 1979.

Porter, M.E., 'Michael Porter on competitive strategy', video film and pamphlet, Harvard Business School Video Series, 1988.

Porter, M.E., 'The competitive advantage of nations', *Harvard Business Review*, March–April 1990.

Prahalad, C.K. and Hamel, G., 'The core competence of the corporation', *Harvard Business Review*, **68** (No. 3), May–June, 1990.

Rees-Mogg, W., 'The old City standards driven out by cowboys', *The Independent*, 6 January 1987.

Reynolds, P.C., 'Corporate culture on the rocks', *Across the Board*, October 1986.

Sikka, P., Puxty, T. and Willmott, H., 'A gaping hole in auditing practice', *The Independent*, 19 April 1994.

Skinner, W, 'The productivity paradox', *Harvard Business Review*, July–August 1986.

Smith, C., 'The new corporate philanthropy', *Harvard Business Review*, May–June 1994.

Stark, A., 'What's the matter with business ethics?' *Harvard Business Review*, May–June 1993.

Stevenson, T. and Cooper, G., 'Promotion to cost Hoover £28m more than planned', *The Independent*, 21 April 1994.

Stiles, P. and Taylor, B., 'Benchmarking corporate governance: the impact of the Cadbury code', *Long Range Planning*, **26** (No. 5), 61–71, 1993.

Thomson, R., 'Bosses lay into Cadbury rules', *The Independent on Sunday*, 8 May 1994.

Trapp, R., 'Competitors click in for a better profile', *The Independent on Sunday*, 29 August 1993.

Trapp, R., 'Non-execs fail to learn the facts of company life', *The Independent on Sunday*, 1 May 1994.

Venkatesan, R., 'Strategic sourcing: to make or not to make', *Harvard Business Review*, November–December 1992.

Virgo, P., *Spring 1991, IT Skills Trends Report*, IT Strategy Services, London; 1991.

Waterhouse, K., 'Atrocity tales from Maxwellia', Life & Times, *The Times*, 7 May 1992.

Waterman, R.H., *The Frontiers of Excellence*, Nicholas Brealey Publishing, 1994.

Weber, M., 1920, *The Protestant Ethic and Spirit of Capitalism*, translated in *Collection of Essays*, (ed. A. Henderson and T. Parsons), The Free Press, New York, 1947.

Webley, S., *Company Philosophies and Codes of Business Ethics*, Institute of Business Ethics, London, 1988.

Webley, S., *Business Ethics and Company Codes*, Institute of Business Ethics, London, 1992.

White, J., 'Corporate culture and corporate success', *Management Decision*, **22**, (No. 4), 1984.

Willcock, J., 'Sexual exchange costs foreign money dealers their Goldman Sachs jobs', *The Independent*, 23 April 1994.

Williams, R., 'Cola taste buds tell the difference', *The Independent*, 19 April 1994.

Williamson, O., 'Managerial discretion and business behaviour', *American Economic Review*, 1963.

Womack, J.P., Jones, D.T. and Ross, D., *The Machine that Changed the World*, Macmillan, London, 1990.

Index